KU-005-230

THE ROUGH GUIDE

SPANISH PHRASEBOOK

Compiled by
LEXUS

www.roughguides.com

Credits

Spanish Phrasebook	Rough Guides Reference
Compiled by: Lexus with Fernando León Solís	Director: Andrew Lockett
Lexus series editor: Sally Davies	Editors: Kate Berens, Tom Cabot, Tracy Hopkins, Matthew Milton, Joe Staines
Layout: Nikhil Agarwal	
Picture research: Nicole Newman	

Publishing information

First edition published in 1995.
This updated edition published August 2011 by
Rough Guides Ltd, 80 Strand, London, WC2R 0RL
Email: mail@roughguides.com

Distributed by the Penguin Group:
Penguin Books Ltd, 80 Strand, London, WC2R 0RL
Penguin Group (USA), 375 Hudson Street, NY 10014, USA
Penguin Group (Australia), 250 Camberwell Road, Camberwell, Victoria 3124, Australia
Penguin Group (New Zealand), Cnr Rosedale and Airborne Roads, Albany, Auckland, New Zealand

Rough Guides is represented in Canada by Tourmaline Editions Inc., 662 King Street West, Suite 304, Toronto, Ontario, M5V 1M7

Printed in Singapore by Toppan Security Printing Pte. Ltd.
The publishers and author have done their best to ensure the accuracy and currency of all information in *The Rough Guide Spanish Phrasebook*; however, they can accept no responsibility for any loss or inconvenience sustained by any reader as a result of its information or advice.

© Lexus Ltd, 2011
Travel tips © Jules Brown

264 pages

A catalogue record for this book is available from the British Library.

978-1-84836-732-6

3 5 7 9 8 6 4 2 1

CONTENTS

How to use this book

The **Rough Guide Spanish phrasebook** is a highly practical introduction to the contemporary language. It gets straight to the point in every situation you might encounter: in bars and shops, on trains and buses, in hotels and banks, on holiday or on business. Laid out in clear A–Z style with easy-to-find, colour-coded sections, it uses key words to take you directly to the phrase you need – so if you want some help booking a room, just look up "room" in the dictionary section.

The phrasebook starts off with **Basics**, where we list some essential phrases, including words for numbers, dates and telling the time, and give guidance on pronunciation, along with a short section on the different regional accents you might come across. Then, to get you started in two-way communication, the **Scenarios** section offers dialogues in key situations such as renting a car, asking directions or booking a taxi, and includes words and phrases for when something goes wrong, from getting a flat tyre or asking to move apartments to more serious emergencies. You can listen to these and download them for free from www.roughguides.com/phrasebooks for use on your computer, MP3 player or smartphone.

Forming the main part of the guide is a double dictionary, first **English–Spanish**, which gives you the essential words you'll need plus easy-to-use phonetic transliterations wherever pronunciation might be a problem. Then, in the **Spanish–English** dictionary, we've given not just the phrases you'll be likely to hear (starting with a selection of slang and colloquialisms) but also many of the signs, labels and

instructions you'll come across in print or in public places. Scattered throughout the sections are travel tips direct from the authors of the Rough Guides guidebook series.

Finally, there's an extensive **Menu reader**. Consisting of separate food and drink sections, each starting with a list of essential terms, it's indispensable whether you're eating out, stopping for a quick drink or looking around a local food market.

¡Buen Viaje!
Have a good trip!

BASICS

Pronunciation

In this phrasebook, the Spanish has been written in a system of imitated pronunciation so that it can be read as though it were English, bearing in mind the notes on pronunciation given below:

air	as in hair
ay	as in may
e	as in get
g	always hard as in goat
H	a harsh 'ch' as in the Scottish way of pronouncing loch
ī	as the 'i' sound in might
ow	as in now
y	as in yes

Letters given in bold type indicate the part of the word to be stressed.

As i and u are always pronounced ee and oo in Spanish, pronunciation has not been given for all words containing these letters unless they present other problems for the learner. Thus María is pronounced maree-a and fútbol is footbol.

Abbreviations

adj	adjective		pl	plural
f	feminine (nouns with la)		pol	polite
fam	familiar		sing	singular
m	masculine (nouns with el)			

Notes

There are two verbs that translate 'to be' – ser and estar – depending on whether the verb is describing a permanent or temporary state. For example, soy inglés **I am English**; estoy cansado **I am tired**.

Where two words are given as a translation, as in **I'm full** estoy lleno/llena, the first is the masculine form, the second the feminine form.

In the Spanish–English and Menu reader sections, the letter ñ is treated as a separate letter that comes after n in the alphabet.

Basic phrases

yes sí

no no

OK vale balay

hello ¡hola! ola

good morning buenos días
bwaynoss

good evening buenas tardes
bwenass tardess

good night buenas noches
nochess

goodbye adiós ad-yoss

hi! ¡hola! ola

see you! ¡hasta luego!
asta lwaygo

please por favor fabor

thanks, thank you gracias
grath-yass

that's OK, don't mention it
no hay de qué ī day kay

yes please sí, por favor

no thanks no gracias

how are you? ¿cómo estás?

I'm fine, thanks bien, gracias
b-yen grath-yass

pleased to meet you
encantado de conocerle
day konothairlay

excuse me (to get past)
con permiso
(to get attention) ¡por favor! fabor
(to say sorry) perdone pairdonay

sorry perdone pairdonay

pardon (me)? (didn't understand/
hear) ¿cómo?

what? ¿qué? kay

what did he say? ¿que ha
dicho? kay a

I see (I understand) ya comprendo

I don't understand no entiendo
ent-yendo

do you speak English?
¿habla inglés? abla

I don't speak Spanish no hablo
español ablo espan-yol

could you say it slowly?
¿podría decirlo despacio?
podree-a detheerlo despath-yo

could you repeat that?
¿puede repetir eso? pwayday
repeteer ayso

could you write it down?
¿puede escribírmelo?
pwayday eskreebeermaylo

I'd like a... quisiera un/una...
kees-yaira...

could I have...? quisiera...
kees-yaira...

how much is it? ¿cuánto es?
kwanto

cheers! (toast) ¡salud! saloo

when? ¿cuando? kwando

where? ¿dónde? donday

Dates

Use the numbers opposite to express the date. In formal Spanish, the ordinal number may be used for 'the first', but not for other dates:

the first of September
el uno/el primero de septiembre
oono/el preemairo day sept-yembray

the second of December
el dos de diciembre
doss day deeth-yembray

the thirtieth of May el treinta
de mayo tray-eenta day ma-yo

the thirty-first of May
el treinta y uno de mayo
tray-eenti oono day ma-yo

Days

Sunday domingo

Monday lunes looness

Tuesday martes martess

Wednesday miércoles
m-yairkoless

Thursday jueves Hwaybess

Friday viernes b-yairness

Saturday sábado

Months

January enero enairo

February febrero febrairo

March marzo martho

April abril

May mayo ma-yo

June junio Hoon-yo

July julio Hool-yo

August agosto

September septiembre
sept-yembray

October octubre oktoobray

November noviembre
nob-yembray

December diciembre
deeth-yembray

Time

what time is it? ¿qué hora es?
kay ora ess

one o'clock la una la oona

two o'clock las dos lass doss

it's one o'clock es la una
ess la oona

it's two o'clock son las dos
son lass doss

it's ten o'clock son las diez
son lass d-yeth

five past one la una y cinco
la oona ee theenko

ten past two las dos y diez
lass doss ee d-yeth

quarter past one la una y
cuarto la oona ee kwarto

quarter past two las dos y
cuarto lass doss ee kwarto

half past ten las diez y media
lass d-yeth ee mayd-ya

twenty to ten las diez menos
veinte lass d-yeth m**ay**noss
ba**y-ee**ntay

quarter to ten las diez menos
cuarto lass d-yeth m**ay**noss
kw**a**rto

at eight o'clock a las ocho
a lass **o**cho

at half past four a las cuatro y
media a lass kw**a**tro ee m**a**yd-ya

2 am las dos de la mañana
lass doss day la man-y**a**na

2 pm las dos de la tarde
lass doss day la t**a**rday

6 am las seis de la mañana
lass say-eess day la man-y**a**na

6 pm las seis de la tarde
lass say-eess day la t**a**rday

noon mediodía m**a**yd-yo d**ee**-a

midnight medianoche m**a**yd-ya
n**o**chay

an hour una hora **oo**na **o**ra

a minute un minuto oon
meen**oo**to

two minutes dos minutos doss
meen**oo**toss

a second un segundo oon
seg**oo**ndo

a quarter of an hour un cuarto
de hora kw**a**rto day **o**ra

half an hour media hora
m**a**yd-ya **o**ra

three quarters of an hour
tres cuartos de hora tress
kw**a**rtoss day **o**ra

Numbers

0 cero th**a**iro

1 uno, una **oo**no, **oo**na

2 dos doss

3 tres tress

4 cuatro kw**a**tro

5 cinco th**ee**nko

6 seis say-eess

7 siete s-y**ay**tay

8 ocho **o**cho

9 nueve nw**ay**bay

10 diez d-yeth

11 once **o**nthay

12 doce d**o**thay

13 trece tr**ay**thay

14 catorce kat**o**rthay

15 quince k**ee**nthay

16 dieciséis d-yethees**ay**-eess

17 diecisiete d-yethees-y**ay**tay

18 dieciocho d-yethee-**o**cho

19 diecinueve d-yetheenw**ay**bay

20 veinte ba**y-ee**ntay

21 veintiuno bay-eentee-**oo**no

22 veintidós bay-eented**o**ss

23 veintitrés bay-eentetr**e**ss

30 treinta tr**ay-ee**nta

31 treinta y uno tr**ay-ee**ntī **oo**no

40 cuarenta kwar**e**nta

50 cincuenta theenkw**e**nta

60 sesenta ses**e**nta

70 setenta setenta

80 ochenta ochenta

90 noventa nobenta

100 cien th-yen

120 ciento veinte th-yento bay-eentay

200 doscientos, doscientas dosth-yentoss, dosth-yentass

300 trescientos, trescientas tresth-yentoss, tresth-yentass

400 cuatrocientos, cuatrocientas kwatroth-yentoss, kwatroth-yentass

500 quinientos, quinientas keen-yentoss, keen-yentass

600 seiscientos, seiscientas say-eesth-yentoss, say-eesth-yentass

700 setecientos, setecientas seteth-yentoss, seteth-yentass

800 ochocientos, ochocientas ochoth-yentoss, ochoth-yentass

900 novecientos, novecientas nobeth-yentoss, nobeth-yentass

1,000 mil meel

2,000 dos mil doss meel

5,000 cinco mil theenko meel

10,000 diez mil d-yeth meel

1,000,000 un millón meel-yon

When uno is used with a masculine noun, the final -o is dropped:

one car un coche oon kochay

una is used with feminine nouns:

one bike una bicicleta oona beetheeklayta

With multiples of a hundred, the -as ending is used with feminine nouns:

300 men trescientos hombres tresth-yentoss ombress

500 women quinientas mujeres keen-yentass mooHairess

Ordinals

1st primero preemairo

2nd segundo segoondo

3rd tercero tairthairo

4th cuarto kwarto

5th quinto keento

6th sexto sesto

7th séptimo septeemo

8th octavo oktabo

9th noveno nobayno

10th décimo detheemo

Regional accents

Castilian Spanish is spoken all over Spain and is regarded by many as standard Spanish. You may also hear (and see signs in) three other official languages. Catalan is spoken in Catalunya (the region around Barcelona) and, with some variations, in Valencia and the Balearic Islands. In Euskadi, the Basque country in northeast Spain, you may hear Basque, and in the northwest of Spain, north of Portugal, you may hear people speaking Galician. But you needn't worry about not being understood: speakers of all of these languages will also speak standard Spanish.

① Madrid
② Around Madrid
③ Castilla-La Mancha & Extremadura
④ Andalucía
⑤ Castilla y León & La Rioja
⑥ Euskal Herria
⑦ Cantabria & Asturias
⑧ Galicia
⑨ Aragon
⑩ Barcelona
⑪ Catalunya
⑫ Valencia & Murcia
⑬ The Balearic Islands

By and large, central, southern and northern Spain (including the Balearics) speak Castilian Spanish, but pronunciation can vary depending on what part of the country you're travelling in. The southern regions of Andalucía, Murcia and Extremadura, plus the Canary Islands, show the most noticeable variations. The key differences are outlined below, and examples are given, region-by-region, in the table that follows.

• The dropping of d and t at the end of a word is common all over Spain. For instance, Madrid is more often than not pronounced madree and felicidad feleetheeda.

	z and c before e and i		s becomes th
	cien	zero	salida
Andalucía	s-yen	sairo	thaleeda
Aragón, Asturias, Balearic Islands, Cantabria, Castilla-La Mancha, Castilla y León, Catalunya, Euskadi (Basque Country), Galicia, La Rioja, Madrid, Valencia	th-yen	thairo	saleeda
Canary Islands	s-yen	sairo	saleeda
Extremadura	s-yen	sairo	saleeda
Murcia	s-yen	sairo	saleeda

- In southern Spain, in Andalucía, Murcia, Extremadura and the Canary Islands, all final consonants may be dropped. So you may hear las niñas pronounced not las neen-yas but la neen-ya or arroz not as arroth but arro.

- It's also common in southern Spain for the strong guttural H of Castilian Spanish (similar to the ch in Scots loch) to be pronounced as a simple h and for a th sound to become an s.

g and j before a, e and i		r and s before a consonant		l before a consonant
gente	jamón	carne	España	algo
hentay	hamon	ka-nay, kan-nay	ep-pan-ya, eh-pan-ya	argo
Hentay	Hamon	karnay	espan-ya	algo
hentay	hamon	ka-nay, kan-nay	ep-pan-ya, eh-pan-ya	algo
Hentay	Hamon	ka-nay, kan-nay	ep-pan-ya, eh-pan-ya	algo
Hentay	Hamon	karnay	espan-ya	algo

SCENARIOS

Download these scenarios as MP3s from
www.roughguides.com/phrasebooks

1. Accommodation

▶ Is there an inexpensive hotel you can recommend?
¿Puede recomendarme un hotel que no sea caro?
pwayday rekomendarmay oon otel kay no say-a karo

▶▶ I'm sorry, they all seem to be fully booked.
Lo siento, parece que todos están completos.
lo s-yento parethay kay todoss estan komplaytoss

▶ Can you give me the name of a good middle-range hotel?
¿Puede decirme un hotel de precio normal?
pwayday detheermay un otel day preth-yo normal

▶▶ Let me have a look, do you want to be in the centre?
Déjeme un momento que mire ¿Prefiere estar en el centro?
dayHaymay oon momento kay meeray pref-yeray estar en el thentro

▶ If possible.
Si es posible.
see ess posseeblay

▶▶ Do you mind being a little way out of town?
¿Le importa estar un poco lejos del centro?
lay eemporta estar oon poko layHoss del thentro

▶ Not too far out.
No demasiado lejos.
no demass-yado layHoss

▶ Where is it on the map?
¿Dónde está en el mapa?
donday esta en el mapa

▶ Can you write the name and address down?
¿Puede escribir el nombre y la dirección?
pwayday eskreebeer el nombray ee la deerekth-yon

▶ I'm looking for a room in a private house.
Estoy buscando una habitación en una casa privada.
estoy booskando oona abeetath-yon en oona kassa preebada

2. Banks

bank account	la cuenta bancaria	kwenta bankar-ya
to change money	cambiar dinero	kamb-yar deenairo
cheque	el cheque	chaykay
to deposit	ingresar	eengressar
euro	el euro	**ay**-ooro
pin number	el pin	peen
pound	la libra	leebra
to withdraw	retirar	reteerar

▶ Can you change this into euros?
¿Puede cambiarme esto a euros?
pwayday kamb-yarmay esto a ay-ooross

> ▶▶ How would you like the money?
> ¿Cómo prefiere el dinero?
> komo pref-yairay el deenairo

▶ Small notes.
Billetes pequeños.
bee-yaytayss pekayn-yoss

▶ Big notes.
Billetes grandes.
bee-yaytayss grandayss

▶ Do you have information in English about opening an account?
¿Tiene información en inglés sobre cómo abrir una cuenta?
t-yaynay eenformath-yon en eenglayss sobray komo abreer oona kwenta

> ▶▶ Yes, what sort of account do you want?
> Sí ¿Qué tipo de cuenta quiere?
> see kay teepo day kwenta k-yayray

▶ I'd like a current account.
Quisiera una cuenta corriente.
keess-yaira oona kwenta korr-yentay

> ▶▶ Your passport, please.
> Permítame su pasaporte, por favor.
> pairmeetamay soo passaportay por fabor

▶ Can I use this card to draw some cash?
¿Puedo sacar dinero con esta tarjeta?
pwaydo sakar deenairo kon esta tarHayta

> ▶▶ You have to go to the cashier's desk.
> Tiene que ir al mostrador de caja.
> t-yaynay kay eer al mostrador day kaHa

▶ I want to transfer this to my account at the Banco Santander.
Quisiera enviar esto a mi cuenta en el Banco Santander.
keess-yaira emb-yar esto a mee kwenta en el banko santandair

▶▶ OK, but we'll have to charge you for the phonecall.
De acuerdo, pero tendremos que cobrarle la llamada.
day akwairdo pairo tendraymoss kay kobrarlay la yamada

3. Booking a room

shower	la ducha	doocha
telephone in	teléfono en	telayfono en
the room	el cuarto	el kwarto
payphone in	teléfono público en	telayfono poobleeko en
the lobby	el vestíbulo	el baysssteeboolo

▶ Do you have any rooms?
¿Tiene habitaciones libres?
t-yaynay abeetath-yonayss leebrayss

▶▶ For how many people?
¿Para cuántas personas?
para kwantass pairsonass

▶ For one/for two.
Para una/para dos.
para oona/para doss

▶▶ Yes, we have rooms.
Sí, tenemos habitaciones libres.
see tenaymoss abeetath-yonayss leebrayss

▶▶ For how many nights?
¿Para cuántas noches?
para kwantass nochayss

▶ Just for one night.
Sólo para una noche.
solo para oona nochay

▶ How much is it?
¿Cuánto es?
kwanto ess

▶▶ 90 euros with bathroom and 70 euros without bathroom.
90 euros con baño y 70 sin baño.
nobenta ay-ooross kon ban-yo ee setenta seen ban-yo

▶ Does that include breakfast?
¿Está incluido el desayuno?
esta eenkl-**wee**do el desa-**yoo**no

▶ Can I see a room with bathroom?
¿Puedo ver una habitación con baño?
pw**ay**do bair **oo**na abeetath-y**o**n kon b**a**n-yo

▶ OK, I'll take it.
Vale, me la quedo.
b**a**lay may la k**ay**do

▶ When do I have to check out?
¿Cuándo tengo que salir?
kw**a**ndo t**e**ngo kay sal**ee**r

▶ Is there anywhere I can leave luggage?
¿Puedo dejar el equipaje en algún sitio?
pw**ay**do dayHar el ekeepa**H**ay en alg**oo**n s**ee**t-yo

4. Car hire

automatic	automático	owtomateeko
full tank	depósito lleno	deposeeto yayno
manual	manual	manwal
rented car	el coche alquilado	kochay alkeelado

▶ I'd like to rent a car.
Quisiera alquilar un coche.
kees-yaira alkeelar oon kochay

▶▶ For how long?
¿Para cuánto tiempo?
para kwanto t-yempo

▶ Two days.
Dos días.
doss dee-ass

▶ I'll take the...
Me llevo el...
may yaybo el...

▶ Is that with unlimited mileage?
¿Es sin límite de kilómetros?
ess seen leemeetay day keelometross

▶▶ Yes.
Sí.
see

▶▶ Can I see your driving licence please?
¿Me permite su carnet de conducir?
may pairmeetay soo karnay day kondootheer

▶▶ And your passport.
Y su pasaporte.
soo pasaportay

▶ Is insurance included?
¿Está incluido el seguro?
esta eenkl-weedo el segooro

▶▶ Yes, but you have to pay the first 100 euros.
Sí, pero usted tendría que pagar los primeros cien euros.
see pairo oostay tendree-a kay pagar loss preemaiross th-yen ay-ooross

▶▶ Can you leave a deposit of 100 euros?
¿Puede dejar una fianza de cien euros?
pwayday dayнar oona fee-antha day th-yen ay-ooross

▶ And if this office is closed, where do I leave the keys?
Y si esta oficina está cerrada, ¿dónde dejo las llaves?
ee see esta ofeetheena esta thairrada donday dayнo lass yabayss

▶▶ You drop them in that box.
Las pone en esa caja.
lass ponay en aysa kaнa

5. Car problems

brakes	los frenos	fraynoss
to break down	tener una avería	tenair oona abairee-a
clutch	el embrague	embragay
diesel	gas-oil	gas-oyl
flat battery	una batería descargada	batairee-a deskargada
flat tyre	una rueda pinchada	rwayda peenchada
petrol	la gasolina	gasoleena

▶ Excuse me, where is the nearest petrol station?
Perdone, ¿dónde está la gasolinera más cercana?
pairdonay donday esta la gasoleenaira mass thairkana

▶▶ In the next town, about 5km away.
En el próximo pueblo, a unos cinco kilómetros.
en el proxeemo pweblo a oonoss theenko keelometross

▶ The car has broken down.
Se me ha averiado el coche.
say may a abair-yado el kochay

▶▶ Can you tell me what happened?
¿Puede decirme que ha pasado?
pwayday detheermay kay a pasado

▶ I've got a flat tyre.
Tengo una rueda pinchada.
tengo oona rwayda peenchada

▶ I think the battery is flat.
Creo que se ha descargado la batería.
kray-o kay say a deskargado la batairee-a

▶▶ Can you tell me exactly where you are?
¿Puede decirme dónde está exactamente?
pwayday detheermay donday esta exaktamentay

▶ I'm about 2km from the border on the A5.
Estoy a unos dos kilómetros de la frontera en la A5.
estoy a oonoss doss keelometross day la frontaira en la a theenko

▶▶ What type of car? What colour?
¿Qué tipo de coche? ¿Qué color?
kay teepo day kochay, kay kolor

▶ Can you send a tow truck?
¿Puede enviar una grúa?
pwayday emb-yar oona groo-a

6. Children

baby	el bebé	baybay
boy	el niño	neen-yo
child	el chico/la chica	cheeko/cheeka
children	los niños/las niñas	neen-yoss/neen-yass
cot	una cuna	koona
formula	la leche en polvo para bebés	lechay en polbo para baybayss
girl	la niña	neen-ya
highchair	una poltrona	poltrona
nappies (diapers)	los pañales	pan-yaless

▶ We need a babysitter for tomorrow evening.
Necesitamos un canguro para mañana.
netheseetamoss oon kangooro para man-yana

▶▶ For what time?
¿Para qué hora?
para kay ora

▶ From 7.30 to 11.00.
De siete y media a once.
day s-yaytay ee mayd-ya a onthay

▶▶ How many children? How old are they?
¿Cuántos niños? ¿Cuántos años tienen?
kwantoss neen-yoss, kwantoss an-yoss t-yaynen

▶ Two children, aged four and eighteen months.
Dos niños, de cuatro y dieciocho meses.
dos neen-yoss day kwatro ee d-yethee-ocho may-sess

▶ Where can I change the baby?
¿Dónde puedo cambiar al bebé?
donday pwaydo kamb-yar al bay-bay

▶ Could you please warm this bottle for me?
¿Me puede calentar este biberón, por favor?
may pwayday kalentar estay beebairon por fabor

▶ Can you give us a child's portion?
¿Puede traernos una ración para niños?
pwayday tra-airnoss oona rath-yon para neen-yoss

▶ We need two child seats.
Necesitamos dos asientos para niños.
netheseetamoss doss see-yass para neen-yoss

▶ Is there a discount for children?
¿Hay descuentos para niños?
i deskwentoss para neen-yoss

7. Communications: Internet

@	arroba	arroba
at sign	la arroba	arroba
computer	un ordenador	ordenador
email	un email	ee-mayl
Internet	Internet	eentairnet
keyboard	el teclado	teklado
mouse	el ratón	raton

▶ Is there somewhere I can check my emails?
¿Puedo leer mis emails en algún sitio?
pwaydo lay-air meess ee-mayls en algoon seet-yo

▶ Do you have Wi-Fi?
¿Tiene wifi?
t-yaynay weefee

▶ Is there an Internet café around here?
¿Hay por aquí un cyber-café?
ī por ak**ee** oon the**e**bair-kaf**ay**

>> Yes, there's one in the shopping centre.
Sí, hay uno en el centro comercial.
see ī **oo**no en el th**e**ntro komairth-y**al**

>> Do you want fifteen minutes, thirty minutes or one hour?
¿Quiere quince minutos, treinta minutos o una hora?
k-y**ai**ray k**ee**nthay meen**oo**toss tr**ay**-e**e**nta meen**oo**toss o **oo**na **o**ra

▶ Thirty minutes, please. Can you help me log on?
Treinta minutos, por favor. ¿Puede ayudarme a conectarme?
tr**ay**-e**e**nta meen**oo**toss por fab**or** pw**ay**day ayood**ar**may a konekt**ar**may

>> OK, here's your password.
Muy bien, aquí tiene su contraseña.
mwee b-yen ak**ee** t-y**ay**nay soo kontras**en**-ya

▶ Can you change this to an English keyboard?
¿Se puede cambiar a teclado inglés?
say pw**ay**day kamb-y**ar** a tekl**a**do eengl**ay**ss

▶ I'll take another quarter of an hour.
¿Puedo estar conectado otro cuarto de hora?
pw**ay**do estar konekt**a**do **o**tro kw**ar**to day **o**ra

▶ Is there a printer I can use?
¿Tiene impresora?
t-y**ay**nay eempres**o**ra

8. Communications: phones

mobile phone (cell phone)	un teléfono móvil	tel**ay**fono m**o**beel
payphone	un teléfono público	tel**ay**fono p**oo**bleeko
phone call	una llamada telefónica	yam**a**da telef**o**neeka
phone card	una tarjeta telefónica	tarH**ay**ta telef**o**neeka
phone charger	un cargador	kargad**or**
SIM card	una tarjeta SIM	tarH**ay**ta seem

▶ Can I call abroad from here?
¿Puedo llamar al extranjero desde aquí?
pw**ay**do yam**ar** al extranH**ai**ro d**e**sday ak**ee**

▶ How do I get an outside line?
¿Me da línea por favor?
may da leenay-a por fabor

▶ What's the code to call the UK/US from here?
¿Cuál es el código para llamar al Reino Unido/a los Estados Unidos?
kwal es el kodeego para yamar al ray-eeno ooneedo/a loss estadoss ooneedoss

▶ Hello, can I speak to Mr Martinez?
Hola, ¿puedo hablar con el señor Martínez?
ola pwaydo ablar kon el sen-yor marteeneth

▶▶ Yes, that's me speaking.
Sí, soy yo.
see soy yo

▶ Do you have a charger for this?
¿Tiene cargador para esto?
t-yaynay kargador para esto

▶ Can I buy a SIM card for this phone?
¿Puedo comprar una tarjeta SIM para este teléfono?
pwaydo komprar oona tarHayta seem para estay telayfono

zero	cero	thairo
one	uno	oono
two	dos	doss
three	tres	tress
four	cuatro	kwatro
five	cinco	theenko
six	seis	say-eess
seven	siete	s-yaytay
eight	ocho	ocho
nine	nueve	nwaybay

9. Directions

▶ Hi, I'm looking for Calle Real.
Hola, estoy buscando la Calle Real.
ola estoy booskando la ka-yay ray-al

▶▶ Sorry, never heard of it.
Lo siento, nunca he oído hablar de ella.
lo s-yento noonka ay oeedo ablar day ay-ya

▶ Hi, can you tell me where Calle Real is?
Hola, ¿puede decirme dónde está la Calle Real?
ola pwayday detheermay donday esta la ka-yay ray-al

▶▶ I'm a stranger here too.
Yo tampoco soy de aquí.
yo tampoko soy day akee

▶ Hi – Calle Real, do you know where it is?
Hola – la Calle Real, ¿sabe dónde está?
ola la ka-yay ray-al sabay donday esta

on the right	a la derecha	a la dairaycha
over there	allí	a-**yee**
back	atrás	atrass
street	calle	ka-yay
near	cerca	thairka
in front of	delante de	daylantay day
opposite	en frente de	en frentay day
turn off	gire	hee-ray
just after	justo después	Hoosto despwess
further	más allá	mass a-ya
past the...	pasado el...	passado el...
next	siguiente	seeg-yentay
straight ahead	todo recto	todo rekto
on the left	a la izquierda	a la eethk-yairda

▶ Where?
¿Dónde?
donday

▶ Which direction?
¿Por dónde?
por donday

▶▶ Left at the second traffic lights.
La izquierda en el segundo semáforo.
la eethk-yairda en el segoondo semaforo

▶▶ Around the corner.
La vuelta de la esquina.
la bwelta day la eskeena

▶▶ Then it's the first street on the right.
Luego es la primera calle a la derecha.
lwaygo ess la preemaira ka-yay a la dairaycha

10. Emergencies

accident	el accidente	aktheedentay
ambulance	la ambulancia	amboolanth-ya
consul	el cónsul	konsool
embassy	la embajada	embaHada
fire brigade	los bomberos	bombaiross
police	la policía	poleethee-a

▶ Help!
¡Socorro!
sokorro

▶ Can you help me?
¿Puede ayudarme?
pwayday ayoodarmay

▶ Please come with me! It's really very urgent.
¡Por favor, venga conmigo! Es de verdad muy urgente.
por fabor baynga konmeego, ess day bairda mwee oorHayntay

▶ I've lost my keys.
He perdido las llaves.
ay pairdeedo lass yabayss

▶ My car is not working.
Mi coche no funciona.
mee kochay no foonth-yona

▶ My purse has been stolen.
Me han robado el monedero.
may an robado el monedairo

▶ I've been mugged.
Me han robado.
may an robado

>> ▶▶ What's your name?
¿Cómo se llama?
komo say yama

>> ▶▶ I need to see your passport.
¿Me permite su pasaporte?
may pairmeetay soo pasaportay

▶ I'm sorry, all my papers have been stolen.
Lo siento, me han robado todos los documentos.
lo s-yento may an robado todoss loss dokoomayntoss

11. Friends

▶ Hi, how're you doing?
Hola, ¿qué tal?
ola kay tal

>> ▶▶ OK, and you?
Muy bien, ¿y tú?
mwee b-yen ee too

▶ Yeah, fine.
Pues bien.
pwess b-yen

▶ Not bad.
No estoy mal.
no estoy mal

▶ D'you know Antonio?
¿Conoces a Antonio?
konothayss a antonio

▶ And this is Marta.
Y ésta es Marta.
ee esta ess marta

▶▶ Yeah, we know each other
Sí, ya nos conocemos.
see ya noss konothaymoss

▶ Where do you know each other from?
¿De qué os conocéis?
day kay oss konothay-eess

▶▶ We met at Gonzalo's place.
Nos conocimos en casa de Gonzalo.
noss konotheemoss en kasa day gonthalo

▶ That was some party, eh?
Menuda fiesta, ¿eh?
maynooda fee-aysta ay

▶▶ The best.
Genial.
Hayn-ya**l**

▶ Are you guys coming for a beer?
¿Venís a tomar una cerveza?
bayn**ee**ss a tomar **oo**na thairb**ay**tha

▶▶ Cool, let's go.
Estupendo, vamos.
estoop**e**ndo b**a**moss

▶▶ No, I'm meeting Lola.
No, he quedado con Lola.
No ay kayd**a**do kon l**o**la

▶ See you at Gonzalo's place tonight.
Nos vemos esta noche en casa de Gonzalo.
noss b**ay**moss esta n**o**chay en k**a**sa day gonth**a**lo

▶▶ See you.
Hasta luego.
asta lw**ay**go

12. Health

antibiotics	el antibiótico	anteeb-**yo**teeko
antiseptic	la pomada	pom**a**da
ointment	antiséptica	anteess**ay**pteeka
cystitis	la cystitis	thees**tee**teess
dentist	el dentista	dent**ee**sta
diarrhoea	la diarrea	d-yarr**ay**-a
doctor	el médico	m**ay**deeko
hospital	el hospital	osp**ee**tal
ill	enfermo	enf**ai**rmo
medicine	la medicina	medeeth**ee**na
painkillers	analgésicos	anal**H**ay**seekoss
pharmacy	la farmacia	farm**a**th-ya
to prescribe	recetar	reth**ay**tar
thrush	las aftas	**a**ftass

▶ I'm not feeling very well.
No me siento bien.
no may s-y**e**nto b-yen

▶ Can you get a doctor?
¿Puede llamar a un médico?
pwayday yamar a oon maydeeko

>> Where does it hurt?
¿Dónde le duele?
donday lay dwaylay

▶ It hurts here.
Me duele aquí.
may dwaylay akee

>> Is the pain constant?
¿Es un dolor constante?
ess oon dolor konstantay

▶ It's not a constant pain.
No es un dolor constante.
no ess oon dolor konstantay

▶ Can I make an appointment?
¿Puedo pedir cita?
pwaydo pedeer theeta

▶ Can you give me something for…?
¿Puede darme algo para…?
pwayday darmay algo para

▶ Yes, I have insurance.
Sí, tengo seguro.
see tengo segooro

13. Hotels

maid	la camarera	kamaraira
manager	el director/	deerektor/
	la directora	deerektora
room service	el servicio de	sairbeeth-yo day
	habitación	abeetath-yon

▶ Hello, we've booked a double room in the name of Cameron.
Hola, hemos reservado una habitación doble a nombre de Cameron.
ola aymoss resairbado oona abeetath-yon doblay a nombray de cameron

▶▶ That was for four nights, wasn't it?
Eran cuatro noches, ¿verdad?
aíran kwatro nochess bairda

▶ Yes, we're leaving on Saturday.
Sí, nos vamos el sábado.
see noss bamoss el sabado

▶▶ Can I see your passport, please?
¿Puede enseñarme el pasaporte, por favor?
pwayday ensen-yarmay el pasaportay por fabor

▶▶ There you are, room 10, on the first floor.
Aquí tiene, habitación 10, en la planta primera.
akee t-yaynay abitath-yon d-yeth en la planta preemaira

▶ I can't get this keycard to work.
No sé cómo funciona esta llave.
no say komo foonth-yona esta yabay

▶▶ Sorry, I need to reactivate it.
Lo siento, tengo que reactivarla.
lo s-yento tengo kay ray-akteebarla

▶ What time is breakfast?
¿A qué hora es el desayuno?
a kay ora ess el desa-yoono

▶ There aren't any towels in my room.
No hay toallas en mi habitación.
no ī to-a-yass en mee abeetath-yon

▶ My flight isn't until this evening, can I keep the room a bit longer?
Mi vuelo no es hasta la tarde ¿Puedo quedarme en la habitación un poco más?
mee bwaylo no ess asta la tarday, pwaydo kaydarmay en la abeetath-yon oon poko mass

▶ Can I settle up? Is this card OK?
¿Puedo pagar? ¿Puedo pagar con esta tarjeta?
pwaydo pagar, pwaydo pagar kon esta tarHayta

14. Language difficulties

a few words	unas palabras	**oo**nass palabrass
interpreter	el intérprete	eent**ai**rpraytay
to translate	traducir	tradoo**thee**r

▶▶ Your credit card has been refused.
Le han rechazado la tarjeta de crédito.
lay an rechathado la tarHayta day kraydeeto

▶ What, I don't understand; do you speak English?
¿Cómo? No comprendo ¿Habla usted inglés?
komo no komprendo abla oostay eenglayss

▶▶ This isn't valid.
Esto no es válido.
esto no ess baleedo

▶ Could you say that again?
¿Puede repetir?
pwayday repeteer

▶ Slowly.
Despacio.
despath-yo

▶ I understand very little Spanish.
Comprendo muy poco español.
komprendo mwee poko espan-yol

▶ I speak Spanish very badly.
Hablo español muy mal.
ablo espan-yol mwee mal

▶▶ You can't use this card to pay.
No puede pagar con esta tarjeta.
no pwayday pagar kon esta tarHayta

▶▶ Do you understand?
¿Comprende?
komprenday

▶ Sorry, no.
No, lo siento.
no lo s-yento

▶ Is there someone who speaks English?
¿Hay alguien que hable inglés?
ī alg-yen kay ablay eenglayss

▶ Oh, now I understand.
Ah, ahora comprendo.
ah a-ora komprendo

▶▶ Is that OK now?
¿Está todo bien ya?
esta todo b-yen ya

15. Meeting people

▶ Hello.
Hola.
ola

    ▶▶ Hello, my name's Blanca.
    Hola, me llamo Blanca.
    ola may yamo blanka

▶ Graham, from England, Thirsk.
Soy Graham, de Thirsk, Inglaterra.
soy graham day thirsk eenglatairra

    ▶▶ Don't know that, where is it?
    No lo conozco, ¿dónde está?
    no lo konothko donday esta

▶ Not far from York, in the north; and you?
No lejos de York, en el norte, ¿y usted?
no layHoss day york en el nortay ee oostay

    ▶▶ I'm from Salamanca; here by yourself?
    Soy de Salamanca, ¿está aquí solo?
    soy day salamanka esta akee solo

▶ No, I'm with my wife and two kids.
No, estoy con mi mujer y mis dos hijos.
no estoy kon mee mooHair ee meess doss eeHoss

▶ What do you do?
¿A qué se dedica?
a kay say daydeeka

    ▶▶ I'm in computers
    A la informática
    a la eenformateeka

▶ Me too.
Yo también.
yo tamb-yen

▶ Here's my wife now.
Aquí está mi mujer.
akee esta mee mooHair

    ▶▶ Nice to meet you.
    Encantada de conocerla.
    enkantada day konothairla

16. Nightlife

heavy metal	el heavy metal	**hay**bee **may**tal
folk	la música folk	**moo**seeka folk
jazz	el jazz	jazz
hip-hop	el hip-hop	hip-hop
electro	la música electronica	**moo**seeka elektro**nee**ka
rock	el rock	rok
dancing	bailar	ba-ee**lar**

▶ What's a good club for...?
¿Puedes decirme una buena discoteca para...?
pw**ay**dess deth**eer**may **oo**na bw**ay**na deeskot**ay**ka para

▶▶ There's going to be a great gig at the square
tomorrow night.
Va a haber un buen concierto en la plaza mañana por la
noche.
ba a ab**air** oon bwen konth-y**air**to en la pl**a**tha man-y**a**na por la n**o**chay

▶ Where can I hear some local music?
¿Dónde se puede escuchar música de aquí?
d**o**nday say pw**ay**day eskoch**ar** m**oo**seeka day ak**ee**

▶ Can you write down the names of the best bars around here?
¿Puedes escribirme los nombres de los mejores bares de por aquí?
pwaydess eskreebeermay loss nombress day loss meHoress baress day por akee?

>> That depends what you're looking for.
Eso depende de lo que busques.
eso dependay day lo kay booskess

▶ The place where the locals go.
Donde vaya la gente de aquí.
donday ba-ya la Hentay day akee

▶ A place for a quiet drink.
Un lugar tranquilo para beber algo.
oon loogar trankeelo para bebair algo

>> The casino across the bay is very good.
El casino al otro lado de la bahía está muy bien.
el kaseeno al otro lado day la ba-ee-a esta mwee b-yen

▶ Is there a dress code?
¿Hay que ir vestido formal?
ī kay eer besteedo formal

>> You can wear what you like.
Puedes vestir como quieras.
pwaydess besteer komo k-yairass

▶ What time does it close?
¿A qué hora cierra?
a kay ora th-yairra

17. Post offices

airmail	correo aéreo	korray-o a-airay-o
post card	la postal	postal
post office	Correos	korray-oss
stamp	el sello	say-yo

▶ What time does the post office close?
¿A qué hora cierra Correos?
a kay ora th-yaira korray-oss

>> Five o'clock weekdays.
A las cinco entre semana.
a lass theenko entray semana

▶ Is the post office open on Saturdays?
¿Correos abre los sábados?
korray-oss abray loss sabadoss

CARTAS	letters
PAQUETES	parcels
LISTA DE	poste
CORREOS	restante

▶▶ Until midday.
Hasta mediodía.
asta med-yodee-a

▶ I'd like to send this registered to England.
Quisiera enviar esto certificado a Inglaterra.
kees-yaira emb-yar esto thairteefeekado a eenglatairra

▶▶ Certainly, that will cost 10 euros.
Sí, claro, van a ser 10 euros.
see klaro ban a sair d-yeth ay-ooross

▶ And also two stamps for England, please.
Y también dos sellos para Inglaterra, por favor.
ee tamb-yen doss say-yoss para eenglatairra por fabor

▶ Do you have some airmail stickers?
¿Tiene pegatinas de correo aéreo?
t-yaynay pegateenass day korray-o a-airay-o

▶ Do you have any mail for me?
¿Tiene correo para mí?
t-yaynay korray-o para mee

18. Restaurants

bill	la cuenta	kwenta
menu	el menú	menoo
table	la mesa	maysa

▶ Can we have a non-smoking table?
¿Nos da una mesa de no fumadores?
noss da oona maysa day no foomadorayss

▶ There are two of us.
Somos dos.
Somoss doss

▶ There are four of us.
Somos cuatro.
Somoss kwatro

▶ What's this?
¿Qué es esto?
kay ess **e**sto

>> It's a type of fish.
Es pescado.
ess pesk**a**do

>> It's a local speciality.
Es una especialidad de la zona.
ess **oo**na espeth-yaleed**a** day la th**o**na

>> Come inside and I'll show you.
Entre y se lo enseño.
entray ee say lo ens**ay**n-yo

▶ We would like two of these, one of these and one of those.
Queremos dos de éstos, uno de éstos y uno de aquéllos.
kair**ay**moss doss day **e**stoss **oo**no day **e**stoss ee **oo**no day ak**ay**-yoss

>> And to drink?
¿Y para beber?
ee p**a**ra beb**ai**r

▶ Red wine.   ▶ White wine.
Vino tinto.   Vino blanco.
b**ee**no t**ee**nto   b**ee**no bl**a**nko

▶ A beer and two orange juices.
Una cerveza y dos zumos de naranja.
oona thairb**ay**tha ee doss th**oo**moss day nar**a**nнa

▶ Some more bread please.
Un poco más de pan, por favor.
oon p**o**ko mass day pan por fab**o**r

>> How was your meal?
¿Les ha gustado la comida?
layss a goost**a**do la kom**ee**da

▶ Excellent, very nice!
¡Estaba estupenda! ¡muy buena!
est**a**ba estoop**ay**nda mwee bw**ay**na

>> Anything else?
¿Algo más?
algo mass

▶ Just the bill thanks.
Sólo la cuenta, gracias.
s**o**lo la kw**e**nta gr**a**th-yass

19. Self-catering accommodation

air-conditioning	el aire acondicionado	**a-ee**ray akondeeth-yonado
apartment	el apartamento	apartam**e**nto
cooker	la cocina	koth**ee**na
fridge	el frigorífico	freegor**ee**feeko
heating	la calefacción	kalefakth-**yo**n
hot water	agua caliente	**a**gwa kal-**ye**ntay
lightbulb	una bombilla	bomb**ee**-ya
toilet	el baño	ban-yo

▶ The toilet's broken, can you get someone to fix it?
El baño está roto, ¿puede venir alguien a arreglarlo?
el ban-yo esta roto p**way**day bayneer **a**lg-yen a arreglarlo

▶ There's no hot water.
No hay agua caliente.
no ī **a**gwa kal-**ye**ntay

▶ Can you show me how the air-conditioning works?
¿Puede enseñarme cómo funciona el aire acondicionado?
p**way**day ensen-y**a**rmay k**o**mo foonth-y**o**na el **a**-eeray akondeeth-yon**a**do

▶▶ OK, what apartment are you in?
Vale, ¿en qué apartamento está?
b**a**lay en kay apartam**e**nto esta

▶ We're in number five.
Estamos en el número cinco.
estam**o**ss en el n**oo**mairo th**ee**enko

▶ Can you move us to a quieter apartment?
¿Puede mudarnos a otro apartamento menos ruidoso?
p**way**day moodarnoss a **o**tro apartam**e**nto m**a**ynoss rw**ee**doso

▶ Is there a supermarket nearby?
¿Hay un supermercado cerca?
ī oon soopairmairk**a**do th**a**irka

▶▶ Have you enjoyed your stay?
¿Lo han pasado bien?
lo an pas**a**do b-yen

▶ Brilliant holiday, thanks!
Unas vacaciones estupendas, ¡gracias!
oonass bakath-**yo**ness estoop**e**ndass gr**a**th-yass

20. Shopping

▶▶ Can I help you?
¿En qué puedo servirle?
en kay pwaydo sairbeerlay

▶ Can I just have a look around?
¿Puedo echar sólo un vistazo?
pwaydo echar solo oon beestatho

▶ Yes, I'm looking for…
Sí, estoy buscando…
see estoy booskando

CAJA	cash desk
CERRADO	closed
CAMBIAR	to exchange
ABIERTO	open
REBAJAS	sale

▶ How much is this?
¿Cuánto es esto?
kwanto ess esto

▶▶ Thirty-two euros.
Treinta y dos euros.
tray-eenta ee doss ay-ooross

▶ OK, I think I'll have to leave it; it's a little too expensive for me.
Vale, creo que tendré que dejarlo; es demasiado caro para mí.
balay kray-o kay tendray kay deHarlo ess demass-yado karo para mee

▶▶ How about this?
¿Y esto?
ee esto

▶ Can I pay by credit card?
¿Puedo pagar con tarjeta de crédito?
pwaydo pagar kon tarHayta day kraydeeto

▶ It's too big.
Es demasiado grande.
ess demass-yado granday

▶ It's too small.
Es demasiado pequeño.
ess demass-yado pekayn-yo

▶ It's for my son – he's about this high.
Es para mi hijo – es más o menos así de alto.
ess para mee eeHo ess mass o maynoss asee day alto

▶▶ Will there be anything else?
¿Va a querer algo más?
ba a kerair algo mass

▶ That's all thanks.
Eso es todo, gracias.
ayso ess todo grath-yass

▶ Make it twenty euros and I'll take it.
Si me lo pone a veinte euros me lo quedo.
see may lo ponay a bay-eentay ay-ooross may lo kaydo

▶ Fine, I'll take it.
Vale, me lo quedo.
balay may lo kaydo

21. Shopping for clothes

to alter	arreglar	arreglar
bigger	más grande	mass granday
just right	perfecto	pairfekto
smaller	más pequeño	mass peken-yo
to try on	probarse	probarsay

▶▶ Can I help you?
¿En qué puedo servirle?
en kay pwaydo sairbeerlay

▶ I'm just looking, thanks.
Gracias, sólo estoy mirando.
grath-yass solo estoy meerando

▶▶ Do you want to try that on?
¿Quiere probárselo?
k-yairay probarsaylo

▶ Yes, and I'll try this one too.
Sí, y me voy a probar esto también.
see ee may boy a probar esto tamb-yen

▶ Do you have it in a bigger size?
¿Tiene una talla más grande?
t-yaynay oona ta-ya mass granday

▶ Do you have it in a different colour?
¿Lo tiene en otro color?
lo t-yaynay en otro kolor

▶▶ That looks good on you.
Le sienta bien
lay s-yenta b-yen

▶ Can you shorten this?
¿Puede acortarme esto?
pwayday akortarmay esto

▶▶ Sure, it'll be ready on Friday, after 12.00.
Claro, estará listo el viernes después de las doce.
klaro estara leesto el b-yairness despwess day lass dothay

22. Sightseeing

art gallery	la galería de arte	galairree-a day artay
bus tour	visita en autobús	beesseeta en owtoboos
city centre	el centro	thentro
closed	cerrado	thairrado
guide	la guía	gee-a
museum	el museo	moossay-o
open	abierto	ab-yairto

▶ I'm interested in seeing the old town.
Quisiera ver el casco antiguo.
kees-yaira bair el kasko anteegwo

▶ Are there guided tours?
¿Hay visitas guiadas?
i beeseetass gee-adass

▶▶ I'm sorry, it's fully booked.
Lo siento, está completo.
lo s-yento esta komplayto

▶ How much would you charge to drive us around for four hours?
¿Cuánto nos cobraría por darnos un paseo de cuatro horas?
kwanto noss kobraree-a por darnoss oon passay-o day kwatro orass

▶ Can we book tickets for the concert here?
¿Podemos reservar aquí las entradas para el concierto?
podaymoss resairbar akee lass entradass para el konth-yairto

▶▶ Yes, in what name?   ▶▶ Which credit card?
Sí ¿A qué nombre?   ¿Qué tarjeta de crédito?
see a kay nombray   kay tarHayta day kraydeeto

▶ Where do we get the tickets?
¿Dónde nos dan las entradas?
donday noss dan lass entradass

>> ▶▶ Pick them up at the entrance.
Recójanlas a la entrada.
rekoнanlass a la entrada

▶ Is it open on Sundays?
¿Abren los domingos?
abrayn loss domeengoss

▶ How much is it to get in?
¿Cuánto cuesta entrar?
kwanto kwesta entrar

▶ Are there reductions for groups of six?
¿Hay descuentos para grupos de seis?
ī deskwentoss para grooposs day say-eess

▶ That was really impressive!
¡Ha estado genial!
a estado нen-yal

23. Taxis

▶ Can you get us a taxi?
¿Nos puede pedir un taxi?
noss pwayday pedeer oon taxi

>> ▶▶ For now? Where are you going?
¿Para ahora? ¿Adónde van?
para a-ora, adonday ban

▶ To the town centre.
Al centro.
al thentro

▶ I'd like to book a taxi to the airport for tomorrow.
Quisiera reservar un taxi para ir al aeropuerto mañana.
kees-yaira resairbar oon taxi para eer al a-airopwairto man-yana

>> ▶▶ Sure, at what time? How many people?
Por supuesto, ¿a qué hora? ¿Cuántas personas?
por soopwesto a kay ora, kwantass pairsonass

▶ How much is it to the cathedral?
¿Cuánto es hasta la catedral?
kwanto ess asta la katedral

▶ Right here is fine, thanks.
Aquí está bien, gracias.
akee esta b-yen grath-yass

▶ Can you wait here and take us back?
¿Puede esperar aquí y llevarnos de vuelta?
pwayday espairar akee ee yebarnoss day bwelta

> ▶▶ How long are you going to be?
> ¿Cuánto van a tardar?
> kwanto ban a tardar

24. Trains

to change trains	hacer transbordo	athair transbordo
platform	el andén	andayn
return	el billete de	bee-yaytay day
	ida y vuelta	eeda ee bwelta
single	el billete de ida	bee-yaytay day eeda
station	la estación	estath-yon
stop	la parada	parada
ticket	el billete	bee-yaytay

▶ How much is...?
¿Cuánto es...?
kwanto ess

▶ A single, second class to...
Un billete de ida, en clase turista a...
oon bee-yaytay day eeda en klasay tooreesta a

▶ Two returns, second class to...
Dos billetes de ida y vuelta, en clase turista a...
doss bee-yaytayss day eeda ee bwelta en klasay tooreesta a

▶ For today.   ▶ For tomorrow.
Para hoy.   Para mañana.
para oy   para man-yana

▶ For next Tuesday.
Para el próximo martes.
para el prokseemo martayss

> ▶▶ There's a supplement for the Talgo.
> El Talgo tiene suplemento.
> el talgo t-yaynay sooplemento

▶▶ Do you want to make a seat reservation?
¿Quiere reservar el asiento?
k-yairay resairbar el as-yento

▶▶ You have to change at Córdoba.
Tiene que hacer transbordo en Córdoba.
t-yaynay kay athair transbordo en kordoba

▶ Is this seat free?
¿Está libre este asiento?
esta leebray estay as-yento

▶ Excuse me, which station are we at?
Perdone, ¿en qué estación estamos?
pairdonay en kay estath-yon estamoss

▶ Is this where I change for Málaga?
¿Es aquí donde tengo que hacer transbordo para Málaga?
es akee donday tengo kay athair transbordo para malaga

ENGLISH
→ **SPANISH**

A

a, an un, *f* una oon, **oo**na

about: about 20 unos veinte

  it's about 5 o'clock son
aproximadamente las cinco
aproxeema**da**mentay

  a film about Spain una
película sobre España **so**bray

above… encima de…
en**thee**ma day

abroad en el extranjero
estran**ʜai**ro

absolutely (I agree) ¡desde luego!
desday l**way**go

accelerator el acelerador
athelai**ra**dor

accept aceptar athep**tar**

accident el accidente
akthee**den**tay

  there's been an accident ha
habido un accidente a a**bee**do

accommodation alojamiento
aloʜam-**yen**to

accurate exacto

ache el dolor

  my back aches me duele la
espalda may d**way**lay

across: across the road al otro
lado de la calle ka-**yay**

adapter el adaptador

address la dirección deerekth-**yon**

  what's your address?
¿cuál es su dirección? kwal

address book la libreta de
direcciones lee**bray**ta day
deerekth-**yon**ess

admission charge la entrada

adult el adulto

advance: in advance por
adelantado

aeroplane el avión ab-**yon**

after después (de) despw**ess** day

  after you usted primero oo**stay**
pree**mai**ro

  after lunch después del
almuerzo

afternoon la tarde **tar**day

  in the afternoon por la tarde

  this afternoon esta tarde

aftershave el aftershave

aftersun cream la crema para
después del sol k**ray**ma para
despw**ess**

afterwards después despw**ess**

again otra vez beth

against contra

age la edad ay**dath**

ago: a week ago hace una
semana **a**thay

  an hour ago hace una hora

agree: I agree estoy de acuerdo
day ak**wai**rdo

AIDS el SIDA **see**da

air el aire a-**ee**ray

  by air en avión ab-**yon**

air-conditioning el aire
acondicionado a-**ee**ray
akondeeth-yo**na**do

airmail: by airmail por avión
ab-**yon**

airmail envelope el sobre aéreo
sobray a-**ai**ray-o

airport el aeropuerto a-airopw**ai**rto

to the airport, please
al aeropuerto, por fav**o**r

airport bus el autobús del
aeropuerto owtob**oo**ss

aisle seat el asiento de pasillo
as-y**e**nto day pas**ee**-yo

alarm clock el despertador

alcohol el alcohol alko-**o**l

alcoholic alcoh**ó**lico

Algeria Argelia ar**H**aylee-a

all: all the boys t**o**dos los chicos

all the girls t**o**das las chicas

all of it t**o**do

all of them todos ellos **ay**-yoss

that's all, thanks eso es todo,
gracias **ay**so

allergic: I'm allergic to... soy
alérgico/alérgica a... ala**ír**Heeko

allowed: is it allowed?
¿est**á** permitido?

all right ¡bien! b-yen

I'm all right est**oy** bien

are you all right? (*fam*)
¿est**á**s bien?

(*pol*) ¿se encuentra bien?
say enkw**ay**ntra

almond la alm**e**ndra

almost c**a**si

alone s**o**lo

alphabet el alfab**e**to

a a	**b** bay	**c** thay
ch chay	**d** day	**e** ay
f ayfay	**g** Hay	**h** achay
i ee	**j** H**o**ta	**k** ka
l aylay	**m** aymay	**n** aynay
ñ ayn-yay	**o** o	**p** pay

q koo	**r** airray	**s** ayssay
t tay	**u** oo	**v** oobay
w oobay doblay		**x** aykeess
y ee gr-y**ay**ga		**z** thayta

already ya

also también tamb-yen

although aunque a-**oo**nkay

altogether del t**o**do

always siempre s-y**e**mpray

am: I am soy; est**oy** (*see note
on p.8*)

am: at 7 am a las siete de la
mañana day la man-y**a**na

amazing (surprising) incre**í**ble
eenkray-**ee**blay

(very good) estup**e**ndo

ambulance la ambulancia
amboolanth-ya

call an ambulance! ¡llame a una ambulancia! yamay

America América

American (*adj*) americano

I'm American (male/female) soy americano/americana

among entre entray

amount la cantidad kanteeda (money) la suma

amp: a 13-amp fuse el fusible de trece amperios fooseeblay day – ampairee-oss

amphitheatre el anfiteatro anfeetay-atro

and y ee

angry enfadado

animal el animal

ankle el tobillo tobee-yo

anniversary (wedding) el aniversario de boda aneebairsar-yo day

annoy: this man's annoying me este hombre me está molestando estay ombray may

annoying molesto

another otro

can we have another room? ¿puede darnos otra habitación? pwayday – abeetath-yon

another beer, please otra cerveza, por favor thairbaytha

antibiotics los antibióticos anteeb-yoteekoss

antifreeze el anticongelante anteekonHelantay

antihistamine el antihistamínico antee-eestameeneeko

antique: is it an antique? ¿es antiguo? anteegwo

antique shop la tienda de antigüedades t-yenda day anteegway-dadess

antiseptic el antiséptico

any: have you got any bread/ tomatoes? ¿tiene pan/ tomates? t-yaynay

do you have any change? ¿tiene cambio? kamb-yo

sorry, I don't have any lo siento, no tengo s-yento

anybody cualquiera kwalk-yaira

does anybody speak English? ¿habla alguien inglés? abla alg-yen eenglayss

there wasn't anybody there allí no había nadie a-yee no abee-a nad-yay

anything algo

apart from aparte de apartay day

apartment el apartamento, el piso

appendicitis la apendicitis apendeetheeteess

appetizer la entrada

aperitif el aperitivo aper*eeteebo*

apology la disculpa

apple la manzana man*thana*

appointment la cita *theeta*

good afternoon, sir, how can I help you? buenas tardes, señor, ¿en qué puedo servirle? *bwenass tardess, sen-yor en kay pwaydo sairbeerlay*

I'd like to make an appointment quisiera pedir hora *kees-yaira pedeer ora*

what time would you like? ¿a qué hora le viene bien? *a kay ora lay b-yaynay b-yen*

three o'clock a las tres

I'm afraid that's not possible, is four o'clock all right? me temo que no será posible, está bien a las cuatro? *may taymo kay no saira poseeblay*

yes, that will be fine sí, está bien

the name was...? ¿su nombre era...? *nombray aira*

apricot el albaricoque albari*kokay*

April abril

are: we are somos; estamos (*see note on p.8*)

you are (*fam*) eres *airess*; estás (*pol*) es; está

they are son; están

area la zona *thona*

area code el prefijo pre*feeho*

arm el brazo *bratho*

arrange: will you arrange it for us? ¿nos lo organiza usted? organ*eetha oostay*

arrival la llegada ye*gada*

arrive llegar ye*gar*

when do we arrive? ¿cuándo llegamos? *kwando yegamoss*

has my fax arrived yet? ¿ha llegado ya mi fax? *a yegado*

we arrived today llegamos hoy *yegamoss oy*

art el arte *artay*

art gallery el museo de bellas artes *moosay-o day bay-yass artess*

(*smaller*) la galería de arte galair*ee-a*

artist (*male/female*) el pintor/la pintora

as: as big as tan grande como gran*day*

as soon as possible lo antes posible *antess poseeblay*

ashtray el cenicero thaynee*thairo*

ask preguntar pregoon*tar*

I didn't ask for this no había pedido eso *abee-a – ayso*

could you ask him to...? ¿puede decirle que...? *pwayday detheerlay kay*

asleep: she's asleep está dormida

aspirin la aspirina

asthma el asma

astonishing increíble
eenkray-**ee**blay

at: at the hotel en el hotel

at the station en la estación

at six o'clock a las seis

at Pedro's en la casa de Pedro

at sign, @ la arroba

athletics el atletismo

Atlantic Ocean el Océano
Atlántico othay-ano

ATM el cajero automático
kaHairo owtomateeko

attractive guapo, atractivo
atrakt**ee**bo

aubergine la berenjena
berenH**ay**na

August agosto

aunt la tía t**ee**-a

Australia Australia owstral-ya

Australian (adj) australiano

I'm Australian (male/female)
soy australiano/australiana

automatic (car) automático
owtomateeko

automatic teller el cajero
automático kaHairo

autumn el otoño oton-yo

in the autumn en otoño

avenue la avenida abeneeda

average (not good) regular regoolar

on average por término
medio t**air**meeno m**ay**d-yo

awake: is he awake?
¿está despierto? desp-y**air**to

away: go away! ¡lárguese!
largays**ay**

is it far away? ¿está lejos?
lay**Hoss**

awful terrible terr**ee**blay

axle el eje **ay**Hay

B

baby el bebé bayb**ay**

baby food la comida de bebé day

baby's bottle el biberón
beebair**on**

> **Travel tip** Baby food,
> disposable nappies and
> formula milk are widely
> available in pharmacies and
> supermarkets, though not
> necessarily with the same
> range you're used to at
> home. Organic baby food is
> hard to find away from the
> big-city supermarkets and
> most Spanish non-organic
> baby foods contain small
> amounts of sugar or salt.

baby-sitter la niñera neen-y**ai**ra

back (of body) la espalda

(back part) la parte de atrás
partay day

at the back en la parte de
atrás

**can I have my money
back?** ¿puede devolverme el
dinero? pw**ay**day daybolb**ai**rmay
el deen**ai**ro

to come/go back volver
bolb**air**

backache el dolor de espalda day

bacon el bacon b**ay**kon,
la panceta panth**e**ta

bad malo

a bad headache un fuerte dolor de cabeza fwa**ir**tay – day kaba**y**tha

badly mal

(injured) gravemente grabema**y**ntay

bag la b**o**lsa

(handbag) el b**o**lso

(suitcase) la maleta mal**a**yta

baggage el equipaje ekeepa**h**ay

baggage check la consigna kons**ee**gna

baggage claim la recogida de equipajes reko**H**e**e**da day ekeepa**H**ess

bakery la panadería panada**ir**ee-a

balcony el balc**ó**n

a room with a balcony una habitación con balcón abeetath-y**o**n

bald calvo k**a**lbo

Balearic Islands las Baleares balay-**a**ress

ball (large) la pel**o**ta

(small) la b**o**la

ballet el ballet

banana el pl**á**tano

band (musical) la orquesta ork**e**sta

(pop) el gr**u**po

bandage la venda b**e**nda

Bandaid la tir**i**ta

bank (money) el b**a**nco

bank account la cuenta banc**a**ria kw**e**nta

bar el bar

bar of chocolate una barra de chocolate day chokol**a**tay

barber's el barbero barb**a**iro

Barcelona Barcelona bartha**y**lona

basket el cesto th**e**sto

(in shop) la c**e**sta

bath el baño ban-yo

can I have a bath? ¿puedo bañarme? pwa**y**do ban-y**a**rmay

bathroom el cuarto de baño kw**a**rto

with a private bathroom con baño privado preeb**a**do

bath towel la toalla de baño to-**a**-ya day

battery la p**i**la

(car) la batería bata**ir**ee-a

bay la bah**í**a ba-**ee**-a

Bay of Biscay el G**o**lfo de Vizcaya day beethka-ya

be ser sair; estar ayst**a**r (see note on p.8)

beach la playa pla-ya

beach mat la esterilla de playa estair**ee**-ya

beach umbrella la sombrilla sombr**ee**-ya

beans las jud**í**as **H**oodee-ass

runner beans las jud**í**as verdes ba**ir**dess

broad beans las h**a**bas **a**bass

beard la b**a**rba

beautiful bon**i**to

because porque p**o**rkay

because of... debido a... debe**e**do

bed la c**a**ma

I'm going to bed now

me voy a acostar ya may boy

bed and breakfast
habitación y desayuno
abeetath-yon ee desa-yoono

bedroom el dormitorio
dormeetor-yo

beef la carne de vaca karnay day
baka

beer la cerveza thairbaytha

two beers, please
dos cervezas, por favor

before antes antess

begin empezar empethar

when does it begin?
¿cuándo empieza?
kwando emp-yetha

beginner el/la principiante
preentheep-yantay

beginning: at the beginning
al principio preentheep-yo

behind detrás

behind me detrás de mí

beige beige bay-eess

Belgium Bélgica baylHeeka

believe creer kray-air

below abajo abaHo

belt el cinturón theentooron

bend (in road) la curva koorba

berth (on ship) el camarote
kamarotay

beside: beside the…
al lado de la…

best el mejor meHor

better mejor

are you feeling better?
¿se siente mejor? say s-yentay

between entre entray

beyond más allá a-ya

bicycle la bicicleta beetheeklayta

big grande granday

too big demasiado grande
demass-yado

it's not big enough no
es suficientemente grande
soofeeth-yentemayntay

bike la bicicleta beetheeklayta
(motorbike) la motocicleta
mototheeklayta

bikini el bikini beekeenee

bill la cuenta kwenta
(banknote) el billete bee-yaytay

**could I have the bill,
please?** la cuenta, por favor

bin el cubo de la basura
koobo day

bin liners las bolsas de basura

binding (ski) la atadura

bird el pájaro paHaro

Biro el bolígrafo

birthday el cumpleaños
koomplayan-yoss

happy birthday! ¡feliz
cumpleaños! feleeth

biscuit la galleta ga-yeta

bit: a little bit un poquito
pokeeto

a big bit un pedazo grande
pedatho granday

a bit of… un pedazo de…

a bit expensive un poco
caro

bite (by insect) la picadura
(by dog) la mordedura

bitter (taste etc) amargo

black negro n**ay**gro

blanket la manta

bleach (for toilet) la lejía le**H**ee-a

bless you! ¡Jesús! **H**ays**oo**ss

blind ciego th-y**ay**go

blinds las persianas pers-y**a**nass

blister la ampolla amp**o**-ya

blocked (road, pipe) obstruido obstrw**ee**do

(sink) atascado

block of flats el bloque de apartamentos bl**o**kay day

blond rubio r**oo**b-yo

blood la sangre s**a**ngray

high blood pressure la tensión alta tenss-y**o**n

blouse la blusa bl**oo**sa

blow-dry (verb) secar a mano

I'd like a cut and blow-dry quisiera un corte y un marcado kees-y**ai**ra oon k**o**rtay ee

blue azul ath**oo**l

blusher el colorete kolor**ay**tay

boarding house la casa de huéspedes w**e**spaydess

boarding pass la tarjeta de embarque tar**H**ayta day embark**ay**

boat el barco

body el cuerpo kw**ai**rpo

boil (water) hervir air**b**eer

boiled egg el huevo pasado por agua w**ay**bo – **a**gwa

boiler la caldera kald**ai**ra

bone el hueso w**ay**so

bonnet (of car) el capó

book el libro l**ee**bro

(verb) reservar resairb**ar**

can I book a seat? ¿puedo reservar un asiento? pw**ay**do – as-y**e**nto

I'd like to book a table for two quisiera reservar una mesa para dos personas kees-y**ai**ra resairb**ar** **oo**na m**ay**sa

what time would you like it booked for? ¿para qué hora le gustaría reservarla? kay **o**ra lay goostar**ee**-a resairb**ar**la

half past seven las siete y media

that's fine de acuerdo day akw**ai**rdo

and your name? ¿y su nombre es…? ee soo n**o**mbray

bookshop, bookstore la librería leebrair**ee**-a

boot (footwear) la bota

(of car) el maletero malet**ai**ro

border (of country) la frontera front**ai**ra

bored: I'm bored estoy abu**rr**ido

boring aburrido

born: I was born in Manchester nací en Manchester nath**ee**

I was born in 1960 nací en mil novecientos sesenta

borrow pedir prestado

    may I borrow...? ¿puede prestarme...? pw**ay**day prest**ar**may

both los dos

bother: sorry to bother you lamento molestarle molest**ar**lay

bottle la botella bot**ay**-ya

    a bottle of house red una botella de tinto de la casa day

bottle-opener el abrebotellas abraybot**ay**-yass

bottom (of person) el trasero trass**ai**ro

    at the bottom of the... (hill/road) al pie del/de la... p-**yay** del/day

box la caja k**a**Ha

box office la taquilla tak**ee**-ya

boy el chico

boyfriend el amigo

bra el sujetador sooHetad**o**r

bracelet la pulsera pools**ai**ra

brake el freno fr**ay**no

brandy el coñac kon-yak

bread el pan

    white bread el pan blanco

    brown bread el pan moreno mor**ay**no

    wholemeal bread el pan integral

break (verb) romper romp**air**

    I've broken the... he roto el... ay

    I think I've broken my... creo que me he roto el... kr**ay**-o kay may

break down averiarse abairee-**ar**say

    I've broken down he tenido una avería ay – ab**air**ee-a

breakdown la avería

breakdown service el servicio de grúa serb**ee**th-yo day gr**oo**-a

breakfast el desayuno desa-y**oo**no

break-in: I've had a break-in han entrado los ladrones en mi casa an – ladr**o**ness

breast el pecho p**ay**cho

breathe respirar

breeze la brisa br**ee**sa

bridge (over river) el puente pw**ent**ay

brief breve br**ay**bay

briefcase el portafolios portaf**o**l-yoss

bright (light etc) brillante bree-y**ant**ay

    bright red rojo vivo r**o**Ho b**ee**bo

brilliant (idea, person) brillante bree-y**ant**ay

bring traer tra-**air**

    I'll bring it back later lo devolveré después lo daybolbair**ay** desp**we**ss

Britain Gran Bretaña bretan-ya

British británico

    I'm British (male/female) soy británico/británica

brochure el folleto fo-y**e**to

broken roto

bronchitis la bronquitis bronk**ee**teess

brooch el broche bro**chay**

broom la escoba

brother el hermano air**ma**no

brother-in-law el cuñado koon-**ya**do

brown mar**rón**

  brown hair el pelo castaño kastan-yo

  brown eyes los ojos castaños **o**Hoss

bruise el cardenal

brush (for hair, cleaning) el cepillo the**pee**-yo

  (artist's) el pincel peenth**el**

bucket el cubo **koo**bo

buffet car el vagón restaurante bag**on** restow**rant**ay

buggy (for child) el cochecito de niño kochay**thee**to day **nee**n-yo

building el edificio edee**feeth**-yo

bulb (light bulb) la bombilla bom**bee**-ya

bull el toro

bullfight la corrida de toros day

bullfighter el torero tor**air**o

bullring la plaza de toros **plath**a day

bumper el parachoques para**chok**ess

bunk la litera lee**tair**a

bureau de change la oficina de cambio ofee**thee**na day **kamb**-yo

burglary el robo con allanamiento de morada a-yanam-**yen**to

burn la quemadura kema**doo**ra

  (*verb*) quemar kem**ar**

burnt: this is burnt está quemado kem**a**do

burst: a burst pipe una cañería rota kan-yair**ee**-a

bus el autobús owto**boos**s

  what number bus is it to...? ¿qué número es para...? kay **noo**mairo

  when is the next bus to...? ¿cuándo sale el próximo autobús para...? kwando sal**ay**

  what time is the last bus? ¿a qué hora es el último autobús? kay **o**ra – **oo**lteemo

  could you let me know when we get there? ¿puede avisarme cuando lleguemos allí? pw**ay**day abees**ar**may kwando yeg**ay**moss a-y**ee**

DIALOGUE

does this bus go to...? ¿este autobús va a...? **e**stay owto**boos**s ba

no, you need a number... no, tiene que coger el... t-**yay**nay kay ko**Hair**

---

business el negocio neg**oth**-yo

bus station la estación de autobuses estath-**yon** day owto**boos**sess

bus stop la parada de autobús

bust el pecho **pay**cho

busy (restaurant etc) concurrido

  I'm busy tomorrow est**oy** ocupado mañana man-**yan**a

but pero **pai**ro

---

butcher's la carnicería
karneethai**ree**-a

butter la mantequilla
mante**kee**-ya

button el botón

buy (*verb*) comprar

  where can I buy…? ¿dónde
puedo comprar…? **don**day
pwaydo

by: by bus/car en autobús/
coche

  written by… escrito por…

  by the window junto a la
ventana Hoonto

  by the sea a orillas del mar
o**ree**-yass

  by Thursday para el jueves

bye ¡adiós! ad-**yoss**

C

cabbage el repollo re**po**-yo

cabin (on ship) el camarote
kama**ro**tay

cable car el teleférico telefai**ree**eko

Cadiz Cádiz **ka**deeth

café la cafetería kafetai**ree**-a

cagoule el chubasquero
choobas**kai**ro

cake el pastel pas**tayl**

cake shop la pastelería
pastelai**ree**-a

call (*verb*) llamar ya**mar**

  (to phone) llamar (por teléfono)

  what's it called? cómo se
llama esto? say **ya**ma

  he/she is called… se llama…

please call the doctor llame
al médico, por favor ya**may**

**please give me a call at
7.30 am tomorrow** por favor,
llámeme mañana a las siete y
media de la mañana ya**ma**may
man-**ya**na

please ask him to call me
por favor, dígale que me llame
deegalay kay may ya**may**

call back: I'll call back later
volveré más tarde bolbai**ray**
mass **tar**day

  (phone back) volveré a llamar
ya**mar**

**call round: I'll call round
tomorrow** me paso mañana
may

camcorder la videocámara
beeday-o ka**mai**ra

camera la máquina de fotos
ma**kee**na

camera shop la tienda de
cámaras fotográficas t-**yen**da
day

camp (*verb*) acampar

  can we camp here? ¿se
puede acampar aquí? say
pwayday – a**kee**

camping gas canister la
bombona de butano boo**ta**no

campsite el camping

can la lata

  a can of beer una lata de
cerveza thairb**ay**tha

can: can you…? ¿puede…?
pwayday

  can I have…? ¿me da…? may

  I can't… no puedo…

Canada el Canadá

Canadian canadiense kanad-yensay

  I'm Canadian soy canadiense

canal el canal

Canary Islands las Islas Canarias eeslass kanar-yass

cancel anular anoolar

candies los caramelos karamayloss

candle la vela bayla

canoe la piragua peeragwa

canoeing el piragüismo peeragweesmo

can-opener el abrelatas

cap (hat) la gorra

  (of bottle) el tapón

car el coche kochay

  by car en coche

carafe la garrafa

  a carafe of house white, please una garrafa de vino blanco de la casa, por favor day beeno

caravan la caravana karabana

caravan site el camping

carburettor el carburador

card (birthday etc) la tarjeta tarHayta

  here's my (business) card aquí tiene mi tarjeta (de visita) akee t-yaynay – day beeseeta

cardigan la rebeca rebayka

cardphone el teléfono de tarjeta telayfono day tarHeta

careful prudente proodentay

  be careful! ¡tenga cuidado! kweedado

caretaker el encargado

car ferry el ferry, el transbordador de coches kochess

car hire el alquiler de coches alkeelair day

car park el aparcamiento aparkam-yento

carpet la moqueta mokayta

carriage (of train) el vagón bagon

carrier bag la bolsa de plástico day plasteeko

carrot la zanahoria thana-or-ya

carry llevar yebar

carry-cot el capazo kapatho

carton el cartón

carwash el lavacoches labakochess

case (suitcase) la maleta malayta

cash el dinero deenairo

  (verb) cobrar

  will you cash this for me? ¿podría hacerme efectivo un cheque? podree-a athairmay efekteebo oon chaykay

cash desk la caja kaHa

cash dispenser el cajero automático kaHairo owtomateeko

cashier (male/female) el cajero/ la cajera

cassette la cassette kaset

cassette recorder el cassette

castanets las castañuelas kastan-ywaylass

Castile Castilla kast**ee**-ya

Castilian castellano kastay-yano

castle el castillo kast**ee**-yo

casualty department las urgencias oorHenth-yass

cat el gato

Catalonia Cataluña kata-loon-ya

catch (*verb*) coger koHair

   where do we catch the bus to...? ¿dónde se coge el autobús a...? **d**onday say ko**H**ay

cathedral la catedral

Catholic (*adj*) católico

cauliflower la coliflor

cave la cueva kw**ay**ba

CD el CD thay-**d**ay

ceiling el techo t**ay**cho

celery el apio **a**p-yo

cellar (for wine) la bodega bod**ay**ga

cell phone el teléfono móvil tel**ay**fono m**o**beel

cemetery el cementerio thement**air**-yo

Centigrade centígrado thent**ee**grado

centimetre el centímetro thent**ee**metro

central central thentral

central heating la calefacción central kalayfakth-y**on**

centre el centro th**e**ntro

   how do we get to the city centre? ¿cómo se llega al centro? say y**ay**ga

cereal los cereales theray-**a**less

certainly desde luego d**e**sday lw**ay**go

   certainly not desde luego que no kay

chair la silla s**ee**-ya

champagne el champán

change (money) el cambio k**a**mb-yo

   (*verb*) cambiar kamb-y**a**r

   can I change this for...? ¿puedo cambiar esto por...? pw**ay**do

   I don't have any change no tengo nada suelto sw**e**lto

   can you give me change for a 20 euro note? ¿puede cambiarme un billete de viente euros? pw**ay**day kamb-y**a**rmay oon bee-y**ay**tay day b**ay**-eentay ay-ooross

---

DIALOGUE

   do we have to change (trains)? ¿tenemos que cambiar de tren? ten**ay**moss kay kamb-y**a**r

   yes, change at Córdoba/ no it's a direct train sí, cambie en Córdoba/no, es un tren directo kamb-y**ay**

---

changed: to get changed cambiarse kamb-y**a**rsay

chapel la capilla kap**ee**-ya

charge (*verb*) cobrar

cheap barato

   do you have anything cheaper? tiene algo más barato? t-y**ay**nay

check (US) el cheque *chaykay*

(US: bill) la cuenta *kwaynta*

see **bill**

(*verb*) revisar *rebeesar*

could you check the…, please? ¿puede revisar el…, por favor? *pwayday*

check book el talonario de cheques *chaykess*

check-in la facturación *faktoorath-yon*

check in facturar

where do we have to check in? ¿dónde se factura? *donday say*

cheek la mejilla *meнee-ya*

cheerio! hasta luego *asta lwaygo*

cheers! (toast) ¡salud! *saloo*

cheese el queso *kayso*

chemist's la farmacia *farmath-ya*

cheque el cheque *chaykay*

do you take cheques? ¿aceptan cheques? *atheptan*

cheque book el talonario de cheques *day*

cheque card la tarjeta de banco *tarнayta*

cherry la cereza *thairaytha*

chess el ajedrez *aнedreth*

chest el pecho *paycho*

chewing gum el chicle *cheeklay*

chicken el pollo *po-yo*

chickenpox la varicela *bareethela*

child (*male/female*) el niño/la niña *neen-yo*

children los niños

child minder la niñera *neen-yaira*

children's pool la piscina infantil *peestheena eenfanteel*

children's portion la ración pequeña (para niños) *rath-yon pekayn-ya – neen-yoss*

chin la barbilla *barbee-ya*

china la porcelana *porthelana*

Chinese (*adj*) chino *cheeno*

chips las patatas fritas

chocolate el chocolate *chokolatay*

milk chocolate el chocolate con leche *lechay*

plain chocolate el chocolate negro *naygro*

a hot chocolate la taza de chocolate *tatha*

choose elegir *eleнeer*

Christian name el nombre de pila *nombray day peela*

Christmas Navidad nabeeda

Christmas Eve Nochebuena nochay-bwayna

Merry Christmas! ¡Feliz Navidad! feleeth

church la iglesia eeglays-ya

cider la sidra seedra

cigar el puro pooro

cigarette el cigarro theegarro, el cigarrillo theegarree-yo

cigarette lighter el encendedor enthendedor

cinema el cine theenay

circle el círculo theerkoolo

(in theatre) el anfiteatro anfeetay-atro

city la ciudad thee-oo-da

city centre el centro de la ciudad thentro day

clean (adj) limpio leemp-yo

can you clean these for me? ¿puede limpiarme estos? pwayday leemp-yarmay

cleaning solution (for contact lenses) el líquido limpiador para las lentillas leekeedo leemp-yador – lentee-yass

cleansing lotion la crema limpiadora krayma leemp-yadora

clear claro

clever listo

cliff el acantilado

climbing el alpinismo

cling film el plástico de envolver day embolbair

clinic la clínica

cloakroom el guardarropa gwardarropa

clock el reloj reloH

close (verb) cerrar therrar

DIALOGUE

what time do you close? ¿a qué hora se cierra? kay ora say th-yairra

we close at 8 pm on weekdays and 1:30 pm on Saturdays cerramos a las ocho de la tarde entre semana y a la una y media los sábados therramoss – day la tarday entray

do you close for lunch? ¿cierra al mediodía? th-yairra – med-yodee-a

yes, between 1 and 3.30 pm sí, entre una y tres y media de la tarde entray – day la tarday

closed cerrado thairrado

cloth (fabric) la tela tayla

(for cleaning etc) el trapo

clothes la ropa

clothes line la cuerda para tender kwairda para tendair

clothes peg la pinza de la ropa peentha day

cloud la nube noobay

cloudy nublado

clutch el embrague embragay

coach (bus) el autocar owtokar

(on train) el vagón bagon

coach station la estación de autobuses estath-yon day owtoboosess

coach trip la excursión (en autobús) eskoorss-**yon**

coast la costa

on the coast en la costa

coat (long coat) el abrigo (jacket) la chaqueta chak**ay**ta

coathanger la percha p**ai**rcha

cockroach la cucaracha kookar**a**cha

cocoa el cacao kak**a**-o

coconut el coco

code (for phoning) el prefijo pref**ee**Ho

what's the (dialling) code for Málaga? ¿cuál es el prefijo de Málaga kwal

coffee el café kaf**ay**

two coffees, please dos cafés, por fav**o**r

coin la moneda mon**ay**da

Coke la Coca-Cola

cold frío fr**ee**-o

I'm cold tengo frío

I have a cold tengo cat**a**rro

collapse: he's collapsed se ha desmayado say a desma-**ya**do

collar el cuello kw**ay**-yo

collect recoger rekoH**ai**r

I've come to collect... he venido a recoger... ay ben**ee**do

collect call la llamada a cobro revertido yam**a**da – rebairt**ee**do

college la Universidad ooneebairseed**a**

colour el color

do you have this in other colours? ¿tiene otros colores? t-**yay**nay

colour film la película en color

comb el peine p**ay**-eenay

come venir bayn**ee**r

come back volver bolb**ai**r

I'll come back tomorrow volveré mañana bolbair**ay**

come in entrar

comfortable cómodo

compact disc el compact disc

company (business) la compañía kompan-**yee**-a

compartment (on train) el compartim**e**nto

compass la brújula br**oo**-Hoola

complain quejarse kayH**a**rsay

complaint la queja k**ay**Ha

I have a complaint tengo una queja

completely completamente kompl**ay**tamentay

computer el ordenador

concert el concierto konth-**yai**rto

concussion la conmoción cerebral kommoth-**yo**n thairebral

conditioner (for hair) el acondicionador de pelo akondeeth-yonad**o**r day p**ay**lo

condom el cond**ó**n

conference el congr**e**so

confirm confirm**a**r

congratulations! ¡enhorabuena! enorab**wa**yna

connecting flight el vuelo de conexión b**way**lo day koneks-**y**on

connection el enlace enla**thay**

conscious consciente konth-**y**entay

constipation el estreñimiento estren-yeem-**y**ento

consulate el consulado konsoo**la**do

contact (*verb*) ponerse en contacto con pon**air**say

contact lenses las lentes de contacto, las lentillas **l**entess – lent**ee**-yass

contraceptive el anticonceptivo anteekonthept**ee**bo

convenient a **ma**no

   that's not convenient eso no viene bien b-**yay**nay b-yen

cook (*verb*) cocinar koth**ee**nar

   not cooked poco hecho **e**cho

cooker la cocina koth**ee**na

cookie la galleta ga-**ya**yta

cooking utensils los utensilios de cocina ooten**see**l-yoss day koth**ee**na

cool fresco fr**ay**sko

cork el corcho

corkscrew el sacac**o**rchos

corner: on the corner en la esquina esk**ee**na

   in the corner en el rinc**ó**n

cornflakes los cornflakes

correct (*right*) corr**e**cto

corridor el pasillo pas**ee**-yo

cosmetics los cosm**é**ticos

cost (*verb*) cost**a**r

   how much does it cost? ¿cuánto cuesta? kw**a**nto kw**e**sta

cot la c**u**na

cotton el algod**ó**n

cotton wool el algod**ó**n

couch (*sofa*) el sof**á**

couchette la litera leet**ai**ra

cough la tos

cough medicine la medicina para la tos medeeth**ee**na

could: could you...? ¿podr**í**a...?

   could I have...? quisiera... kees-**ya**ira...

   I couldn't... (*wasn't able to*) no podía...

country (*nation*) el país pa-**ee**ss

   (*countryside*) el c**a**mpo

countryside el c**a**mpo

couple (*two people*) la pareja par**ay**Ha

   a couple of... un par de...

courgette el calabacín kalabath**ee**n

courier el/la guía turístico g**ee**-a

course (*main course etc*) el pl**a**to

   of course por supuesto soop**we**sto

   of course not ¡claro que no! kay

cousin (*male/female*) el primo pr**ee**mo/la pr**i**ma

cow la vaca b**a**ka

crab el cangrejo kangr**ay**Ho

cracker la galleta salada ga-**ya**yta

craft shop la tienda de artesanía
t-yenda day artesanee-a

crash el accidente aktheedentay

  I've had a crash he tenido un
  accidente ay teneedo

crazy loco

cream (on milk, in cake) la nata

  (lotion) la crema krayma

  (colour) color crema

creche la guardería infantil
gwardairee-a

credit card la tarjeta de crédito
tarHayta day

  can I pay by credit card?
  ¿puedo pagar con tarjeta?
  pwaydo

  **which card do you want
  to use?** ¿qué tarjeta quiere
  usar? kay – k-yairay oosar

  yes, sir sí, señor sen-yor

  what's the number? ¿qué
  número es? noomairo

  and the expiry date? ¿y la
  fecha de caducidad? fecha
  day kadootheeda

credit crunch la crisis
hipotecaria kreeseess
eepotekar-ya

crisps las patatas fritas (de bolsa)

crockery la loza lotha

crossing (by sea) la travesía
trabesee-a

crossroads el cruce kroothay

crowd la muchedumbre
moochay-doombray

crowded lleno yayno

crown (on tooth) la funda foonda

cruise el crucero kroothairo

crutches la muleta moolayta

cry (verb) llorar yorar

cucumber el pepino

cup la taza tatha

  a cup of…, please una taza
  de…, por favor

cupboard el armario armar-yo

cure la cura koora

curly rizado reethado

current la corriente korr-yentay

curtains las cortinas

cushion el cojín koHeen

custom la costumbre
kostoombray

Customs la aduana adwana

cut el corte kortay

  (verb) cortar

  I've cut myself me he cortado
  may ay

cutlery los cubiertos koob-yairtoss

cycling el ciclismo theekleesmo

cyclist el/la ciclista theekleesta

D

dad el papá

daily el periódico pair-yodeeko

damage: damaged estropeado
estropay-ado

  **I'm sorry, I've damaged
  this** lo siento, he estropeado
  esto s-yento – ay

damn! ¡maldita sea! say-a

damp (adj) húmedo oomaydo

dance el baile ba-**ee**lay

(*verb*) bailar ba-**ee**lar

would you like to dance?
¿quiere bailar? k-y**ai**ray

dangerous peligroso

Danish el danés dan**ay**ss

dark (*adj*: colour) oscuro osk**oo**ro

(hair) moreno mor**ay**no

it's getting dark está
oscureciendo oskooreth-y**e**ndo

date: what's the date today?
¿qué día es hoy? kay – oy

**let's make a date for next
Monday** vamos a quedar para
el lunes que viene ba**moss** a
kedar – kay b-y**ay**nay

dates (fruit) los dátiles d**a**teeless

daughter la hija **ee**Ha

daughter-in-law la nuera nw**ai**ra

dawn el amanecer amaneth**ai**r

at dawn al amanecer

day el día

the day after el día siguiente
seeg-y**e**ntay

the day after tomorrow
pasado mañana man-y**a**na

the day before el día anterior
antair-y**o**r

the day before yesterday
anteayer antay-a-y**ai**r

every day todos los días

all day todo el día

in two days' time dentro de
dos días

have a nice day! ¡que pase un
buen día! kay pasay oon bwen
día

day trip la excursión exkoors-y**o**n

dead muerto mw**ai**rto

deaf sordo

deal (business) la transacción
transakth-y**o**n

it's a deal trato hecho **ay**cho

death la muerte mw**ai**rtay

decaffeinated coffee el café
descafeinado kaf**ay** deskafay-
eenado

December diciembre
deeth-y**e**mbray

decide decidir detheed**ee**r

**we haven't decided
yet** todavía no hemos
decidido todab**ee**-a no **ay**moss
detheed**ee**edo

decision la decisión detheess-y**o**n

deck (on ship) la cubierta
koob-y**ai**rta

deckchair la tumbona

deduct descontar

deep profundo

definitely claramente, ¡desde
luego! klaram**e**ntay d**e**sday
lw**ay**go

definitely not desde luego que
no kay

degree (qualification) la carrera
karr**ai**ra

delay el retraso

deliberately a propósito

delicatessen la charcutería
charkootair**ee**-a

delicious delicioso deleeth-y**o**so

deliver repartir

delivery (of mail) el reparto

Denmark Dinamarca

dental floss el hilo dental eelo

dentist el/la dentista

it's this one here es ésta de aquí day akee

this one? ¿ésta?

no, that one no, esa aysa

here? ¿aquí?

yes sí

dentures la dentadura postiza posteetha

deodorant el desodorante desodorantay

department el departamento

department store los grandes almacenes grandess almathayness

departure la salida

departure lounge la sala de embarque day embarkay

depend: it depends depende dependay

it depends on... depende de... day

deposit (as security) la fianza fee-antha

(as part payment) el depósito

description la descripción deskreepth-yon

dessert el postre postray

destination el destino

develop (photos) revelar rebelar

diabetic (*male/female*) el diabético dee-abayteeko/la diabética

diabetic foods la comida para diabéticos

dial marcar

dialling code el prefijo prefeeHo

diamond el diamante d-yamantay

diaper el pañal pan-yal

diarrhoea la diarrea d-yarray-a

diary (business etc) la agenda aHenda

(for personal experiences) el diario d-yar-yo

dictionary el diccionario deekth-yonar-yo

didn't

see **not**

die morir

diesel el gasoil

diet la dieta d-yayta

I'm on a diet estoy a dieta

I have to follow a special diet tengo que seguir una dieta especial kay segeer – espeth-yal

difference la diferencia deefairenth-ya

what's the difference? ¿cuál es la diferencia? kwal

different diferente deefairentay

this one is different éste es diferente estay

a different table otra mesa maysa

difficult difícil deefeetheel

difficulty la dificultad deefeekoolta

dinghy el bote botay

dining room el comedor komaydor

dinner (evening meal) la cena
th**ay**na

to have dinner cenar

> Travel tip Friends are more
> likely to meet in restaurants
> for meals, but if you are
> invited to someone's house
> for dinner, you should take
> a small gift for any children,
> along with chocolates, a
> bottle of wine or some
> flowers (though avoid
> dahlias, chrysanthemums
> and flowers in odd numbers
> as these would only be
> given at funerals).

direct (*adj*) directo

is there a direct train?
¿hay un tren directo? ī

direction la dirección
deerekth-y**o**n

which direction is it?
¿en qué dirección está? kay

is it in this direction?
¿es por aquí? ak**ee**

directory enquiries
información eenformath-y**o**n

dirt la suciedad sooth-yayd**a**

dirty sucio s**oo**th-yo

disabled minusválido
meenoosb**a**leedo

**is there access for the
disabled?** ¿hay acceso para
minusv**á**lidos? ī akth**ay**so

disappear desaparecer
desapareth**ai**r

it's disappeared ha
desaparecido a desapareth**ee**do

disappointed desilusionado
deseelooss-yon**a**do

disappointing decepcionante
dethepth-yon**a**ntay

disaster el desastre des**a**stray

disco la discot**e**ca

discount el descuento
deskw**e**nto

is there a discount? ¿hacen
descuento? **a**then

disease la enfermedad
enfairmed**a**

disgusting repugnante
repoogn**a**ntay

dish (meal) el pl**a**to

dishcloth el paño de cocina
pan-yo day koth**ee**na

disinfectant el desinfectante
deseenfekt**a**ntay

disk (for computer) el diskette
deesk**ay**tay

disposable diapers/nappies
los pañales (braguita)
pan-y**a**less brag**ee**ta

distance la distancia deestanth-ya

in the distance a lo lejos
lay**H**oss

distilled water el agua destil**a**da
agwa

district el distr**i**to

disturb molest**a**r

diversion (detour) el desvío
desb**ee**-o

diving board el trampol**i**n

divorced divorciado
deeborth-y**a**do

dizzy: I feel dizzy est**oy**
mareado maray-**a**do

do hacer athair

what shall we do? ¿qué hacemos? kay athaymoss

how do you do it? ¿cómo se hace? say athay

will you do it for me? ¿me lo puede hacer usted? pwayday athair oostay

DIALOGUE

how do you do? ¿qué tal? kay

nice to meet you encantado de conocerle day konothairlay

what do you do? (work) ¿a qué se dedica? say

I'm a teacher, and you? soy profesor, ¿y usted? ee oostay

I'm a student soy estudiante estood-yantay

what are you doing this evening? ¿qué hace esta tarde? athay

we're going out for a drink; do you want to join us? vamos a salir a tomar una copa; ¿nos acompaña? bamoss – akompan-ya

do you want cream? ¿quiere crema? k-yairay krayma

I do, but she doesn't yo sí, pero ella no pairo ay-ya

doctor el/la médico

we need a doctor necesitamos un médico naytheseetamoss

please call a doctor por favor, llame a un médico yamay

DIALOGUE

where does it hurt? ¿dónde le duele? donday lay dwaylay

right here justo aquí Hoosto akee

does that hurt now? ¿le duele ahora? lay dwaylay a-ora

yes sí

take this to the chemist's lleve esto a la farmacia yaybay – farmath-ya

document el documento dokoomento

dog el perro pairro

doll la muñeca moon-yayka

domestic flight el vuelo nacional bwaylo nath-yonal

donkey el burro boorro

don't! ¡no lo haga! aga

don't do that! ¡no haga eso! ayso

see **not**

door la puerta pwairta

doorman el portero portairo

double doble doblay

double bed la cama de matrimonio matreemon-yo

double room la habitación doble abeetath-yon doblay

doughnut el dónut donoot

down: down here aquí abajo akee abaHo

put it down over there
póngalo ahí a-**ee**

it's down there on the right
está ahí a la derecha dair**e**cha

it's further down the road está
bajando la calle baHando la ka-yay

downhill skiing el esquí alpino
aysk**ee** alp**ee**no

download (*verb*) descargar

downmarket bar**a**to

downstairs abajo ab**a**Ho

dozen la docena doth**ay**na

  half a dozen media docena
  mayd-ya

drain el desagüe des**a**gway

draught beer la cerveza de grifo
thairb**ay**tha day

draughty: it's draughty hay
corriente ī korr-y**e**ntay

drawer el cajón kaH**o**n

drawing el dibujo deeb**oo**Ho

dreadful horrible orr**ee**blay

dream el sueño sw**ay**n-yo

dress el vestido best**ee**do

dressed: to get dressed
  vestirse best**ee**rsay

dressing (for cut) el vendaje
  bend**a**Hay

  salad dressing el aliño
  al**ee**n-yo

dressing gown la bata

drink (alcoholic) la copa
  (non-alcoholic) la bebida
  (*verb*) beber beb**ai**r

  a cold drink una bebida fría
  can I get you a drink?
  ¿quiere beber algo? k-y**ai**ray

what would you like (to drink)? ¿qué le apetece beber? kay lay apet*ay*thay

no thanks, I don't drink no gracias, no bebo gr*ath*-yass no b*ay*bo

I'll just have a drink of water voy a beber sólo agua boy – *a*gwa

drinking water agua potable *a*gwa pot*a*blay

is this drinking water? ¿esto es agua potable?

drive (*verb*) conducir kondoot*heer*

we drove here vinimos en coche been*e*moss en k*o*chay

I'll drive you home te llevaré a casa en el coche tay yebar*ay* – k*o*chay

driver (*male/female*) el conductor kondo*oktor*/la conduct*o*ra

Travel tip An EU driver's licence is sufficient to drive in Spain. US, Canadian, Australian and New Zealand licences should also be enough, though you may want to get an International Driver's Licence as well, just to be on the safe side.

driving licence el permiso de conducir pairm*ee*so day kondoot*heer*

drop: just a drop, please (of drink) un poquito pok*ee*to

drug la medicina maydeeth*ee*na

drugs (narcotics) la dr*o*ga

drunk (*adj*) borr*a*cho

drunken driving conducir en estado de embriaguez kondoot*heer* – embr-yag*eth*

dry (*adj*) seco s*ay*ko

(sherry) f*ee*no

dry-cleaner la tintorería teentorair*ee*-a

duck el p*a*to

due: he was due to arrive yesterday tenía que llegar ayer ten*ee*-a kay yegar a-y*air*

when is the train due? ¿cuándo tiene el tren la llegada? kw*a*ndo t-y*ay*nay – yeg*a*da

dull (pain) s*o*rdo

(weather) gris greess

dummy (baby's) el chupete choop*ay*tay

during durante door*a*ntay

dust el polvo p*o*lbo

dusty polvoriento polbor-y*e*nto

dustbin el cubo de la basura k*oo*bo day

duty-free (goods) (los productos) duty free

duty-free shop la tienda de duty free t-y*e*nda day

duvet el edredón

DVD el DVD day-oobay-d*a*y

E

each c*a*da

how much are they each? ¿cuánto es cada uno? kw*a*nto

ear la oreja or*ay*нa

earache: I have earache
tengo dolor de oídos o-**ee**doss

early temprano

early in the morning por la
mañana temprano man-yana

I called by earlier vine antes
beenay antess

earring el pendiente pend-yentay

east este estay

in the east en el este

Easter la Semana Santa

easy fácil fatheel

eat comer komair

**we've already eaten,
thanks** ya hemos comido,
gracias aymoss

eau de toilette el agua de baño
agwa day ban-yo

EC la CE thay-ay

economy class la clase turista
klasay

Edinburgh Edimburgo
edeemboorgo

egg el huevo waybo

eggplant la berenjena berenHayna

either: either... or... o... o...

either of them cualquiera de
ellos kwalk-yaira day ay-yoss

elastic el elástico

elastic band la goma elástica

elbow el codo

electric eléctrico

electrical appliances los
electrodomésticos

electric fire la estufa eléctrica

electrician el electricista
elektreetheesta

electricity la electricidad
elektreetheeda

elevator el ascensor asthensor

else: something else algo más

somewhere else en otra
parte partay

DIALOGUE

**would you like anything
else?** ¿quiere algo más?
k-yairay

no, nothing else, thanks
nada más, gracias

email el email

(*verb:* person) enviar un email a
emb-yar

(*verb:* text, file) enviar por email

embassy la embajada embaHada

emergency la emergencia
emairHenth-ya

this is an emergency! ¡es
una emergencia!

emergency exit la salida de
emergencia

empty vacío bathee-o

end el final feenal

(*verb*) terminar tairmeenar

at the end of the street
al final de la calle day la ka-yay

when does it end? ¿cuándo
termina? kwando tairmeena

engaged (toilet) ocupado

(telephone) comunicando

(to be married) prometido

engine (car) el motor

England Inglaterra eenglata**i**rra

English inglés eenglayss

I'm English (*male/female*) soy inglés/inglesa

do you speak English? ¿habla inglés? abla

enjoy: to enjoy oneself divertirse deebairteersay

DIALOGUE

how did you like the film? ¿le gustó la película? lay goosto

I enjoyed it very much, did you enjoy it? me gustó mucho, ¿le gustó a usted? may – moocho – lay – oostay

enjoyable entretenido

enlargement (of photo) la ampliación ampl-yath-yon

enormous enorme enormay

enough suficiente soofeeth-yentay

there's not enough no hay bastante ī bastantay

it's not big enough no es suficientemente grande soofeeth-yentementay

that's enough es suficiente

entrance la entrada

envelope el sobre sobray

epileptic epiléptico

equipment el equipo ekeepo

especially especialmente espeth-yalmentay

essential imprescindible eemprestheendeeblay

it is essential that... es imprescindible que... kay

EU UE oo-ay

euro el euro ay-ooro

Eurocheque el eurocheque ay-oorochekay

Eurocheque card la tarjeta eurocheque tarнayta

Europe Europa ay-ooropa

European europeo ay-ooropay-o

European Union la Unión Europea oon-yon

even (including) incluso eenklooso

even if... incluso si...

evening (early evening) la tarde tarday

(after nightfall) la noche nochay

this evening esta tarde/noche

in the evening por la tarde/noche

evening meal la cena thayna

eventually finalmente feenalmentay

ever alguna vez beth

DIALOGUE

have you ever been to Barcelona? ¿ha estado alguna vez en Barcelona? a

yes, I was there two years ago sí, estuve allí hace dos años estoobay a-yee athay – an-yoss

every cada

every day todos los días

everyone todos

everything todo

everywhere en todas partes partess

exactly! ¡exactamente! exaktamentay

exam el examen

example el ejemplo eHaymplo

   for example por ejemplo

excellent excelente esthelentay

   excellent! ¡estupendo!

except excepto esthepto

excess baggage el exceso de
   equipaje esthayso day ekeepaHay

exchange rate el cambio
   kamb-yo

exciting emocionante emoth-
   yonantay

excuse me (to get past) con
   permiso
   (to get attention) ¡por favor! fabor
   (to say sorry) perdone pairdonay

exhaust (pipe) el tubo de escape
   toobo day eskapay

exhausted (tired) agotado

exhibition la exposición
   exposeeth-yon

exit la salida

   where's the nearest exit?
   ¿cuál es la salida más próxima?
   kwal

expect esperar espairar

expensive caro

experienced con experiencia
   espair-yenth-ya

explain explicar espleekar

   can you explain that?
   ¿puede explicármelo?
   pwayday

express (mail) urgente oorHentay
   (train) expreso esprayso

extension (phone) extensión
   estens-yon

extension 221, please
   extensión doscientos veintiuno,
   por favor

extension lead el alargador

**extra: can we have an extra
   one?** ¿nos puede dar otro?
   pwayday

   **do you charge extra for
   that?** ¿esto tiene recargo?
   t-yaynay

extraordinary extraordinario
   estra-ordeenar-yo

extremely extremadamente
   estremadamentay

eye el ojo oHo

   **will you keep an eye on my
   suitcase for me?** ¿puede
   cuidarme la maleta? pwayday
   kweedarmay la malayta

eyebrow pencil el lápiz de cejas
   lapeeth day thayHass

eye drops el colirio koleer-yo

eyeglasses las gafas

eyeliner el lápiz de ojos lapeeth
   day oHoss

eye make-up remover el
   desmaquillador de ojos
   desmakee-yador

eye shadow la sombra de ojos

F

face la cara

factory la fábrica

Fahrenheit Fahrenheit

faint (verb) desmayarse desmayarsay

she's fainted se ha desmayado say a desma-yado

I feel faint estoy mareado maray-ado

fair la feria fair-ya

(*adj*) justo Hoosto

fairly bastante bastantay

fake la falsificación falseefeekath-yon

fall el otoño oton-yo

see **autumn**

fall caerse ka-airsay

she's had a fall se ha caído say a ka-eedo

false falso fal-so

family la familia fameel-ya

famous famoso

fan (electrical) el ventilador benteelador

(hand held) el abanico

(sports) el/la hincha eencha

fan belt la correa del ventilador korray-a del benteelador

fantastic fantástico

far lejos layHoss

fare el precio prayth-yo

farm la granja granHa

fashionable de moda

fast rápido

fat (person) gordo

(on meat) la grasa

father el padre padray

father-in-law el suegro swaygro

faucet el grifo greefo

fault el defecto

sorry, it was my fault lo siento, fue culpa mía s-yento fway koolpa mee-a

it's not my fault no es culpa mía

faulty defectuoso dayfektwoso

favourite favorito faboreeto

fax el fax

(*verb*: person) mandar un fax a

(document) mandar por fax

February febrero febrairo

feel sentir

I feel hot tengo calor

I feel unwell no me siento bien may s-yento b-yen

I feel like going for a walk me apetece dar un paseo apetaythay – pasay-o

how are you feeling today? ¿qué tal se encuentra hoy? kay tal say enkwentra oy

I'm feeling better me siento mejor mayHor

felt-tip (pen) el rotulador

fence la valla ba-ya

fender el parachoques parachokess

ferry el ferry

festival el festival festeebal

fetch: I'll fetch him yo iré a recogerle ee**ray** a raykoH**air**lay

will you come and fetch me later? ¿quiere venir a buscarme más tarde? k-y**air**ay ben**eer** a boosk**ar**may mass t**ar**day

feverish con fiebre f-y**ay**bray

few: a few unos pocos

a few days unos pocos días

fiancé el novio n**ob**-yo

fiancée la n**o**via

field el c**a**mpo

fight la pelea pel**ay**-a

figs los higos ee**goss**

file el archivo arch**ee**bo

fill (*verb*) llenar yen**ar**

fill in rellenar ray-yen**ar**

do I have to fill this in? ¿tengo que rellenar esto? kay

fill up llenar yen**ar**

fill it up, please lleno, por favor y**ay**no

filling (in cake, sandwich) el relleno ray-y**ay**no

(in tooth) el empaste emp**a**stay

film (movie, for camera) la película

film processing el revelado rebel**a**do

filter coffee el café de filtro kaf**ay** day f**ee**ltro

filter papers los filtros

filthy sucísimo sooth**ee**seemo

find (*verb*) encontrar

I can't find it no lo encuentro enk**we**ntro

I've found it lo he encontrado ay

find out enterarse enter**ar**say

could you find out for me? ¿me lo puede preguntar? may lo pw**ay**day pregoont**ar**

fine (weather) bueno bw**ay**no

(*noun*) la multa m**oo**lta

finger el dedo d**ay**do

finish (*verb*) terminar tairmeen**ar**, acab**ar**

I haven't finished yet no he terminado todavía ay tairmeen**a**do todab**ee**-a

when does it finish? ¿cuándo termina? kw**a**ndo term**ee**na

fire: fire! ¡fuego! fw**ay**go

can we light a fire here? ¿se puede encender fuego aquí? say pw**ay**day enthend**air** – ak**ee**

it's on fire está ardiendo ard-y**e**ndo

fire alarm la alarma de incendios day eenthend-y**o**ss

fire brigade los bomberos bomb**air**oss

fire escape la salida de incendios day eenthend-y**o**ss

fire extinguisher el extintor esteent**o**r

first primero preem**ai**ro

  I was first fui el primero
fwee

  at first al principio preenth**ee**p-
yo

  the first time la prim**e**ra vez
beth

  first on the left la primera a la
izquierda eethk-y**ai**rda

first aid prim**e**ros auxilios
owks**ee**l-yoss

first aid kit el botiquín
bootek**ee**n

first class (travel etc) de primera
(clase) preem**ai**ra kl**a**say

first floor la primera pl**a**nta
(US) la planta baja b**a**Ha

first name el nombre de p**i**la
n**o**mbray day

fish el pez peth
  (food) el pesc**a**do

fishing village el pueblo
de pescadores pw**e**blo day
peskad**o**ress

fishmonger's la pescadería
peskad**ai**ree-a

fit (attack) el ataque at**a**kay

fit: it doesn't fit me no me
viene bien b-y**ay**nay b-yen

fitting room el probad**o**r

fix (verb) arregl**a**r
  (arrange) fijar feeH**a**r

  can you fix this? ¿puede
arreglar esto? pw**ay**day

fizzy con gas

flag la bandera band**ai**ra

flannel la man**o**pla

flash (for camera) el flash

flat (noun: apartment) el p**i**so
  (adj) llano y**a**no

  I've got a flat tyre tengo un
pinchazo peench**a**tho

flavour el sab**o**r

flea la p**u**lga

flight el vuelo bw**ay**lo

flight number el número de
vuelo n**oo**mairo day

flippers las aletas al**ay**tass

flood la inundación eenoondath-
y**o**n

floor (of room) el suelo sw**ay**lo
  (of building) el p**i**so

  on the floor en el suelo

florist la floristería floreestair**ee**-a

flour la harina ar**ee**na

flower la flor

flu la gripe gr**ee**pay

**fluent: he speaks fluent
Spanish** domina el castellano
kastay-y**a**no

fly la m**o**sca
  (verb) volar bol**a**r

  can we fly there?
¿podemos ir en avión allí?
pod**ay**moss eer en ab-y**o**n
a-y**ee**

fly in llegar en avión yeg**a**r

fly out irse en avión **ee**rsay

fog la niebla n-y**e**bla

foggy: it's foggy hay niebla ī

folk dancing el baile tradicional
ba-**ee**lay tradeeth-y**o**nal

folk music la música popular
m**oo**seeka popo**o**lar

follow seguir seg**ee**r

  follow me sígame s**ee**gamay

food la comida

food poisoning la intoxicación alimenticia eentoxeekath-yon aleement**ee**th-ya

food shop/store la tienda de comestibles t-y**e**nda day komest**ee**bless

foot el pie p-yay

  on foot a pie

football (game) el fútbol

  (ball) el balón

football match el partido de fútbol

for p**a**ra, por

  do you have something for…? (headache/diarrhoea etc) ¿tiene **a**lgo para…? t-y**ay**nay

  who's the chicken paella for? ¿para quién es la paella con pollo? k-yen ess la pa-**ay**-ya con p**o**-yo

  that's for me es para mí

  and this one? ¿y ésta? ee

  that's for her ésa es para ella **ay**sa – **ay**-ya

  where do I get the bus for Granada? ¿dónde se coge el autobús p**a**ra Granada? donday say ko**H**ay

  the bus for Granada leaves from Plaza de España el autobús para Granada sale de la Pl**a**za de España salay day

how long have you been here for? ¿cuánto tiempo lleva aquí? kwanto t-yempo y**ay**ba akee

I've been here for two days, how about you? llevo aquí dos días, ¿y usted? y**ay**bo – ee oost**ay**

I've been here for a week llevo aquí una semana

forehead la frente fr**e**ntay

foreign extranjero estran**H**airo

foreigner (*male/female*) el extranjero/la extranj**e**ra

forest el bosque b**o**skay

forget olvidar olbeed**a**r

  I forget no me acuerdo no may akw**a**irdo

  I've forgotten me he olvidado ay olbeed**a**do

fork el tenedor

  (in road) la bifurcación beefoorkath-y**o**n

form (document) el impreso eempr**ay**so

formal (dress) de etiqueta day eteek**ay**ta

fortnight quince días k**ee**nthay

fortunately afortunadamente afortoonadam**e**ntay

forward: could you forward my mail? ¿puede enviarme el correo? pw**ay**day emb-y**a**rmay el korr**ay**-o

forwarding address la nueva dirección nw**ay**ba deerekth-y**o**n

foundation (make-up) la crema base kr**ay**ma b**a**say

fountain la fuente fw**e**ntay

foyer (of hotel, theatre) el hall Hol

fracture la fractura frakt**oo**ra

France Francia fr**a**nth-ya

free libre l**ee**bray

(no charge) gratuito gratw**ee**to

is it free (of charge)? ¿es gratis?

freeway la autopista owtop**ee**sta

freezer el congelador konHayl**a**dor

French francés fr**a**nthess

French fries las patatas fritas

frequent frecuente frek**wé**ntay

how frequent is the bus to Seville? ¿cada cuánto tiempo hay autobús a Sevilla? kw**a**nto t-y**e**mpo ī

fresh fr**e**sco

fresh orange el zumo de naranja natural th**oo**mo day nar**a**nHa nator**a**l

Friday viernes b-y**ai**rness

fridge el frigorífico

fried fr**i**to

fried egg el huevo frito w**a**ybo

friend (male/female) el amigo/ la amiga

friendly simpático

from de, desde day, d**e**sday

when does the next train from Tarragona arrive? ¿cuándo llega el próximo tren de Tarragona? kw**a**ndo y**a**yga

from Monday to Friday de lunes a viernes day

from next Thursday desde el próximo jueves

where are you from? ¿de dónde es usted? day d**o**nday ess oost**ay**

I'm from Brighton soy de Brighton soy day

front la parte delantera p**a**rtay delant**ai**ra

in front delante del**a**ntay

in front of the hotel delante del hotel

at the front delante

frost la escarcha

frozen congelado konHayl**a**do

frozen food los congelados

fruit la fruta

fruit juice el zumo de frutas th**oo**mo

fry freír fray-**eer**

frying pan la sartén

full lleno y**a**yno

it's full of... está lleno de... day

I'm full estoy lleno/llena

full board pensión completa pens-y**o**n kompl**ay**ta

fun: it was fun fue muy divertido fway mwee deebairt**ee**do

funeral el funeral foon**ai**ral

funny (strange) raro

(amusing) gracioso grath-y**o**so

furniture los muebles mw**ay**bless

further más allá a-y**a**

it's further down the road está más adelante adel**a**ntay

how much further is it to Cáceres? ¿cuánto queda para Cáceres? kw**a**nto k**ay**da

about 5 kilometres unos cinco kil**ó**metros

fuse el fusible foos**ee**blay

the lights have fused se han fundido los pl**o**mos say an

fuse box la caja de fusibles k**a**Ha day foos**ee**bless

fuse wire el pl**o**mo

future el futuro foot**oo**ro

in the future en lo sucesivo soothes**ee**bo

G

gallon el gal**ó**n

game (cards etc) el juego Hw**ay**go

(match) el partido

(meat) la caza k**a**tha

garage (for fuel) la gasolinera gasoleen**ai**ra

(for repairs) el taller (de reparaciones) ta-y**ai**r day reparath-y**o**ness

(for parking) el garaje gar**a**Hay

garden el jardín Hard**ee**n

garlic el ajo **a**Ho

gas el gas

(US) la gasolina

gas cylinder (camping gas) la bomb**o**na de gas

gasoline la gasolina

gas permeable lenses las lentillas por**o**sas lent**ee**-yass

gas station la gasolinera gasoleen**ai**ra

gate la puerta pw**ai**rta

(at airport) la puerta de embarque emb**a**rkay

gay el gay

Travel tip Gay and lesbian life in Spain has come a long way in the last three decades, and Spanish attitudes have changed dramatically. Same-sex marriages were made legal in 2005, giving same-sex couples the same rights as heterosexual couples, including the right to adopt, and the age of consent is 16 – the same as for hetero-sexual couples.

---

gay bar el bar gay

gears la marcha

gearbox la caja de cambios k**a**Ha day k**a**mb-yoss

gear lever la palanca de velocidades beloth**ee**dadess

general general Hen**e**ral

gents (toilet) el aseo de caballeros as**ay**-o day kaba-y**ai**ross

genuine (antique etc) genuino Henw**ee**no

German alemán

German measles la rubéola
roobay-ola

Germany Alemania aleman-ya

Gerona Gerona Herona

get (fetch) traer tra-air

will you get me another one, please? me quiere traer otro, por favor may k-yairay

how do I get to...? ¿cómo se va a...? say ba

do you know where I can get them? ¿sabe dónde las puedo comprar? sabay donday lass pwaydo

can I get you a drink? ¿puedo ofrecerle algo de beber? pwaydo ofrethair-lay – day bebair

no, I'll get this one; what would you like? no, ésta la pago yo; ¿qué le apetece? kay lay apaytaythay

a glass of red wine un vaso de vino tinto baso day beeno teento

get back (return) volver bolbair

get in (arrive) llegar yegar

get off bajarse baHarsay

where do I get off? ¿dónde tengo que bajarme? donday – kay baHarmay

get on (to train etc) subirse soobeersay

get out (of car etc) bajarse baHarsay

get up (in the morning) levantarse lebantarsay

gift el regalo

gift shop la tienda de regalos t-yenda

gin la ginebra Heenaybra

a gin and tonic, please un gintónic, por favor Heentoneek

girl la chica cheeka

girlfriend la novia nob-ya

give dar

can you give me some change? ¿me puede dar cambio? may pwayday – kamb-yo

I gave it to him se lo dí a él say

will you give this to...? ¿podría entregarle esto a...? entregarlay

how much do you want for this? ¿cuánto quiere por esto? kwanto k-yairay

10 euros diez euros d-yeth ay-ooross

I'll give you 8 euros le doy ocho euros lay

give back devolver debolbair

glad alegre alegray

glass (material) el cristal kreestal
(tumbler) el vaso baso
(wine glass) la copa

glasses las gafas

gloves los guantes gwantess

glue el pegamento

go (*verb*) ir eer

  we'd like to go to the swimming-pool nos gustaría ir a la piscina peestheena

  where are you going? ¿adónde va? adonday ba

  where does this bus go? ¿adónde va este autobús? estay

  let's go! ¡vamos! bamoss

  she's gone (left) se ha marchado say a

  where has he gone? ¿dónde se ha ido? donday – eedo

  I went there last week fui allí la semana pasada fwee a-yee

go away irse eersay

  go away! ¡váyase! ba-yasay

go back (return) volver bolbair

go down (the stairs etc) bajar baнar

go in entrar

go out salir

  do you want to go out tonight? ¿quiere salir esta noche? k-yairay – nochay

go through pasar por

go up (the stairs etc) subir

goat la cabra

God Dios d-yoss

goggles las gafas protectoras

gold el oro

golf el golf

golf course el campo de golf

good bueno bwayno

  good! ¡muy bien! mwee b-yen

  it's no good es inútil eenooteel

goodbye adiós ad-yoss

good evening buenas tardes bwenass tardess

Good Friday el Viernes Santo b-yairness

good morning buenos días bwaynoss

good night buenas noches nochess

goose el ganso

got: we've got to... tenemos que... taynaymoss kay

have you got any apples? ¿tiene manzanas? t-yaynay

government el gobierno gob-yairno

gradually gradualmente gradwalmentay

grammar la gramática

gram(me) el gramo

granddaughter la nieta n-yayta

grandfather el abuelo abwaylo

grandmother la abuela abwela

grandson el nieto n-yayto

grapefruit el pomelo pomaylo

grapefruit juice el zumo de pomelo thoomo

grapes las uvas oobass

grass la hierba yairba

grateful agradecido agradetheedo

gravy la salsa

great (excellent) muy bueno mwee bwayno

that's great! ¡estupendo! estoopendo

a great success un gran éxito

Great Britain Gran Bretaña bretanya

Greece Grecia grayth-ya

greedy comilón

Greek (*adj*) griego gr-yaygo

green verde bairday

green card (car insurance) la carta verde

greengrocer's la frutería frootairee-a

grey gris

grill la parrilla parree-ya

grilled a la parrilla

grocer's (la tienda de) comestibles t-yenda day komesteebless

ground el suelo swaylo

on the ground en el suelo

ground floor la planta baja baHa

group el grupo

guarantee la garantía

is it guaranteed? ¿está garantizado? garanteethado

guest (*male/female*) el invitado eembeetado/la invitada

guesthouse la casa de huéspedes day wespedess

guide el/la guía gee-a

guidebook la guía

guided tour la visita con guía beeseeta

guitar la guitarra geetarra

gum (in mouth) la encía enthee-a

gun la pistola

gym el gimnasio Heemnas-yo

H

hair el pelo *paylo*

hairbrush el cepillo para el pelo
thepee-yo

haircut el corte de pelo *kortay*

hairdresser's (men's) la barbería
(women's) la peluquería
pelookairee-a

hairdryer el secador de pelo *day
paylo*

hair gel el fijador (para el pelo)
feeHador

hairgrips la horquilla *orkee-ya*

hair spray la laca

half la mitad la *meeta*

   half an hour media hora
mayd-ya ora

   half a litre medio litro

   about half that
aproximadamente la mitad
de eso *aproximadamentay –
day ayso*

half board la media pensión
pens-yon

half-bottle la botella pequeña
botay-ya pekayn-ya

half fare el medio billete *mayd-yo
bee-yaytay*

half price la mitad del precio
meeta del preth-yo

ham el jamón *Hamon*

hamburger la hamburguesa
amboorgaysa

hammer el martillo *martee-yo*

hand la mano

handbag el bolso

handbrake el freno de mano
frayno day

handkerchief el pañuelo
pan-ywaylo

handle (on door) la manilla
manee-ya
(on suitcase etc) el asa

hand luggage el equipaje de
mano *ekeepaHay*

hang-gliding el ala delta

hangover la resaca

   I've got a hangover tengo
resaca

happen suceder *soothedair*

   what's happening? ¿qué
pasa? *kay*

   what has happened? ¿qué
ha pasado? *a*

happy contento

   I'm not happy about this
esto no me agrada *may*

harbour el puerto *pwairto*

hard duro *dooro*
(difficult) difícil *deefeetheel*

hard-boiled egg el huevo duro
waybo

hard lenses las lentillas duras
lentee-yass

hardly apenas *apaynass*

   hardly ever casi nunca

hardware shop la ferretería
fairretairee-a

hat el sombrero

hate (verb) odiar

have tener *tenair*

   can I have a...? ¿me da...?
may

do you have...? ¿tiene...? t-yaynay

what'll you have? ¿qué va a tomar? kay ba

I have to leave now tengo que dejarle ahora dayнarlay a-ora

do I have to...? ¿tengo que...?

can we have some...? ¿nos pone...? ponay

hayfever la alergia al polen alairнee-a al polayn

hazelnut la avellana abay-yana

he él

head la cabeza kabaytha

headache el dolor de cabeza

headlights el faro

headphones los auriculares owreekoolaress

health food shop la tienda naturista t-yenda natooreesta

healthy sano

hear oír o-eer

DIALOGUE

can you hear me? ¿me oye? may oy-ay

I can't hear you, could you repeat that? no le oigo, podría repetirlo lay oygo podree-a

hearing aid el aparato del oído o-eedo

heart el corazón korathon

heart attack el infarto

heat el calor

heater (in room) el calefactor

(in car) la calefacción kalayfakth-yon

heating la calefacción

heavy pesado

heel (of foot) el talón

(of shoe) el tacón

could you heel these? ¿podría cambiarles los tacones? kamb-yarless – takoness

heel bar el zapatero thapatairo

height la altura

helicopter el helicóptero

hello ¡hola! ola

(answer on phone) ¡dígame! deegamay

helmet el casco

help la ayuda a-yooda

(verb) ayudar a-yoodar

help! ¡socorro!

can you help me? ¿puede ayudarme? pwayday a-yoodarmay

thank you very much for your help gracias por su ayuda

helpful amable amablay

hepatitis la hepatitis epateeteess

her: I haven't seen her no la he visto ay

to her a ella ay-ya

with her con ella

for her para ella

that's her ésa es (ella) aysa

that's her towel ésa es su toalla

herbal tea el té de hierbas tay day yairbass

herbs las hierbas

here aquí akee

here is/are… aquí está/están…

here you are (offering) tenga

hers (el) suyo soo-yo, (la) suya

that's hers es de ella day ay-ya, es suyo/suya

hey! ¡oiga!

hi! (hello) ¡hola! ola

hide (verb) esconder eskondair

high alto

highchair la silla alta para bebés see-ya – baybayss

highway la autopista owtopeesta

hill la colina

him: I haven't seen him no le he visto lay ay

to him a él

with him con él

for him para él

that's him ése es (él) aysay

hip la cadera kadaira

hire (verb) alquilar alkeelar

for hire de alquiler alkeelair

where can I hire a bike? ¿dónde puedo alquilar una bicicleta? donday pwaydo

his: it's his car es su coche

that's his eso de él ayso day, eso es suyo soo-yo

hit (verb) golpear golpay-ar

hitch-hike hacer autostop athair owtostop

hobby el pasatiempo pasat-yempo

hold (verb) sostener sostaynair

hole el agujero agooнairo

holiday las vacaciones bakath-yoness

on holiday de vacaciones

home la casa

at home (in my house) en casa (in my country) en mi país pa-eess

we go home tomorrow volvemos a casa mañana bolbaymoss

honest honrado onrado

honey la miel m-yel

honeymoon la luna de miel loona day

hood (of car) el capó

hope la esperanza espairantha

I hope so espero que sí espairo kay

I hope not espero que no

hopefully it won't rain no lloverá, eso espero no yobaira ayso

horn (of car) la bocina botheena

horrible horrible orreeblay

horse el caballo kaba-yo

horse riding la equitación ekeetath-yon

hospital el hospital ospeetal

hospitality la hospitalidad ospeetaleeda

thank you for your hospitality gracias por su hospitalidad soo

hot caliente kal-yentay

(spicy) picante peekantay

I'm hot tengo calor

it's hot today hoy hace calor oy athay

hotel el hotel otel

hotel room: in my hotel room en mi habitación del hotel abeetath-yon

hour la hora ora

house la casa

house wine el vino de la casa beeno day

hovercraft el aerodeslizador a-airodesleethador

how como

how many? ¿cuántos? kwantoss

how do you do? ¡mucho gusto! moocho

how are you? ¿cómo está?
fine, thanks, and you? bien gracias, y usted b-yen – ee oostay

how much is it? ¿cuánto es? kwanto

10 euros diez euros d-yeth ay-ooross

I'll take it me lo quedo may lo kaydo

humid húmedo oomedo

humour el humor oomor

hungry hambriento ambr-yento

I'm hungry tengo hambre ambray

are you hungry? ¿tiene hambre? t-yaynay

hurry (*verb*) darse prisa darsay preesa

I'm in a hurry tengo prisa

there's no hurry no hay prisa ī

hurry up! ¡dese prisa! daysay

hurt doler dolair

it really hurts me duele mucho may dwaylay moocho

husband mi marido

hydrofoil la hidroala eedro-ala

hypermarket el hipermercado eepairmairkado

I

I yo

ice el hielo yaylo

with ice con hielo

no ice, thanks sin hielo, gracias seen

ice cream el helado elado

ice-cream cone el cucurucho de helado kookooroochoo

iced coffee el café helado

ice lolly el polo

idea la idea eeday-a

idiot el/la idiota eed-yota

if si

ignition el encendido enthendeedo

ill enfermo enfairmo

I feel ill me encuentro mal may enkwentro

illness la enfermedad enfairmayda

imitation (leather etc)
de imitación day eemeetath-
yon

immediately ahora mismo a-ora
meesmo

important importante
eemportantay

it's very important es muy
importante mwee

it's not important no
tiene importancia t-yaynay
eemportanth-ya

impossible imposible
eemposeeblay

impressive impresionante
eempres-yonantay

improve mejorar mayHorar

**I want to improve my
Spanish** quiero mejorar
mi español k-yairo –
espan-yol

in: it's in the centre está en el
centro

in my car en mi coche

in Córdoba en Córdoba

in two days from now
dentro de dos días day

in five minutes dentro de
cinco minutos

in May en mayo

in English en inglés

in Spanish en español?

is he in? ¿está?

inch la pulgada poolgada

include incluir eenklweer

does that include meals?
¿eso incluye las comidas? ayso
eenkloo-yay

is that included? ¿está
eso incluido en el precio?
eenklweedo en el prayth-yo

inconvenient inoportuno
eenoportoono

incredible increíble eenkray-
eeblay

Indian (adj) indio eend-yo

indicator el intermitente
eentairmeetentay

indigestion la indigestión
eendeeHest-yon

indoor pool la piscina cubierta
peestheena koob-yairta

indoors dentro

inexpensive barato

infection la infección
eenfekth-yon

infectious infeccioso
eenfekth-yoso

inflammation la inflamación
eenflamath-yon

informal (occasion, meeting)
informal eenformal

(dress) de sport day

information la información
eenformath-yon

**do you have any
information about...?** ¿tiene
información sobre… ? t-yaynay
– sobray

information desk la
información

injection la inyección een-yekth-
yon

injured herido ereedo

she's been injured está
herida

in-laws la familia política
fam**eel**-ya

inner tube (for tyre) la cámara de
aire a-**ee**ray

innocent inocente eenoth**entay**

insect el ins**e**cto

insect bite la picad**u**ra de
insecto day

   **do you have anything for
   insect bites?** ¿tiene algo
   para la picadura de insectos?
   t-**yay**nay

insect repellent el repelente de
insectos repel**en**tay day

inside d**e**ntro de day

   inside the hotel dentro del
   hotel

   let's sit inside vamos a
   sentarnos ad**e**ntro bam**o**ss

insist insistir eenseest**eer**

   I insist ins**i**sto

insomnia el insomnio
eens**o**mn-yo

instant coffee el café
instantáneo kaf**ay**
eenstant**a**nay-o

**instead: give me that one
instead** deme ese **o**tro
d**ay**may **ay**say

   instead of... en lugar de...
   day

intersection el cruce kr**oo**thay

insulin la insulina eensool**ee**na

insurance el seguro seg**oo**ro

intelligent inteligente
eentelee**Hen**tay

interested: I'm interested in...
est**oy** interes**a**do en...

interesting interesante
eenteres**a**ntay

   that's very interesting eso es
   muy interesante **ay**so ess mwee

international internacional
internath-y**o**nal

Internet el Internet eentair**net**

interpret actuar de intérprete
aktoo-**ar** day eent**air**pretay

interpreter el/la intérprete

interval (at theatre) el desc**a**nso

into en

   I'm not into... no me gusta...
   may g**oo**sta

introduce present**ar**

   may I introduce...? le
   pres**e**nto a...

invitation la invitación
eembeetath-y**on**

invite invitar eembeet**ar**

Ireland Irlanda eerl**a**nda

Irish irlandés eerland**ay**ss

   I'm Irish (male/female) soy
   irlandés/irland**e**sa

iron (for ironing) la pl**a**ncha

   **can you iron these for
   me?** ¿puede planch**ár**melos?
   pw**ay**day

is es; está (see note on p.8)

island la isla e**e**ssla

it ello, lo **ay**-yo

   it is... es...; está...

   is it...? ¿es...?; ¿está...?

   where is it? ¿dónde está?
   d**o**nday

   it's him es él

   it was... era...; estaba... **ai**ra

Italian (*adj*) italiano eetal-yano

Italy Italia

itch: it itches me pica may

J

jack (for car) el gato

jacket la chaqueta chakayta

jar el tarro

jam la mermelada mairmaylada

jammed: it's jammed está atascado

January enero enairo

jaw la mandíbula mandeeboola

jazz el jazz

jealous celoso theloso

jeans los vaqueros bakaiross

jellyfish la medusa medoosa

jersey el jersey Hairsay

jetty el muelle mway-yay

Jewish judío Hoodee-o

jeweller's la joyería Ho-yeree-a

jewellery las joyas Hoyass

job el trabajo trabaHo

jogging el footing

   to go jogging hacer footing athair

joke el chiste cheesstay

journey el viaje b-yaHay

   have a good journey! ¡buen viaje! bwen b-yaHay

jug la jarra Harra

   a jug of water una jarra de agua agwa

juice el zumo thoomo

July julio Hool-yo

jump (*verb*) saltar

jumper el jersey Hairsay

jump leads las pinzas (para la batería) peenthass – batairee-a

junction el cruce kroothay

June junio Hoon-yo

just (only) solamente solamentay

   just two sólo dos

   just for me sólo para mí

   just here aquí mismo akee meesmo

   not just now ahora no a-ora

   we've just arrived acabamos de llegar yegar

K

keep quedarse kedarsay

   keep the change quédese con el cambio kay-daysay – kamb-yo

   can I keep it? ¿puedo quedármelo? pwaydo kedarmelo

   please keep it por favor, quédeselo kaydayselo

ketchup el ketchup

kettle el hervidor airbeedor

key la llave yabay

   the key for room 201, please la llave de la habitacion doscientos uno, por favor day la abeetath-yon

key ring el llavero yabairo

kidneys los riñones reen-yoness

kill matar

kilo el kilo

kilometre el kilómetro

**how many kilometres is it
to…?** ¿cuántos kilómetros hay
a…? kwantoss – ī

kind (nice) amable amablay

that's very kind es muy
amable mwee

DIALOGUE

which kind do you want?
¿qué tipo quiere? kay teepo
k-yairay

I want this/that kind quiero
este/aquel tipo k-yairo estay/
akel

king el rey ray

kiosk el quiosco kee-osko

kiss el beso bayso

(verb) besarse baysarsay

kitchen la cocina kotheena

kitchenette la cocina pequeña
pekwayn-ya

Kleenex el kleenex

knee la rodilla rodee-ya

knickers las bragas

knife el cuchillo koochee-yo

knitwear los géneros de punto
Henaiross

knock (verb: on door) llamar
yamar

knock down atropellar atropay-
yar

he's been knocked down
le han atropellado lay an
atropay-yado

knock over (object) volcar bolkar
(pedestrian) atropellar atropay-yar

know (somebody, a place) conocer
konothair

(something) saber sabair

I don't know no sé say

I didn't know that no lo sabía

**do you know where I can
find…?** ¿sabe dónde puedo
encontrar…? sabay donday
pwaydo

DIALOGUE

**do you know how this
works?** ¿sabe cómo
funciona esto? foonth-yona

sorry, I don't know lo
siento, no sé s-yento – say

L

label la etiqueta eteekayta

ladies' (toilets) el aseo de
señoras asay-o day sen-yorass

ladies' wear la ropa de señoras

lady la señora sen-yora

lager la cerveza thairbaytha

lake el lago

lamb (meat) el cordero kordairo

lamp la lámpara

lane (motorway) el carril karreel
(small road) la callejuela ka-yay-
Hwayla

language el idioma eed-yoma

language course el curso de
idiomas koorso day

laptop el ordenador portátil
ordenador portateel

large grande granday

last último **oo**lteemo

   last week la semana pasada

   last Friday el viernes pasado

   last night anoche an**o**chay

   what time is the last train to Toledo? ¿a qué hora es el último tren a Toledo? kay **o**ra

late tarde t**a**rday

   sorry I'm late siento llegar tarde s-y**ay**nto yeg**a**r

   the train was late el tren llegó con retraso yayg**o**

   we must go – we'll be late debemos irnos – llegaremos tarde deb**ay**moss **ee**rnoss – yegar**ay**moss

   it's getting late se hace tarde say **a**thay

later más tarde

   I'll come back later volveré más tarde bolbair**ay**

   see you later hasta luego **a**sta lw**ay**go

   later on más tarde

latest lo último **oo**lteemo

   by Wednesday at the latest para el miércoles lo más tarde

laugh (*verb*) reirse r**ay**-**ee**rsay

launderette/laundromat la lavandería labandair**ee**-a

laundry (clothes) la ropa sucia s**oo**th-ya

   (place) la lavandería

> **Travel tip** You'll find a few self-service laundries (*lavanderías automáticas*) in the major cities, but you normally have to leave your clothes for a service wash and dry. By law you're not allowed to leave laundry hanging out of windows over a street, and many pensiones and hostales expressly forbid washing clothes in the sink.

lavatory el lavabo lab**a**bo

law la ley lay

lawn el césped th**e**sped

lawyer (*male/female*) el abog**a**do/ la abog**a**da

laxative el laxante lax**a**ntay

lazy perezoso pair**e**th**o**so

lead (electrical) el cable k**a**blay

lead (*verb*) conducir kond**oo**th**ee**r

   where does this lead to?
   ¿adónde va esta carretera? ad**o**nday ba – karrayt**ai**ra

leaf la hoja **o**Ha

leaflet el folleto fo-y**ay**to

leak (in roof) la gotera got**ai**ra

   (gas, water) el escape esk**a**pay

   (*verb*) filtrar feeltr**a**r

   the roof leaks el tejado tiene goteras teH**a**do t-y**ay**nay got**ai**rass

learn aprender aprend**ai**r

least: not in the least de ninguna manera day neeng**oo**na man**ai**ra

   at least por lo menos m**ay**noss

leather (fine) la piel p-yel

   (heavy) el cuero kw**ai**ro

leave (*verb*) irse **ee**rsay

   I am leaving tomorrow me marcho mañana may

   he left yesterday se marchó ay**e**r say

   may I leave this here?
   ¿puedo dejar esto aquí? pw**ay**do dayH**a**r – ak**ee**

   I left my coat in the bar me he dejado el abrigo en el bar ay dayH**a**do

leek el puerro pw**ai**rro

left izquierda eethk-y**ai**rda

   on the left a la izquierda

   to the left a la izquierda

   turn left gire a la izquierda H**ee**ray

   there's none left no queda ninguno k**ay**da

left-handed zurdo th**oo**rdo

left luggage (office) la consigna kons**ee**gna

leg la pierna p-y**ai**rna

lemon el limón leem**o**n

lemonade la limonada leemon**a**da

lemon tea el té con limón tay

lend prestar

   will you lend me your...?
   ¿podría prestarme su...? prest**a**rmay

lens (of camera) el objetivo obHet**ee**bo

lesbian la lesbiana

less menos m**ay**noss

   less expensive menos caro

   less than 10 menos de diez

   less than you menos que tú kay too

lesson la lección lekth-y**o**n

let (allow) dejar dayHar

will you let me know? ¿me lo dirá? may lo deeray

I'll let you know se lo diré say lo deeray

let's go for something to eat vamos a comer algo bamoss a komair

let off: will you let me off at…? ¿me para en…? may

letter la carta

do you have any letters for me? ¿tiene cartas para mí? t-yaynay

letterbox el buzón boothon

lettuce la lechuga lechooga

lever la palanca

library la biblioteca beebl-yotayka

licence el permiso

lid la tapa

lie (verb: tell untruth) mentir

lie down acostarse akostarsay, echarse aycharsay

life la vida beeda

lifebelt el salvavidas salbabeedass

lifeguard el/la socorrista

life jacket el chaleco salvavidas chalayko salbabeedass

lift (in building) el ascensor asthensor

could you give me a lift? ¿podría llevarme en su coche? yebarmay – kochay

would you like a lift? ¿quiere que le lleve? k-yairay kay lay yaybay

lift pass el forfait forfa-ee

a daily/weekly lift pass un forfait de un día/una semana

light la luz looth

(not heavy) ligero leeHairo

do you have a light? (for cigarette) ¿tiene fuego? t-yaynay fwaygo

light green verde claro bairday

light bulb la bombilla bombee-ya

I need a new light bulb necesito una bombilla nueva netheseeto – nwayba

lighter (cigarette) el encendedor enthendedor

lightning el relámpago

like (verb) gustar goostar

I like it me gusta may

I like going for walks me gusta pasear pasay-ar

I like you me gustas

I don't like it no me gusta

do you like…? ¿le gusta…? lay

I'd like a beer quisiera una cerveza kees-yaira oona thairbaytha

I'd like to go swimming me gustaría ir a nadar

would you like a drink? ¿le apetece beber algo? apaytaythay bebair

would you like to go for a walk? ¿le apetece dar un paseo? lay – pasay-o

what's it like? ¿cómo es?

I want one like this quiero uno como éste k-yairo – estay

lime la lima *leema*

lime cordial el zumo de lima *thoomo day*

line la línea *leenay-a*

could you give me an outside line? ¿puede darme línea? *pwayday darmay*

lips el labio *lab-yo*

lip salve la crema de labios *krayma*

lipstick el lápiz de labios *lapeeth*

liqueur el licor

listen escuchar *eskoochar*

litre el litro *leetro*

a litre of white wine un litro de vino blanco *day beeno*

little pequeño *paykayn-yo*

just a little, thanks sólo un poco, gracias *grathee-as*

a little milk un poco de leche *lechay*

a little bit more un poquito más *pokeeto*

live (*verb*) vivir *beebeer*

we live together vivimos juntos *beebeemoss Hoontoss*

where do you live? ¿dónde vive? *donday beebay*

I live in London vivo en Londres *beebo*

lively alegre *alaygray*

liver el hígado *eegado*

loaf el pan

lobby (in hotel) el vestíbulo *besteeboolo*

lobster la langosta

local local

can you recommend a local wine/restaurant? puede recomendarme un vino/ un restaurante local *pwayday rekomendarmay oon beeno/oon restowrantay*

lock la cerradura *thairradoora* (*verb*) cerrar *thairrar*

it's locked está cerrado con llave *thairrado kon yabay*

lock in dejar encerrado *day-Har enthairrado*

lock out: I've locked myself out he cerrado la puerta con las llaves dentro *ay – la pwairta – yabayss*

locker (for luggage etc) la consigna automática *konseegna owtomateeka*

lollipop el Chupa-Chups *choopa-choopss*

London Londres *londress*

long largo

how long will it take to fix it? ¿cuánto tiempo llevará arreglarlo? *kwanto t-yempo yaybara*

how long does it take? ¿cuánto tiempo se tarda? *say*

a long time mucho tiempo *moocho*

one day/two days longer un día/dos días más

long distance call la conferencia *konfairenth-ya*

look: I'm just looking, thanks sólo estoy mirando, gracias

you don't look well no tienes buen aspecto t-yayness bwen

look out! ¡cuidado! kweedado

can I have a look? ¿puedo mirar? pwaydo

look after cuidar kweedar

look at mirar

look for buscar

I'm looking for... estoy buscando...

look forward to: I'm looking forward to it tengo muchas ganas moochass

loose (handle etc) suelto swelto

lorry el camión kam-yon

lose perder pairdair

I've lost my way me he perdido may ay pairdeedo

I'm lost, I want to get to... estoy perdido/perdida, quiero ir a... k-yairo

I've lost my bag he perdido el bolso ay

lost property (office) (la oficina de) objetos perdidos ofeetheena day obHaytoss pairdeedoss

lot: a lot, lots mucho, muchos moocho

not a lot no mucho

a lot of people mucha gente Hentay

a lot bigger mucho mayor

I like it a lot me gusta mucho may goosta

lotion la loción loth-yon

loud fuerte fwairtay

lounge (in house, hotel) el salón

(in airport) la sala de espera day espaira

love el amor

(*verb*) querer kairair

I love Spain me encanta España may

lovely encantador

low bajo baHo

luck la suerte swairtay

good luck! ¡buena suerte! bwayna

luggage el equipaje ekeepaHay

luggage trolley el carrito portaequipaje porta-ekeepaHay

lump (on body) la hinchazón eenchathon

lunch el almuerzo almwairtho

lungs los pulmones poolmoness

luxurious (hotel, furnishings) de lujo looHo

luxury el lujo

M

machine la máquina makeena

mad (insane) loco

(angry) furioso foor-yoso

Madrid Madrid madree

magazine la revista rebeesta

maid (in hotel) la camarera kamaraira

maiden name el nombre de soltera nombray day soltaira

mail el correo korray-o

  is there any mail for me?
  ¿hay correspondencia para
  mí? ī korrespond**e**nth-ya

  see **post**

mailbox el buzón booth**o**n

main principal preenth**ee**pal

main course el plato principal

main post office la oficina
  central de correos ofeeth**ee**na
  thentr**a**l day korray-oss

main road (in town) la calle
  principal ka-yay preenth**ee**pal
  (in country) la carretera principal
  karret**ai**ra

mains (for water) la llave de paso
  yabay day

mains switch (for electricity) el
  interruptor de la red eléctrica
  eentairroopt**o**r day

Majorca Mallorca ma-y**o**rka

make (brand name) la marca
  (*verb*) hacer ath**ai**r

  I make it 50 euros creo
  que son cincuenta euros
  kra**yo** kay – theenkw**e**nta
  ay-ooross

  what is it made of?
  ¿de qué está hecho? day kay
  – **ay**cho

make-up el maquillaje makee-
  ya**Ha**y

man el hombre **o**mbray

manager el gerente Hair**e**ntay

  can I see the manager?
  ¿puedo ver al gerente? pw**ay**do
  bair

manageress la gerente

manual (car with manual gears) el
  coche de marchas k**o**chay

many muchos m**oo**choss

  not many no muchos

map (city plan) el plano
  (road map, geographical) el m**a**pa

March marzo m**a**rtho

margarine la margarina

market el mercado mairk**a**do

marmalade la mermelada
  de naranja mairmel**a**da day
  nar**a**nHa

married: I'm married (said by
  a man/woman) est**oy** cas**a**do/
  cas**a**da

  are you married? (said to
  a man/woman) ¿est**á** cas**a**do/
  cas**a**da?

mascara el rímel

match (football etc) el partido

matches las cerillas thair**ee**-yass

material (fabric) el tejido teH**ee**do

matter: it doesn't matter no
  imp**o**rta

  what's the matter? ¿qué
  pasa? kay

mattress el colchón

May mayo ma-yo

**may: may I have another
  one?** ¿me da **o**tro? may

  may I come in? ¿se puede
  entrar? say pw**ay**day

  may I see it? ¿puedo verlo?
  pw**ay**do ba**ir**lo

  may I sit here? ¿puedo
  sentarme aquí? sentarmay ak**ee**

maybe tal vez beth

mayonnaise la mayonesa
ma-yon**ay**sa

me: that's for me eso es para
mí **ay**so

   send it to me envíemelo
embee-**ay**melo

   me too yo también tamb-**yen**

meal la comida

did you enjoy your meal?
¿te ha gustado la comida?
tay a goost**a**do

**it was excellent, thank
you** estaba riquísima,
gracias reek**ee**seema

mean (*verb*) querer decir kair**air**
deth**eer**

   what do you mean? ¿qué
quiere decir? kay k-y**ai**ray

**what does this word
mean?** ¿qué significa esta
palabra? kay

it means… in English
significa… en inglés
eengl**ay**ss

measles el sarampión saramp-
yon

meat la carne k**ar**nay

mechanic el mecánico

medicine la medicina
medeeth**ee**na

Mediterranean el Mediterráneo
medeeta**irra**nay-o

medium (*adj:* size) medio
mayd-yo

medium-dry semi-seco s**ay**ko
(sherry) amontillado amontee-
y**a**do

medium-rare poco hecho
aycho

medium-sized de tamaño
medio tam**an**-yo m**ay**d-yo

meet encontrar
(for the first time) conocer
konoth**air**

   nice to meet you encantado
de conocerle day konoth**air**lay

   where shall I meet you?
¿dónde nos vemos? d**o**nday noss
b**ay**moss

meeting la reunión ray-oon-y**on**

meeting place el lugar de
reunión l**oo**gar

melon el melón

memory stick el lápiz de
memoria lapeeth day mem**o**r-ya

men los hombres **o**mbress

mend arreglar

   **could you mend this for
me?** ¿puede arreglarme esto?
pw**ay**day arregl**ar**may

men's room el servicio de
caballeros sairbeeth-yo day
kaba-y**ai**ross

menswear la ropa de caballero

mention (*verb*) mencionar
menth-y**o**nar

   don't mention it de nada day

menu el menú men**oo**

   **may I see the menu,
please?** ¿puede traerme el
menú? pw**ay**day tra-**air**may
see Menu reader

message: are there any messages for me? ¿hay algún recado para mí? ī

I want to leave a message for... quisiera dejar un recado para... kees-yaira day-Har

metal el metal

metre el metro

microwave (oven) el (horno) microondas orno meekro-ondass

midday el mediodía mayd-yodee-a

at midday al mediodía

middle: in the middle en el medio mayd-yo

in the middle of the night a mitad de la noche meeta day la nochay

the middle one el del medio

midnight la medianoche mayd-ya-nochay

at midnight a medianoche

might: I might es posible poseeblay

I might not puede que no pwayday kay

I might want to stay another day quizás decida quedarme otro día keethass detheeda kedarmay

migraine la jaqueca Hakayka

mild (taste) suave swabay

(weather) templado

mile la milla mee-ya

milk la leche lechay

milkshake el batido

millimetre el milímetro

minced meat la carne picada karnay

mind: never mind ¡qué más da! kay

I've changed my mind he cambiado de idea ay kamb-yado day eeday-a

DIALOGUE

do you mind if I open the window? ¿le importa si abro la ventana? lay eemporta – bentana

no, I don't mind no, no me importa may

mine: it's mine es mío

mineral water el agua mineral agwa meenairal

mint-flavoured con sabor a menta

mints los caramelos de menta karamayloss day

minute el minuto meenooto

in a minute en seguida segeeda

just a minute un momento

mirror el espejo espayнo

Miss Señorita sen-yoreeta

miss: I missed the bus he perdido el autobús ay pairdeedo

missing: one of my... is missing me falta uno de mis... may — day

there's a suitcase missing falta una maleta

mist la niebla n-yaybla

mistake el error

I think there's a mistake
me parece que hay una
equivocación may parethay kay ī
oona ekeebokath-yon

sorry, I've made a mistake
perdón, me he equivocado may
ay ekeebokado

misunderstanding el
malentendido

**mix-up: sorry, there's been
a mix-up** perdón ha habido
una confusión a abeedo oona
konfoos-yon

mobile phone el teléfono móvil
telayfono mobeel

> **Travel tip** Most European
> mobile phones will work
> in Spain, though it's worth
> checking with your provider
> whether you need to get
> international access turned
> on and whether there are
> any extra charges. Even
> though prices are coming
> down, it's still expensive
> to use your own mobile
> extensively while abroad:
> you'll pay to receive
> incoming calls, for example.

modern moderno modairno

modern art gallery la galería
de arte moderno galairee-a
day artay

moisturizer la crema hidratante
krayma eedratantay

**moment: I won't be a
moment** vuelvo enseguida
bwelbo ensegeeda

monastery el monasterio
monastair-yo

Monday lunes looness

money el dinero deenairo

month el mes

monument el monumento
monoomento

(statue) la estatua estatwa

moon la luna

moped el ciclomotor theeklomotor

more más

**can I have some more
water, please?** más agua, por
favor

more expensive/interesting
más caro/interesante

more than 50 más de
cincuenta

more than that más que eso
kay ayso

a lot more mucho más
moocho

**would you like some
more?** ¿quiere más?
k-yairay

**no, no more for me,
thanks** no, para mí no,
gracias

how about you? ¿y usted?
ee oostay

**I don't want any more,
thanks** no quiero más,
gracias k-yairo

morning la mañana man-yana

this morning esta mañana

in the morning por la mañana

Morocco Marruecos
marrwaykoss

mosquito el mosquito

mosquito repellent el repelente
de mosquitos repelentay

**most: I like this one most
of all** éste es el que más me
gusta estay – kay mass may
goosta

most of the time la mayor
parte del tiempo ma-yor partay
del t-yempo

most tourists la mayoría de
los turistas ma-yoree-a day

mostly generalmente
Haynairalmentay

mother la madre madray

motorbike la moto

motorboat la (lancha) motora

motorway la autopista
owtopeesta

mountain la montaña montan-ya

  in the mountains en las
  montañas

mountaineering el montañismo
montan-yeesmo

mouse el ratón

moustache el bigote beegotay

mouth la boca

mouth ulcer la llaga yaga

**move: he's moved to another
room** se ha cambiado a otra
habitación say a kamb-yado –
abeetath-yon

  could you move your car?
  ¿podría cambiar de sitio su
  coche? podree-a kamb-yar day
  seet-yo

  could you move up a little?
  ¿puede correrse un poco?
  pwayday corrairsay

  where has it moved to?
  ¿adónde se ha trasladado?
  adonday say a

movie la película peleekoola

movie theater el cine theenay

MP3 format el formato MP3
formato emay pay tress

Mr Señor sen-yor

Mrs Señora sen-yora

Ms Señorita sen-yoreeta

much mucho moocho

  much better/worse
  mucho mejor/peor ma-yor/
  pay-or

  much hotter mucho más
  caliente kal-yentay

  not (very) much no mucho

  I don't want very much no
  quiero mucho k-yairo

mud el barro

mug (for drinking) la taza tatha

  I've been mugged me han
  asaltado may an

mum la mamá

mumps las paperas papairass

museum el museo moosay-o

mushrooms los champiñones
champeen-yoness

music la música mooseeka

musician el/la músico

Muslim (adj) musulmán
moosoolman

mussels los mejillones
meHeeyoness

must: I must tengo que kay

I mustn't drink alcohol no debo beber alcohol d**ay**bo beb**air** alko-**ol**

mustard la mostaza most**a**tha

my mi; (pl) mis

myself: I'll do it myself lo haré yo mismo ar**ay** yo m**ee**smo

by myself yo solo

N

nail (finger) la uña **oo**n-ya

(metal) el clavo kl**a**bo

nailbrush el cepillo para las uñas thep**ee**-yo – **oo**n-yass

nail varnish el esmalte para uñas esm**a**ltay

name el nombre n**o**mbray

my name's John me llamo John may y**a**mo

what's your name? ¿cómo se llama usted? say – oost**ay**

what is the name of this street? ¿cómo se llama esta calle?

napkin la servilleta sairbee-y**ay**ta

nappy el pañal pan-y**al**

narrow (street) estrecho estr**ay**cho

nasty (person) desagradable desagrad**a**blay

(weather, accident) m**a**lo

national nacional nath-y**o**nal

nationality la nacionalidad nath-yonal**ee**da

natural natural nat**oo**ral

nausea la nausea n**o**wsay-a

navy (blue) azul marino ath**oo**l mar**ee**no

near cerca th**ai**rka

is it near the city centre? ¿está cerca del centro? th**e**ntro

do you go near Las Ramblas? ¿pasa usted cerca de Las Ramblas? oost**a** – day

where is the nearest...? ¿dónde está el... más cercano? d**o**nday – th**ai**rkano

nearby por aquí cerca ak**ee**

nearly c**a**si

necessary necesario nethesar-yo

neck el cuello kw**ay**-yo

necklace el collar ko-y**ar**

necktie la corb**a**ta

need: I need... necesito un... neseth**ee**to

do I need to pay? ¿necesito pagar?

needle la aguja ag**oo**Ha

negative (film) el negativo
negate**ee**bo

neither: neither (one) of them
ninguno (de ellos) neen**goo**no
day **ay**-yoss

neither... nor... ni... ni...

nephew el sobrino

Nerja Nerja n**air**Ha

net (in sport) la red

Netherlands Los Países Bajos
pa-**ee**sess ba**Hoss**

network map el mapa

never nunca n**oo**nka

**have you ever been to
Seville?** ¿ha estado alguna
vez en Sevilla? a – beth

**no, never, I've never been
there** no, nunca, nunca he
estado allí ay – a-**yee**

new nuevo nw**ay**bo

news (radio, TV etc) las noticias
not**ee**th-yass

newsagent's el kiosko de prensa
day

newspaper el periódico pair-
yodeeko

newspaper kiosk el kiosko de
prensa day

New Year el Año Nuevo **an**-yo
nw**ay**bo

Happy New Year! ¡Feliz Año
Nuevo fel**ee**th

New Year's Eve Nochevieja
n**o**chay-b-y**ay**Ha

New Zealand Nueva Zelanda
nw**ay**ba thel**a**nda

**New Zealander: I'm a New
Zealander** (*male/female*) soy
neozelandés/neozeland**e**sa
nayo-theland**ay**ss

next pr**ó**ximo

**the next turning/street on
the left** la siguiente calle a la
izquierda seeg-y**e**ntay ka-yay a
la eethk-y**air**da

at the next stop en la
siguiente par**a**da

next week la pr**ó**xima semana

next to al lado de day

nice (food) bueno bw**ay**no
(looks, view etc) bonito
(person) simp**á**tico

niece la sobrina

night la noche n**o**chay

at night por la noche

good night buenas noches
bw**ay**nass

**do you have a single room
for one night?** ¿tiene una
habitación individual para
una noche? t-**ay**nay **oo**na
abeetath-yon eendeebeedw**al**

yes, madam sí, señora
sen-**yo**ra

how much is it per night?
¿cuánto es la noche? kw**a**nto

it's 65 euros for one night
son sesenta y cinco euros
la noche ses**e**nti th**ee**nko
ay-ooross

thank you, I'll take it
gracias, me la quedo may
la k**ay**do

nightclub la discoteca deeskot**ay**ka

nightdress el camis**ó**n

night porter el portero port**ai**ro

no no

I've no change no t**e**ngo cambio kamb-yo

there's no… left no queda… k**ay**da

no way! ¡ni hablar! abl**a**r

oh no! (upset, annoyed) ¡Dios m**í**o!

nobody nadie n**a**d-yay

there's nobody there no hay nadie ahí ī – a-**ee**

noise el ruido rw**ee**do

noisy: it's too noisy hay demasiado ruido ī daymass-y**a**do

non-alcoholic sin alcohol alko-**o**l

none ning**u**no

non-smoking compartment no fumadores foomad**o**ress

noon el mediodía m**ay**d-yo-d**ee**-a

no-one nadie n**a**d-yay

nor: nor do I yo tamp**o**co

normal norm**a**l

north norte n**o**rtay

in the north en el norte

north of Girona al norte de Gir**o**na

northeast nordeste nord**e**stay

northern del norte n**o**rtay

northwest noroeste noro-**e**stay

Northern Ireland Irlanda del Norte eerl**a**nda del n**o**rtay

Norway Noruega norw**ay**ga

Norwegian (adj) noru**e**go

nose la nariz nar**ee**th

nosebleed la hemorragia nasal emorraн-ya

not no

no, I'm not hungry no, no tengo hambre **a**mbray

I don't want any, thank you no quiero ninguno, gracias k-y**ai**ro

it's not necessary no es necesario nethes**a**r-yo

I didn't know that no lo sab**í**a

not that one – this one ése no – éste **ay**sa – **e**stay

note (banknote) el billete bee-**ay**tay

notebook el cuaderno kwad**ai**rno

notepaper (for letters) el papel de c**a**rta

nothing n**a**da

nothing for me, thanks para mí nada, gracias

nothing else nada más

novel la novela nob**ay**la

November noviembre nob-y**e**mbray

now ahora a-**o**ra

number el número n**oo**mairo

I've got the wrong number me he equivocado de número may ay ekeebok**a**do day

what is your phone number? ¿cuál es su número de teléfono? kwal – tel**ay**fono

number plate la matrícula

nurse (male/female) el enfermero enfairm**ai**ro/la enferm**e**ra

nursery slope la pista de principiantes day preentheep-yantess

nut (for bolt) la tuerca twairka

nuts los frutos secos

O

o'clock en punto poonto

occupied (toilet) ocupado okoopado

October octubre oktoobray

odd (strange) raro

of de day

off (lights) apagado

　it's just off calle Corredera está cerca de calle Corredera thairka day ka-yay

　we're off tomorrow nos vamos mañana bamoss

offensive (language, behaviour) insultante eensooltantay

office (place of work) la oficina ofeetheena

officer (said to policeman) señor sen-yor

often a menudo

　not often pocas veces baythess

　how often are the buses? ¿cada cuánto son los autobuses? kwanto

oil el aceite athay-eetay

ointment la pomada

OK vale balay

　are you OK? ¿está bien? b-yen

　is that OK with you? ¿le parece bien? lay paraythay

　is it OK to...? ¿se puede...? say pwayday

　that's OK thanks (it doesn't matter) está bien, gracias

　I'm OK (nothing for me) yo no quiero k-yairo

　(I feel OK) me siento bien may s-yento

　is this train OK for...? ¿este tren va a...? estay – ba

　I said I'm sorry, OK? he dicho que lo siento, ¿vale? ay – kay – balay

old viejo b-yayHo

DIALOGUE

　how old are you? ¿cuántos años tiene? kwantoss an-yoss t-yaynay

　I'm twenty-five tengo veinticinco

　and you? ¿y usted? ee oostay

old-fashioned pasado de moda day

old town (old part of town) el casco antiguo anteegwo

　in the old town en el casco antiguo

olive la aceituna athay-eetoona, la oliva

　black/green olives las aceitunas negras/verdes bairdess

olive oil el aceite de oliva athay-eetay day oleeba

omelette la tortilla tortee-ya

on en

on the street/beach en la calle/la playa

is it on this road? ¿está en esta calle?

on the plane en el avión ab-yon

on Saturday el sábado

on television en la tele taylay

I haven't got it on me no lo llevo encima yaybo entheema

this one's on me (drink) ésta va de mi cuenta ba day mee kwenta

the light wasn't on la luz no estaba encendida looth – enthendeeda

what's on tonight? ¿qué ponen esta noche? kay ponen esta noche

once (one time) una vez oona beth

at once (immediately) en seguida segeeda

one uno oono, una

the white one el blanco, la blanca

one-way: a one-way ticket to… un billete de ida para… bee-yaytay day eeda

onion la cebolla thebo-ya

online (book, check) en línea en leenay-a

only sólo

only one sólo uno

it's only 6 o'clock son sólo las seis

I've only just got here acabo de llegar yegar

on/off switch el interruptor eentairrooptor

open (adj) abierto ab-yairto

(verb) abrir abreer

when do you open? ¿a qué hora abre? kay ora abray

I can't get it open no puedo abrirlo pwaydo

in the open air al aire libre a-eeray leebray

opening times el horario orar-yo

> Travel tip Almost everything in Spain – shops, museums, churches, tourist offices – closes for a siesta of at least two hours in the middle of the day. There's a lot of variation across the country, but you'll get far less aggravated if you accept that the early afternoon is best spent asleep, or in a bar, or both.

open ticket el billete abierto bee-yaytay ab-yairto

opera la ópera

operation (medical) la operación opairath-yon

operator (telephone: male/female) el operador/la operadora

opposite: the opposite direction la dirección contraria deerekth-yon kontrar-ya

the bar opposite el bar de enfrente day enfrentay

opposite my hotel enfrente de mi hotel

optician el óptico

or o

orange (fruit) la naranja naranHa
(colour) (color) naranja

orange juice (fresh) el zumo de naranja thoomo day
(fizzy, diluted) la naranjada naranHada

orchestra la orquesta orkesta

order: can we order now?
(in restaurant) ¿podemos pedir ya? podaymoss

I've already ordered, thanks ya he pedido, gracias ay

I didn't order this no he pedido eso ayso

out of order averiado, fuera de servicio abair-yado, fwaira day sairbeeth-yo

ordinary corriente korr-yentay

other otro

the other one el otro

the other day el otro día

I'm waiting for the others estoy esperando a los demás

do you have any others? ¿tiene usted otros? t-yaynay oostay

otherwise de otra manera manaira

our nuestro nwestro, nuestra; (pl) nuestros, nuestras

ours (el) nuestro, (la) nuestra

out: he's out no está

three kilometres out of town a tres kilómetros de la ciudad

outdoors fuera de casa fwaira day

outside... fuera de...

can we sit outside? ¿podemos sentarnos fuera? podaymoss

oven el horno orno

over: over here por aquí akee

over there por allí a-yee

over 500 más de quinientos

it's over se acabó say

overcharge: you've overcharged me me ha cobrado de más may a – day

overcoat el abrigo

overlook: I'd like a room overlooking the courtyard querría una habitación que dé al patio kairree-a oona abeetath-yon kay day

overnight (travel) de noche day nochay

overtake adelantar

owe: how much do I owe you? ¿cuánto le debo? kwanto lay daybo

own: my own... mi propio... prop-yo

are you on your own? (to a man/woman) ¿está solo/sola?

I'm on my own (male/female) estoy solo/sola

owner (male/female) el propietario prop-yetar-yo/la propietaria

P

pack: a pack of... un paquete de... pak**ay**tay day

(*verb*) hacer las maletas mal**ay**tass

package el paquete pak**ay**tay

package holiday el viaje organizado b-ya**Hay** organeeth**a**do

packed lunch la b**o**lsa con la comida

packet: a packet of cigarettes un paquete de cigarrillos pak**ay**tay day theegar**ee**-yoss

padlock el cand**a**do

page (of book) la página pa**Hee**na

could you page Mr...? ¿podría llamar al Señor (por altav**o**z)...? yam**a**r

pain el dol**o**r

I have a pain here me duele aquí may dw**ay**lay ak**ee**

painful dolor**o**so

painkillers los analgésicos anal**Hay**seekoss

paint la pint**u**ra

painting el cuadro kw**a**dro

pair: a pair of... un par de... day

Pakistani (*adj*) paquistaní pakeestan**ee**

palace el palacio pal**a**th-yo

pale p**á**lido

pale blue azul claro ath**oo**l

pan la cazuela kath**way**la

panties las br**a**gas

pants (underwear: men's) los calzoncillos kalthonth**ee**-yoss

(women's) las br**a**gas

(trousers) los pantalones pantal**o**ness

pantyhose los panties

paper el pap**e**l

(newspaper) el periódico pair-y**o**deeko

a piece of paper un trozo de papel tr**o**tho day

paper handkerchiefs los Kleenex

parcel el paquete pak**ay**tay

pardon (me)? (didn't understand/ hear) ¿c**ó**mo?

parents: my parents mis padres p**a**dress

parents-in-law los suegros sw**e**gross

park el parque p**a**rkay

(*verb*) aparc**a**r

can I park here? ¿puedo aparcar aquí? pw**ay**do – ak**ee**

parking lot el aparcamiento aparkam-y**e**nto

part la parte p**a**rtay

partner (boyfriend, girlfriend etc) el compañero kompan-y**ai**ro

party (group) el grupo

(celebration) la fiesta

pass (in mountains) el puerto pw**ai**rto

passenger (*male/female*) el pasajero pasa**Hai**ro/la pasaj**e**ra

passport el pasaporte pasap**o**rtay

password la contraseña kontras**e**n-ya

past: in the past antiguamente anteegwamentay

just past the information office justo después de la oficina de información Hoosto despwayss day

path el camino

pattern el dibujo deebooHo

pavement la acera athaira

on the pavement en la acera

pavement café el café terraza terratha

pay (*verb*) pagar

can I pay, please? la cuenta, por favor kwenta

it's already paid for ya está pagado

who's paying? ¿quién paga? k-yen

I'll pay pago yo

no, you paid last time, I'll pay no, usted pagó la última vez, yo pago oostay – oolteema beth

pay phone el teléfono público telayfono poobleeko

peaceful tranquilo trankeelo

peach el melocotón

peanuts los cacahuetes kakawaytess

pear la pera paira

peas los guisantes geesantess

peculiar (taste, custom) raro

pedestrian crossing el paso de peatones pay-atoness

pedestrian precinct la calle peatonal ka-yay pay-atonal

peg (for washing) la pinza peentha

(for tent) la estaca

pen la pluma plooma

pencil el lápiz lapeeth

penfriend (*male/female*) el amigo/ la amiga por correspondencia korrespondenth-ya

penicillin la penicilina peneetheeleena

penknife la navaja nabaHa

pensioner el/la pensionista pens-yoneesta

people la gente Hentay

the other people in the hotel los otros huéspedes del hotel wespedess

too many people demasiada gente daymas-yada

pepper (spice) la pimienta peem-yenta

(vegetable) el pimiento

peppermint (sweet) el caramelo de menta karamaylo day

per: per night por noche nochay

how much per day? ¿cuánto es por noche? kwanto

per cent por ciento th-yento

perfect perfecto pairfekto

perfume el perfume pairfoomay

perhaps quizás keethass

perhaps not quizás no

period (of time, menstruation) el período pairee-odo

perm la permanente pairmanentay

permit el permiso pairmeeso

person la persona pairs**o**na

petrol la gasol**i**na

petrol can la lata de gasolina
day

petrol station la gasolinera
gasoleen**ai**ra

pharmacy la farmacia farmath-ya

phone el teléfono tel**ay**fono

  (*verb*) llamar por teléfono
yam**a**r

phone book la guía telefónica
g**ee**-a

phone box la cabina telefónica
kab**ee**na

phonecard la tarjeta de teléfono
tarH**ay**ta day tayl**ay**fono

phone charger el cargador
kargad**o**r

phone number el número de
teléfono n**oo**mairo

photo la f**o**to

  **excuse me, could you take
  a photo of us?** ¿le importaría
  hacernos una foto? lay –
  ath**ai**rnoss

phrasebook el libro de frases
day fr**a**sess

piano el piano p-y**a**no

pickpocket el/la carterista

**pick up: will you be there to
pick me up?** ¿va a ir
  a recogerme?
  ba – rekoH**ai**rmay

picnic el picnic

picture el cuadro kw**a**dro

pie (meat) la empanada
  (fruit) la tarta

piece el pedazo ped**a**tho

  a piece of... un pedazo de…
  day

pill la p**í**ldora

  I'm on the pill est**oy** tomando
  la píldora

pillow la almohada almo-**a**da

pillow case la funda (de
almohada) f**oo**nda

pin el alfiler alfeel**ai**r

pineapple la piña p**ee**n-ya

pineapple juice el zumo de piña
th**oo**mo

pink r**o**sa

pipe (for smoking) la pipa p**ee**pa
  (for water) el tubo t**oo**bo

pipe cleaners los limpiapipas
leemp-yap**ee**pass

pity: it's a pity es una l**á**stima

pizza la p**i**zza

place el sitio s**ee**t-yo

  is this place taken? ¿está
  ocup**a**do este sitio? est**ay**

  at your place en tu c**a**sa

  at his place en su c**a**sa

plain (not patterned) liso

plane el avión ab-y**on**

  by plane en avión

plant la pl**a**nta

plaster cast la escayola
eska-y**o**la

plasters las tir**i**tas

plastic pl**á**stico

  (credit cards) las tarjetas de
  crédito tarH**ay**tass day kr**ay**deeto

plastic bag la b**o**lsa de plástico

plate el pl**a**to

platform el andén

which platform is it for Saragossa, please? ¿qué andén para Zaragoza, por favor? kay andén para Zaragoza, por fabor? kay

play (in theatre) la obra

(*verb*) jugar Hoogar

playground el patio de recreo pat-yo day rekray-o

pleasant agradable agradablay

please por favor fabor

yes please sí, por favor

could you please...? ¿podría hacer el favor de...? athair – day

please don't no, por favor

pleased to meet you encantado de conocerle day konothairlay

pleasure: my pleasure es un placer plathair

plenty: plenty of... mucho... moocho

there's plenty of time tenemos mucho tiempo taynaymoss – t-yempo

that's plenty, thanks es suficiente, gracias soofeeth-yentay

pliers los alicates aleekatess

plug (electrical) el enchufe enchoofay

(for car) la bujía booHee-a

(in sink) el tapón

plumber el fontanero fontanairo

pm de la tarde day la tarday

poached egg el huevo escalfado waybo

pocket el bolsillo bolsee-yo

point: two point five dos coma cinco

there's no point no merece la pena mairaythay la payna

points (in car) los platinos

poisonous venenoso benenoso

police la policía poleethee-a

call the police! ¡llame a la policía! yamay

policeman el (agente de) policía aHentay day

police station la comisaría de policía

policewoman la policía

polish el betún betoon

polite educado edookado

polluted contaminado

pony el poney

pool (for swimming) la piscina peestheena

poor (not rich) pobre pobray

(quality) de baja calidad day baHa kaleeda

pop music la música pop mooseeka

pop singer el/la cantante de música pop kantantay

population la población poblath-yon

pork la carne de cerdo karnay day thairdo

port (for boats) el puerto pwairto

(drink) el Oporto

porter (in hotel) el conserje konsairHay

portrait el retrato

Portugal Portugal

Portuguese (adj) portugués portoogayss

posh (restaurant) de lujo looHo

(people) pijo peeHo

possible posible poseeblay

is it possible to…? ¿es posible…?

as… as possible tan… como sea posible say-a

post (mail) el correo korray-o

(verb) echar al correo

could you post this for me? ¿podría enviarme esto por correo? emb-yarmay

postbox el buzón boothon

postcard la postal

poster el poster postair, el cartel

post office Correos korray-oss

poste restante la lista de Correos leesta

potato la patata

potato chips las patatas fritas (de bolsa)

pots and pans (ie cooking implements) los cacharros de cocina day kotheena

pottery (objects) la cerámica thairameeka

pound (money, weight) la libra

power cut el apagón

power point la toma de corriente day korr-yentay

practise: I want to practise my Spanish quiero practicar el español k-yairo – espan-yol

prawns las gambas

prefer: I prefer… prefiero… pref-yairo

pregnant embarazada embarathada

prescription (for chemist) la receta rethayta

present (gift) el regalo

president (of country) el/la
presidente *preseedentay*

pretty *mono*

it's pretty expensive es
bastante caro *bastantay*

price el precio *preth-yo*

priest el sacerdote *sathairdotay*

prime minister (*male/female*) el
primer ministro *preemair*/la
primera ministra

printed matter los impresos
eempraysoss

priority (in driving) la preferencia
prefairenth-ya

prison la cárcel *karthel*

private privado *preebado*

private bathroom el baño
privado *ban-yo*

probably probablemente
probablementay

problem el problema *problayma*

no problem! ¡con mucho
gusto! *moocho goosto*

program(me) el programa

promise: I promise lo prometo
promayto

**pronounce: how is this
pronounced?** ¿cómo se
pronuncia esto? *say pronoonth-ya*

properly (repaired, locked etc)
bien *b-yen*

protection factor (of suntan
lotion) el factor de protección
protekth-yon

Protestant (*adj*) protestante
protestantay

public convenience los aseos
públicos *asay-oss poobleekoss*

public holiday el día de fiesta
day

pudding (dessert) el postre *postray*

pull tirar

pullover el jersey *Hairsay*

puncture el pinchazo *peenchatho*

purple morado

purse (for money) el monedero
monedairo

(US: handbag) el bolso

push empujar *empooHar*

pushchair la sillita de ruedas
see-yeeta day rwaydass

put poner *ponair*

where can I put...? ¿dónde
puedo poner...? *donday pwaydo*

**could you put us up for the
night?** ¿podría alojarnos esta
noche? *aloHarnoss – nochay*

pyjamas el pijama *peeHama*

Pyrenees los Pirineos *peereenay-
oss*

Q

quality la calidad *kaleeda*

quarantine la cuarentena
kwarentayna

quarter la cuarta parte *kwarta
partay*

quayside: on the quayside en
el muelle *mway-yay*

question la pregunta *pregoonta*

queue la cola

quick rápido

that was quick sí que ha sido
rápido *kay a*

what's the quickest way there? ¿cuál es el camino más rápido? kwal

fancy a quick drink? ¿te apetece algo rápido de beber? tay apetaythay – day bebair

quickly rápidamente rapeedamentay

quiet (place, hotel) tranquilo trankeelo

quiet! ¡cállese! ka-yesay

quite (fairly) bastante bastantay

(very) muy mwee

that's quite right eso es cierto th-yairto

quite a lot bastante

R

rabbit el conejo konayHo

race (for runners, cars) la carrera karraira

racket (tennis etc) la raqueta rakayta

radiator (of car, in room) el radiador rad-yador

radio la radio rad-yo

on the radio por la radio

rail: by rail en tren

railway el ferrocarril

rain la lluvia yoob-ya

in the rain bajo la lluvia baHo

it's raining está lloviendo yob-yendo

raincoat el impermeable eempairmay-ablay

rape la violación b-yolath-yon

rare (steak) (muy) poco hecho mwee – aycho

rash (on skin) la erupción cutánea airoopth-yon kootanay-a

raspberry la frambuesa frambwaysa

rat la rata

rate (for changing money) el cambio kamb-yo

rather: it's rather good es bastante bueno bastantay bwayno

I'd rather... prefiero... pref-yairo

razor la maquinilla de afeitar makeenee-ya day afay-eetar

(electric) la máquina de afeitar eléctrica makeena

razor blades las hojas de afeitar oHass

read leer lay-air

ready preparado

are you ready? ¿estás listo? leesto

I'm not ready yet aún no estoy listo a-oon

DIALOGUE

when will it be ready? ¿cuándo estará listo? kwando

it should be ready in a couple of days estará listo dentro de un par de días day

real verdadero bairdadairo

really realmente ray-almentay

that's really great eso es estupendo ayso

really? (doubt) ¿de verdad? day bairda

(polite interest) ¿sí?

rearview mirror el (espejo) retrovisor espayнo retrobeesor

reasonable (prices etc) razonable rathonablay

receipt el recibo retheebo

recently recientemente rethyentementay

reception la recepción rethepth-yon

at reception en recepción

reception desk la recepción

receptionist el/la recepcionista rethepth-yoneesta

recognize reconocer rekonothair

recommend: could you recommend...? ¿puede usted recomendar...? pwayday oostay

record (music) el disco deesko

red rojo roнo

red wine el vino tinto beeno teento

refund el reembolso ray-embolso

can I have a refund? ¿puede devolverme el dinero? pwayday debolbairmay el deenairo

region la zona thona, la región reн-yon

registered: by registered mail por correo certificado korray-o thairteefeekado

registration number el número de la matrícula noomairo day

relatives los parientes par-yentess

religion la religión releeн-yon

remember: I don't remember no recuerdo rekwairdo

I remember recuerdo

do you remember? ¿recuerda? rekwairda

rent (for apartment etc) el alquiler alkeelair

(verb) alquilar

to/for rent de alquiler

rented car el coche alquilado kochay alkeelado

repair (verb) reparar

can you repair it? ¿puede arreglarlo? pwayday

repeat repetir

could you repeat that? ¿puede repetir eso? pwayday – ayso

reservation la reserva resairba

I'd like to make a reservation quisiera hacer una reserva kees-yaira athair

DIALOGUE

I have a reservation tengo una reserva

yes sir, what name please? sí, señor, ¿a qué nombre, por favor? sen-yor a kay nombray

reserve reservar resairbar

DIALOGUE

can I reserve a table for tonight? ¿puedo reservar una mesa para esta noche? pwaydo – maysa – nochay

yes madam, for how many people? sí, señora, ¿para cuántos? sen-**y**ora – kwant**o**ss

for two para dos

and for what time? ¿y para qué hora? kay **o**ra

for eight o'clock para las **o**cho

and could I have your name please? ¿me dice su nombre, por favor? may d**ee**thay soo n**o**mbray

see **alphabet** *for spelling*

rest: I need a rest necesito un descanso neth**e**s**ee**to

the rest of the group el r**e**sto del grupo gr**oo**po

restaurant el restaurante restowr**a**ntay

restaurant car el vagón-cafetería bag**o**n kafetair**ee**-a

rest room los servicios sairb**ee**th-yoss

see **toilet**

retired: I'm retired est**oy** jubilado/jubil**a**da ноobeel**a**do

return (ticket) el billete de ida y vuelta bee-y**e**tay day **ee**da ee bw**e**lta

reverse charge call la llamada a cobro revertido yam**a**da – rebert**ee**do

reverse gear la m**a**rcha atr**á**s

revolting asqueroso ask**a**ir**o**so

rib la costilla kost**ee**-ya

rice arroz arr**o**th

rich (person) rico r**ee**ko

(food) sustancial soostanth-y**a**l

ridiculous ridículo reed**ee**k**oo**lo

right (correct) corr**e**cto

(not left) der**e**cho

you were right tenía razón rath**o**n

that's right eso es **a**yso

this can't be right esto no puede ser así pw**a**yday sair

right! ¡bien! b-yen

is this the right road for…? ¿por aquí se va bien a…? ak**ee** say ba b-yen

on the right a la der**e**cha

turn right gire a la derecha н**ee**ray

right-hand drive con el volante a la derecha bol**a**ntay

ring (on finger) la sortija sort**ee**на

I'll ring you te llamaré tay yamar**ay**

ring back volver a llamar bolb**a**ir a yamar

ripe (fruit) mad**u**ro

rip-off: it's a rip-off es un t**i**mo

rip-off prices los precios alt**í**simos pr**a**yth-yoss

risky arriesgado arr-yesg**a**do

river el río

road la carretera karret**a**ira

is this the road for…? ¿es ésta la carretera que va a…? kay ba

down the road en **e**sta calle ka-yay

road accident el accidente automovilístico *aktheedentay owtomobeeleesteeko*

road map el mapa de carreteras

roadsign la señal de tráfico *sen-yal day*

rob: I've been robbed ¡me han robado! *may an robado*

rock la roca

(music) el rock

on the rocks (with ice) con hielo *yaylo*

roll (bread) el bollo *bo-yo*

roof el tejado *teнado*

roof rack la baca

room la habitación *abeetath-yon*

in my room en mi habitación

room service el servicio de habitaciones *sairbeeth-yo day*

rope la cuerda *kwairda*

rosé (wine) vino rosado *beeno*

roughly (approximately) aproximadamente *–mentay*

round: it's my round es mi turno *toorno*

roundabout (for traffic) la rotonda

round trip ticket el billete de ida y vuelta *bee-yaytay day eeda ee bwelta*

route la ruta *roota*

what's the best route? ¿cuál es la mejor ruta? *kwal ess la mayнor*

rubber (material) la goma

(eraser) la goma de borrar

rubber band la goma elástica

rubbish (waste) la basura

(poor quality goods) las porquerías *porkaire-ass*

rubbish! (nonsense) ¡tonterías! *tontairee-ass*

rucksack la mochila

rude grosero *grosairo*

ruins las ruinas *rweenass*

rum el ron

rum and Coke el ron con Coca-Cola

run (*verb:* person) correr *korrair*

how often do the buses run? ¿cada cuánto pasan los autobuses? *kwanto*

I've run out of money se me ha acabado el dinero *say may a – deenairo*

rush hour la hora punta *ora poonta*

S

sad triste *treestay*

saddle (for horse) la silla de montar *see-ya day*

(on bike) el sillín *see-yeen*

safe seguro *segooro*

safety pin el imperdible *eempairdeeblay*

sail la vela *bayla*

sailboard el windsurf

sailboarding el windsurf

salad la ensalada

salad dressing el aliño para la ensalada *aleen-yo*

sale: for sale en venta *em baynta*

salmon el salmón *sal-mon*

salt la sal

same: the same mismo m**ee**smo

  the same as this igual que éste eegw**a**l kay **e**stay

  the same again, please lo mismo **o**tra vez, por fav**o**r beth

  it's all the same to me me es igual may – eegw**a**l

sand la arena ar**a**yna

sandals las sandalias sand**a**l-yass

sandwich el sandwich

sanitary napkin la compresa kompr**a**ysa

sanitary towel la compresa

Saragossa Zaragoza tharag**o**tha

sardines las sardinas

Saturday sábado

sauce la salsa

saucepan el cazo k**a**tho

saucer el platillo plat**ee**-yo

sauna la sauna s**ow**na

sausage la salchicha

say: how do you say… in Spanish? ¿cómo se dice… en español? say d**ee**thay en espan-y**o**l

  what did he say? ¿que ha dicho? kay a

  I said… he dicho… ay

  he said… ha dicho…

  could you say that again? ¿podría repetirlo?

scarf (for neck) la bufanda

  (for head) el pañuelo pan-yw**ay**lo

scenery el paisaje pa-eesa**н**ay

schedule el horario or**a**r-yo

scheduled flight el vuelo regular bw**ay**lo reg**oo**lar

school la escuela eskw**ay**la

scissors: a pair of scissors las tijeras teeн**ai**rass

scotch el whisky

Scotch tape la cinta adhesiva th**ee**nta ades**ee**ba

Scotland Escocia esk**o**th-ya

Scottish escocés esk**o**th**a**yss

  I'm Scottish (male/female) soy escocés/escoc**e**sa

scrambled eggs los huevos revueltos w**ay**boss rebw**ay**ltoss

scratch el rasguño rasg**oo**n-yo

screw el tornillo torn**ee**-yo

screwdriver el destornillador destornee-yad**o**r

sea el mar

  by the sea junto al mar н**oo**nto

seafood los mariscos

seafood restaurant la marisquería mareeskair**ee**-a

seafront el paseo marítimo pas**ay**-o mar**ee**teemo

  on the seafront en línea de playa l**ee**nay-a day pl**a**-ya

seagull la gaviota gab-y**o**ta

search (verb) buscar

seashell la concha marina

seasick: I feel seasick est**o**y mareado maray-**a**do

  I get seasick me mareo may mar**a**y-o

seaside: by the seaside en la playa pl**a**-ya

seat el asiento as-yento

is this anyone's seat? ¿es de alguien este asiento? day alg-yen estay

seat belt el cinturón de seguridad theentooron day segooreeda

sea urchin el erizo de mar aireetho

seaweed el alga

secluded apartado

second (*adj*) segundo segoondo

(of time) el segundo

just a second! ¡un momento!

second class (travel) en segunda clase klasay

secondhand de segunda mano day

see ver bair

can I see? ¿puedo ver? pwaydo

have you seen...? ¿ha visto...? a beesto

I saw him this morning le vi esta mañana lay bee

see you! ¡hasta luego! asta lwaygo

I see (I understand) ya comprendo

self-catering apartment el apartamento

self-service autoservicio owtosairbeeth-yo

sell vender bendair

do you sell...? ¿vende...? benday

Sellotape la cinta adhesiva theenta adeseeba

send enviar emb-yar

I want to send this to England quiero enviar esto a Inglaterra k-yairo emb-yar

senior citizen el/la pensionista pens-yoneesta

separate separado

separated: I'm separated estoy separado/separada

separately (pay, travel) por separado

September septiembre sept-yembray

septic séptico

serious serio sair-yo

service charge el servicio sairbeeth-yo

service station la estacion de servicio estath-yon day

serviette la servilleta sairbee-yayta

set menu el menu del día menoo

several varios bar-yoss

Seville Sevilla sebee-ya

sew coser kosair

could you sew this back on? ¿podría coserme esto? kosairmay

sex el sexo

sexy sexy

shade: in the shade a la sombra

shake: let's shake hands choque esa mano chokay aysa

shallow (water) poco profundo profoondo

shame: what a shame! ¡que lástima! kay

shampoo el champú

a shampoo and set un lavado y marcado labado ee

share (verb: room, table etc) compartir

sharp (knife) afilado

(taste) ácido atheedo

(pain) agudo

shattered (very tired) agotado

shaver la máquina de afeitar makeena day afay-eetar

shaving foam la espuma de afeitar

shaving point el enchufe (para la máquina de afeitar) enchoofay – makeena

she ella ay-ya

is she here? ¿está (ella) aquí? akee

sheet (for bed) la sábana

shelf la estantería estantairee-a

shellfish los mariscos

sherry el jerez Hereth

ship el barco

by ship en barco

shirt el camisa

shit! ¡mierda! m-yairda

shock el susto soosto

I got an electric shock me ha dado calambre may a – kalambray

shock-absorber el amortiguador amorteegwador

shocking escandaloso

shoes los zapatos thapatoss

a pair of shoes un par de zapatos

shoelaces los cordones para zapatos kordoness

shoe polish la crema para los zapatos krayma

shoe repairer's la zapatería thapatairee-a

shop la tienda t-yenda

shopping: I'm going shopping voy de compras boy

shopping centre el centro comercial thentro komairth-yal

shop window el escaparate eskaparatay

shore la orilla oree-ya

short (time, journey) corto

(person) bajo baнo

it's only a short distance queda bastante cerca kayda bastantay thairka

shortcut el atajo ataнo

shorts los pantalones cortos pantaloness

should: what should I do? ¿que hago? kay ago

he shouldn't be long no tardará mucho moocho

you should have told me debiste habérmelo dicho debeestay abairmelo

shoulder el hombro ombro

shout (verb) gritar

show (in theatre) el espectáculo espektakoolo

could you show me? ¿me lo enseña? may lo ensen-ya

shower (in bathroom) la ducha doocha

with shower con ducha

shower gel el gel de ducha Hel

shut (*verb*) cerrar thairrar

  when do you shut? ¿a qué hora cierran? a kay ora th-yairran

  when do they shut? ¿a qué hora cierran?

  they're shut está cerrado thairrado

  I've shut myself out he cerrado y he dejado la llave dentro ay – ee ay dayHado la yabay

  shut up! ¡cállese! ka-yesay

shutter (on camera) el obturador (on window) la contraventana kontrabentana

shy tímido teemeedo

sick (ill) enfermo enfairmo

  I'm going to be sick (vomit) voy a vomitar boy a bomeetar

side el lado

  on the other side of town al otro lado de la ciudad day la th-yooda

side lights las luces de posición loothess day poseeth-yon

side salad la ensalada aparte apartay

side street la callejuela ka-yay-Hwayla

sidewalk la acera athaira

sight: the sights of... los lugares de interés de... loogaress day eentairess

sightseeing: we're going sightseeing vamos a hacer un recorrido turístico bamoss a athair

sightseeing tour el recorrido turístico

sign (notice) el letrero letrairo

(road sign) la señal de tráfico
sen-yal day

**signal: he didn't give a
signal** no hizo ninguna señal
no **eetho**

signature la firma feerma

signpost el letrero letrairo

silence el silencio seelenth-yo

silk la seda sayda

silly tonto

silver la plata

silver foil el papel de aluminio
aloomeen-yo

similar parecido paretheedo

simple (easy) sencillo
senthee-yo

since: since yesterday desde
ayer desday a-yair

since I got here desde que
llegué aquí kay yegay akee

sing cantar

singer el/la cantante kantantay

single: a single to... un billete
para... bee-yaytay

I'm single soy soltero soltairo

single bed la cama individual
eendeebeedwal

single room la habitación
individual abeetath-yon

sink (in kitchen) el fregadero
fregadairo

sister la hermana airmana

sister-in-law la cuñada
koon-yada

sit: can I sit here? ¿puedo
sentarme aquí? pwaydo
sentarmay akee

sit down sentarse sentarsay

sit down! ¡siéntese!
s-yentaysay

is anyone sitting here? ¿está
ocupado este asiento? estay
as-yento

size el tamaño taman-yo

(of clothes) la talla **ta**-ya

ski el esquí eskee

(verb) esquiar esk-yar

a pair of skis un par de esquís
day

ski boots las botas de esquiar

skiing el esquí eskee

we're going skiing vamos a
esquiar bamoss – esk-yar

ski instructor (male/female) el
monitor/la monitora de esquí

ski-lift el telesquí teleskee

skin la piel p-yel

skin-diving el buceo boothay-o

skinny flaco

ski-pants los pantalones de
esquí pantaloness day eskee

ski-pass el abono

ski pole el bastón de esquí day

skirt la falda

ski run la pista de esquí eskee

ski slope la pista de esquí

ski wax la cera de esquís thaira

sky el cielo th-yaylo

sleep (verb) dormir

did you sleep well? ¿ha
dormido bien? a – b-yen

I need a good sleep
necesito dormir bien
netheseeto

sleeper (on train) el coche-cama kochay-kama

sleeping bag el saco de dormir day

sleeping car el coche-cama kochay-kama

sleeping pill la pastilla para dormir pastee-ya

sleepy: I'm feeling sleepy tengo sueño swayn-yo

sleeve la manga

slide (photographic) la diapositiva d-yaposeeteeba

slip (under dress) la combinación kombeenath-yon

slippery resbaladizo resbaladeetho

slow lento

slow down! ¡más despacio! despath-yo

slowly despacio

could you say it slowly? ¿podría decirlo despacio? detheerlo

very slowly muy despacio mwee

small pequeño peken-yo

smell: it smells! (smells bad) ¡apesta!

smile (verb) sonreír sonray-eer

smoke el humo oomo

do you mind if I smoke? ¿le importa si fumo? lay – foomo

I don't smoke no fumo

do you smoke? ¿fuma?

snack: I'd just like a snack quisiera una tapa solamente kees-yaira – solamentay

sneeze el estornudo

snorkel el tubo de buceo toobo day boothay-o

snow la nieve n-yaybay

it's snowing está nevando

so: it's so good es tan bueno bwayno

not so fast no tan de prisa preesa

so am I yo también tamb-yen

so do I yo también

so-so más o menos maynoss

soaking solution (for contact lenses) el líquido preservador leekeedo

soap el jabón Habon

soap powder el jabón en polvo em polbo

sober sobrio sobr-yo

sock el calcetín kaltheteen

socket (electrical) el enchufe enchoofay

soda (water) la soda

sofa el sofá

soft (material etc) suave swabay

soft-boiled egg el huevo pasado por agua waybo – agwa

soft drink el refresco

soft lenses las lentes blandas lentess

sole (of shoe, of foot) la suela swayla

could you put new soles on these? ¿podría cambiarles las suelas? kamb-yarless

some: can I have some water? ¿me da un poco de agua? may – day

can I have some rolls? ¿me da unos bollos? bo-yoss

can I have some? ¿me da un poco?

somebody, someone alguien alg-yen

something algo

something to drink algo de beber bebair

sometimes a veces baythess

somewhere en alguna parte partay

son el hijo eeHo

song la canción kanth-yon

son-in-law el yerno yairno

soon pronto

I'll be back soon volveré pronto bolbairay

as soon as possible lo antes posible antess poseeblay

sore: it's sore me duele may dwaylay

sore throat el dolor de garganta

sorry: (I'm) sorry perdone pairdonay

sorry? (didn't understand) ¿cómo?

sort: what sort of...? ¿qué clase de...? kay klasay day

soup la sopa

sour (taste) ácido atheedo

south el sur soor

in the south en el sur

South Africa Sudáfrica

South African (*adj*) sudafricano

I'm South African (*male/female*) soy sudafricano/ sudafricana

southeast el sudeste sood-estay

southwest el sudoeste soodo-estay

souvenir el recuerdo rekwairdo

Spain España espan-ya

Spaniard (*male/female*) el español espan-yol/la española

Spanish español

the Spanish los españoles espan-yoless

spanner la llave inglesa yabay eenglaysa

spare part el repuesto repwesto

spare tyre la rueda de repuesto rwayda day

spark plug la bujía booHee-a

speak: do you speak English? ¿habla inglés? abla

I don't speak... no hablo... ablo

DIALOGUE

can I speak to Pablo? ¿puedo hablar con Pablo? pwaydo

who's calling ¿quién llama? k-yen yama

it's Patricia soy Patricia

I'm sorry, he's not in, can I take a message? lo siento, no está, ¿quiere dejar algún recado? s-yento – k-yairay dayHar

---

no thanks, I'll call back later no gracias, llamaré más tarde yamaray mass tarday

please tell him I called por favor, dígale que he llamado deegalay kay ay yamado

speciality la especialidad espeth-yaleeda

spectacles las gafas

speed la velocidad belotheeda

speed limit el límite de velocidad leemeetay day

speedometer el velocímetro belotheemetro

spell: how do you spell it? ¿cómo se escribe? say eskreebay

see **alphabet**

spend gastar

spider la araña aran-ya

spin-dryer la secadora

splinter la astilla astee-ya

spoke (in wheel) el radio rad-yo

spoon la cuchara

sport el deporte dayportay

sprain: I've sprained my… me he torcido el… may ay tortheedo

spring (season) la primavera preemabaira

(of car, seat) el muelle mway-yay

square (in town) la plaza platha

stairs las escaleras eskalairass

stale (bread, taste) pasado

stall: the engine keeps stalling el motor se para a cada rato say

stamp el sello say-yo

a stamp for England, please un sello para Inglaterra, por favor

what are you sending? ¿qué es lo que envía? kay – embee-a

this postcard esta postal

standby el vuelo standby bwaylo

star la estrella estray-ya

(in film) el/la protagonista

start el principio preentheep-yo

(*verb*) comenzar komenthar

when does it start? ¿cuándo empieza? kwando emp-yaytha

the car won't start el coche no arranca kochay

starter (of car) el motor de arranque arrankay

(food) la entrada

starving: I'm starving me muero de hambre may mwairo day ambray

state (in country) el estado

the States (USA) los Estados Unidos ooneedoss

station la estación del ferrocarril estath-yon

statue la estatua estatwa

stay: where are you staying? ¿dónde se hospedan? donday say ospaydan

I'm staying at… me hospedo en… may osp**ay**do

I'd like to stay another two nights me gustaría quedarme otras dos noches may – kedar**may** – **no**chess

steak el filete feel**ay**tay

steal robar

my bag has been stolen me han robado el bolso may an

steep (hill) empin**a**do

steering la dirección deerekth-**yon**

step: on the steps en las escaleras eskala**ai**rass

stereo el estéreo est**ai**ray-o

sterling las libras esterlinas estairl**ee**nass

steward (on plane) el auxiliar de vuelo owkseel-**yar** day b**way**lo

stewardess la azafata atha**fa**ta

sticking plaster la tirita

still: I'm still waiting todavía est**oy** esperando todab**ee**-a

is he still there? ¿está todavía ahí? a-**ee**

keep still! ¡quédese quieto! k**ay**daysay k-y**ay**to

sting: I've been stung algo me ha picado may a

stockings las medias m**ay**d-yass

stomach el estómago

stomach ache el dolor de estómago day

stone (rock) la piedra p-y**e**dra

stop (verb) parar

please, stop here (to taxi driver etc) pare aquí, por favor paray ak**ee**

do you stop near…? ¿para cerca de…? tha**ir**ka day

stop doing that! ¡deje de hacer eso! d**ay**Hay day ath**air** **ay**so

stopover la escala, la parada

storm la tormenta

straight: it's straight ahead todo derecho dair**e**cho

a straight whisky un whisky solo

straightaway en seguida seg**ee**da

strange (odd) extraño estran-yo

stranger (male/female) el forastero forast**air**o/la forast**e**ra

I'm a stranger here no soy de aquí day ak**ee**

strap la correa korr**ay**-a

strawberry la fresa fr**ay**sa

stream el arroyo arr**o**-yo

street la calle ka-y**ay**

on the street en la calle

streetmap el mapa de la ciudad thy**oo**da

string la cuerda kw**air**da

strong fuerte fw**air**tay

stuck atascado

the key's stuck la llave se ha atascado yabay say a

student el/la estudiante estood-y**an**tay

stupid estúpido esto**o**peedo

subway el metro

suburb el suburbio soobo**o**rb-yo

suddenly de repente rep**en**tay

suede el ante **an**tay

sugar el azúcar ath**oo**kar

suit el traje tra**H**ay

  it doesn't suit me (jacket etc) no me sienta bien no may s-y**e**nta b-yen

  it suits you te sienta muy bien tay – mw**ee**

suitcase la maleta mal**ay**ta

summer el verano bair**a**no

  in the summer en el verano

sun el sol

  in the sun en el sol

  out of the sun en la sombra

sunbathe tomar el sol

sunblock (cream) la crema protect**o**ra kr**ay**ma

sunburn la quemadura de sol kemad**oo**ra

sunburnt quemado kem**a**do

Sunday dom**i**ngo

sunglasses las g**a**fas de sol

sun lounger la tumb**o**na

sunny: it's sunny hace sol ath**ay**

sun roof (in car) el techo corredizo korrayd**ee**tho

sunset la puesta de sol pw**e**sta day

sunshade la sombrilla sombr**ee**-ya

sunshine la luz del sol looth

sunstroke la insolación eensolath-yon

suntan el bronceado bronthay-**a**do

suntan lotion la loción bronceadora loth-y**o**n bronthay-**a**do**ra**

suntanned bronce**a**do

suntan oil el aceite bronceador ath**ay**-ee**t**ay

super fabul**o**so

supermarket el supermercado soopairmairk**a**do

supper la cena th**a**yna

supplement (extra charge) el suplem**e**nto

sure: are you sure? ¿está seguro?

  sure! ¡por supuesto¡ soopw**e**sto

surname el apellido apay-y**ee**do

swearword la palabr**o**ta

sweater el suéter sw**e**tair

sweatshirt la sudadera soodad**ai**ra

Sweden Suecia sw**ay**th-ya

Swedish (adj) sueco sw**ay**ko

sweet (dessert) el postre p**o**stray

  (adj: taste) dulce d**oo**lthay

  (sherry) olor**o**so

sweets los caramelos karam**ay**loss

swelling la hinchazón eenchath**o**n

swim (verb) nadar

  I'm going for a swim voy a nadar boy

  let's go for a swim vamos a nadar bam**o**ss

swimming costume el bañador ban-yad**o**r

swimming pool la piscina peesth**ee**na

swimming trunks el traje de baño tra**H**ay day b**a**nyo

switch el interruptor eentairooptor

switch off apagar

switch on encender enthendair

swollen inflamado

T

table la mesa maysa

a table for two una mesa para dos

tablecloth el mantel

table tennis el ping-pong

table wine el vino de mesa beeno day maysa

tailback (of traffic) la caravana de coches karabana day kochess

tailor el sastre sastray

take (lead) coger koHair

(accept) aceptar atheptar

can you take me to the airport? ¿me lleva al aeropuerto? may yayba al a-airopwairto

do you take credit cards? ¿acepta tarjetas de crédito? athepta tarHaytass day kraydeeto

fine, I'll take it está bien, lo compro b-yen

can I take this? (leaflet etc) ¿puedo llevarme esto? pwaydo yebarmay

how long does it take? ¿cuánto se tarda? kwanto say

it takes three hours se tarda tres horas orass

is this seat taken? ¿está ocupado este asiento? estay as-yento

a hamburger to take away una hamburguesa para llevar yebar

can you take a little off here? (to hairdresser) ¿puede quitarme un poco de aquí? pwayday keetarmay – day akee

talcum powder el talco

talk (verb) hablar ablar

tall alto

tampons los tampones tampon-ess

tan el bronceado bronthay-ado

to get a tan broncearse bronthay-arsay

tank (of car) el depósito deposeeto

tap el grifo

tape (for cassette) la cinta theenta

(sticky) la cinta adhesiva adeseeba

tape measure la cinta métrica

tape recorder el casete kaset

taste el sabor

can I taste it? ¿puedo probarlo? pwaydo

taxi el taxi

will you get me a taxi? ¿podría conseguirme un taxi? konsegeermay

where can I find a taxi? ¿dónde puedo coger un taxi? donday pwaydo koHair

DIALOGUE

to the airport/to Hotel Sol please al aeropuerto/ al hotel Sol, por favor a-airopwairto/otel

how much will it be?
¿cuánto costará? kwanto

20 euros viente euros bay-
eentay ay-ooross

**that's fine, right here,
thanks** está bien, aquí
mismo, gracias b-yen akee
meesmo

taxi-driver el/la taxista

taxi rank la parada de taxis day

tea (drink) el té tay

  tea for one/two please un
  té/dos tés, por favor

teabags las bolsas de té

teach: could you teach me?
¿podría enseñarme? ensen-
yarmay

teacher (primary: *male/female*) el
maestro ma-estro/la maestra
(secondary: *male/female*) el
profesor/la profesora

team el equipo ekeepo

teaspoon la cuchara de té day tay

tea towel el paño de cocina pan-
yo day kotheena

teenager el/la adolescente
adolesthentay

telephone el teléfono telayfono
  see **phone**

television la televisión telebees-
yon

tell: could you tell him…?
¿podría decirle…? detheerlay

temperature (weather) la
temperatura temperatoora
(fever) la fiebre f-yebray

tennis el tenis

tennis ball la pelota de tenis day

tennis court la pista de tenis

tennis racket la raqueta de tenis
rakayta

tent la tienda de campaña t-yenda
day kampan-ya

term (at university, school) el
trimestre treemestray

terminus (rail) la estación
terminal estath-yon tairmeenal

terrible terrible terreeblay

terrific fabuloso fabooloso

text (*verb*) enviar un mensaje de
texto a emb-yar oon mensaHay
day teksto a

text (message) el mensaje
(de texto) mensaHay

than que kay

  smaller than más pequeño
  que pekayn-yo

thanks, thank you gracias
grath-yass

  thank you very much
  muchas gracias moochass

  thanks for the lift gracias por
  traerme tra-airmay

  no thanks no gracias

thanks gracias
**that's OK, don't mention
it** no hay de qué ī day
kay

DIALOGUE

that: that man ese hombre aysay
ombray

  that woman esa mujer
mooHair

The Rough Guide Spanish Phrasebook > **ENGLISH→SPANISH** 131

that one ése

I hope that... espero que... espairo kay

that's nice (clothes, souvenir etc) es bonito

is that...? ¿es ése...? aysay

that's it (that's right) eso es

the el, la; (pl) los, las

theatre el teatro tay-atro

their su; (pl) sus sooss

theirs su, sus; (pl) suyos soo-yoss, suyas; de ellos day ay-yoss, de ellas

them (things) los, las

(people) les

for them para ellos ay-yoss/ ellas

with them con ellos/ellas

I gave it to them se lo di a ellos/ellas say

who? – them ¿quién? – ellos/ ellas k-yen

then entonces entonthess

there allí a-yee

over there allí

up there allí arriba

is/are there...? ¿hay...? ī

there is/are... hay...

there you are (giving something) aquí tiene akee t-yaynay

thermometer el termómetro tairmometro

thermos flask el termo tairmo

these: these men estos hombres

these women estas mujeres

can I have these? ¿me puedo llevar éstos? may pwaydo yebar

they (male) ellos ay-yoss (female) ellas ay-yass

thick grueso grwayso

(stupid) estúpido estoopeedo

thief (male/female) el ladrón/la ladrona

thigh el muslo mooslo

thin delgado

thing la cosa

my things mis cosas meess

think pensar

I think so creo que sí kray-o kay

I don't think so no lo creo

I'll think about it lo pensaré pensaray

third party insurance el seguro contra terceros tairthaiross

thirsty: I'm thirsty tengo sed seth

this: this man este hombre estay

this woman esta mujer

this one éste/ésta

this is my wife ésta es mi mujer

is this...? ¿es éste/ésta...?

those: those men aquellos hombres akay-yoss

those women aquellas mujeres akay-yass

which ones? – those ¿cuáles? – aquéllos/aquéllas kwaless

thread el hilo eelo

throat la garganta

throat pastilles las pastillas para la garganta pastee-yass

through a través de day

does it go through…? (train, bus) ¿pasa por…?

throw (*verb*) tirar

throw away (*verb*) tirar

thumb el dedo pulgar daydo

thunderstorm la tormenta

Thursday jueves Hwaybess

ticket el billete bee-yaytay

a return to Salamanca un billete de ida y vuelta a Salamanca day eeda ee bwelta

coming back when? ¿cuándo piensa volver? kwando p-yensa bolbair

today/next Tuesday hoy/el martes que viene oy/el martess kay b-yaynay

that will be 12 euros son doce euros dothay ay-ooross

ticket office (bus, rail) la taquilla takee-ya

tide la marea maray-a

tie (necktie) la corbata

tight (clothes etc) ajustado aHoostado

it's too tight es demasiado estrecho daymass-yado

tights los panties

till la caja kaHa

time el tiempo t-yempo

what's the time? ¿qué hora es? kay ora

this time esta vez beth

last time la última vez oolteema

next time la próxima vez

four times cuatro veces bethess

timetable el horario orar-yo

tin (can) la lata

tinfoil el papel de aluminio aloomeen-yo

tin opener el abrelatas

tiny diminuto

tip (to waiter etc) la propina

tired cansado

I'm tired estoy cansado/cansada

tissues los Kleenex

to: to Barcelona/London a Barcelona/Londres

to Spain/England a España/Inglaterra

to the post office a la oficina de Correos

toast (bread) la tostada

today hoy **oy**

toe el dedo del pie **day**do del p-yay

together junto Ho**on**to

 we're together (in shop etc)
 venimos juntos ben**ee**moss

 can we pay together?
 ¿podemos pagar to**d**o junto,
 por favor? pod**ay**moss

toilet los servicios sairb**ee**th-yoss

 where is the toilet? ¿dónde
 están los servicios? d**on**day

 I have to go to the toilet
 tengo que ir al servicio kay

toilet paper el papel higiénico
 eeH-y**ay**neeko

tomato el tomate tom**a**tay

tomato juice el zumo de tomate
 th**oo**mo

tomato ketchup el ketchup

tomorrow mañana man-**ya**na

 tomorrow morning mañana
 por la mañana

 the day after tomorrow
 pas**a**do mañana

toner (for skin) el tonificador
 facial fath-**yal**

tongue la lengua l**e**ngwa

tonic (water) la t**ó**nica

tonight esta noche n**o**chay

tonsillitis las anginas anH**ee**nass

too (excessively) demasiado
 demass-**ya**do

 (also) también tamb-y**e**n

 too hot demasiado caliente
 kal-y**e**ntay

 too much demasiado

 me too yo también

tooth el diente d-y**e**ntay

toothache el dolor de muelas
 day mw**ay**lass

toothbrush el cepillo de dientes
 thepee-yo day d-y**e**ntess

toothpaste la pasta de dientes

top: on top of... encima de...
 enth**ee**ma day

 at the top en lo alto

top floor el último piso **oo**lteemo

topless t**o**pless

torch la linterna leent**ai**rna

total el total

tour el viaje b-ya**H**ay

 is there a tour of...? ¿hay
 una gira por...? ī **oo**na H**ee**ra

tour guide el guía turístico, la
 guía turística g**ee**-a

tourist el/la turista

tourist information office la
 oficina de información turística
 ofeeth**ee**na day eenformath-y**on**

tour operator la agencia de
 viajes aH**e**nth-ya day b-ya**H**ess

towards hacia **a**th-ya

towel la toalla to-**a**-ya

town la ciudad th-y**oo**da

 in town en el centro th**e**ntro

 just out of town en las
 afueras de la ciudad afw**ai**rass

town centre el centro de la
 ciudad

town hall el ayuntamiento
 a-yoontam-y**e**nto

toy el juguete Hoog**ay**tay

track (US) el and**é**n

tracksuit el chándal

traditional tradicional tradeeth-yonal

traffic el tráfico

traffic jam el embotellamiento de tráfico embotayam-yento day

traffic lights los semáforos

trailer (for carrying tent etc) el remolque remolkay
la caravana karabana

trailer park el camping

train el tren

by train en tren

DIALOGUE

is this the train for…? ¿es éste el tren para…? estay

sure exacto

no, you want that platform there no, tiene que ir a aquel andén de allí t-yaynay kay eer a akayl – day a-yee

trainers (shoes) las zapatillas de deporte thapatee-yass day deportay

train station la estación de trenes estath-yon day trayness

tram el tranvía trambee-a

translate traducir tradootheer

could you translate that? ¿podría traducir eso? ayso

translation la traducción tradookth-yon

translator (male/female) el traductor/la traductora

trashcan el cubo de la basura koobo day la basoora

travel (verb) viajar b-yaHar

we're travelling around estamos viajando b-yaHando

travel agent's la agencia de viajes aHenth-ya day b-yaHess

traveller's cheque el cheque de viaje chaykay day b-yaHay

tray la bandeja bandayHa

tree el árbol

tremendous tremendo

trendy moderno modairno

trim: just a trim please (to hairdresser) córtemelo sólo un poco, por favor kortaymelo

trip (excursion) la excursión eskoors-yon

I'd like to go on a trip to… me gustaría hacer una excursión a… may – athair

trolley el carrito

trouble problemas problaymass

I'm having trouble with… tengo problemas con…

sorry to trouble you perdone que le moleste pairdonay kay lay molestay

trousers los pantalones pantaloness

true verdadero bairdadairo

that's not true no es verdad bairda

trunk (car) el maletero maletairo

trunks (swimming) el bañador ban-yador

try (verb) intentar

can I have a try? ¿puedo probarlo? pwaydo

try on: can I try it on? ¿puedo probármelo?

T-shirt la camiseta kamees**ay**ta

Tuesday martes m**a**rtess

tuna el atún at**oo**n

tunnel el túnel t**oo**nel

turn: turn left/right gire a la izqui**e**rda/der**e**cha H**ee**ray

turn off: where do I turn off? ¿dónde me desvío? d**o**nday may desb**ee**-o

can you turn the heating off? ¿puede apagar la calefacción? pw**ay**day – kalefakth-y**o**n

turn on: can you turn the heating on? ¿puede encender la calefacción? enthend**air**

turning (in road) el desvío desb**ee**-o

TV la tele t**ay**lay

tweezers las pinzas p**ee**nthass

twice dos veces b**ay**thess

twice as much el doble d**o**blay

twin beds las camas gemelas Haym**ay**lass

twin room la habitación doble abeetath-y**o**n d**o**blay

twist: I've twisted my ankle me he torcido el tobillo may ay torth**ee**do el tob**ee**-yo

type el tipo

a different type of... un tipo diferente de... deefair**ay**ntay day

typical t**í**pico

tyre la rueda rw**ay**da

ugly (person, building) feo f**ay**-o

UK el Reino Unido r**ay-ee**no oon**ee**do

ulcer la úlcera **oo**lthaira

umbrella el paraguas par**a**gwass

uncle el tío

unconscious inconsciente eenkonsth-y**e**ntay

under (position) debajo de deb**a**Ho day

(less than) menos de maynoss

underdone (meat) poco hecha aycha

underground (railway) el metro

underpants los calzoncillos kalthonthee-yoss

understand: I understand lo entiendo ent-yendo

I don't understand no entiendo

do you understand? ¿entiende usted? ent-yenday oostay

unemployed desempleado desemplay-ado

United States los Estados Unidos ooneedoss

university la universidad ooneebairseeda

unleaded petrol la gasolina sin plomo gasoleena seen

unlimited mileage sin límite de kilometraje seen leemeetay day keelometraHay

unlock abrir abreer

unpack deshacer las maletas desathair lass malaytass

until hasta que asta kay

unusual poco común komoon

up arriba

up there allí arriba a-yee

he's not up yet (not out of bed) todavía no se ha levantado todabee-a no say a laybantado

what's up? (what's wrong?) ¿qué pasa? kay

upmarket de lujo day looHo

upset stomach el malestar de estómago

upside down al revés rebayss

upstairs arriba

urgent urgente oorHentay

us: with us con nosotros

for us para nosotros

USA EE. UU., Estados Unidos ooneedoss

use (*verb*) usar oosar

may I use…? ¿podría usar…?

useful útil ooteel

usual habitual abeetwal

the usual (drink etc) lo de siempre day s-yempray

V

vacancy: do you have any vacancies? (hotel) ¿tiene habitaciones libres? t-yaynay abeetath-yoness leebress

vacation las vacaciones bakath-yoness

see **holiday**

vaccination la vacuna bakoona

vacuum cleaner la aspiradora

valid (ticket etc) válido baleedo

how long is it valid for? ¿hasta cuándo tiene validez? asta kwando t-yaynay baleedeth

valley el valle ba-yay

valuable (*adj*) valioso bal-yoso

can I leave my valuables here? ¿puedo dejar aquí mis objetos de valor? pwaydo dayHar akee meess obHaytoss day balor

value el valor

van la furgoneta foorgon**ay**ta

vanilla vainilla ba-een**ee**-ya

  a vanilla ice cream un
  helado de vainilla el**a**do

vary: it varies depende
  day**pe**nday

vase el florero flor**ai**ro

veal la ternera tair**nai**ra

vegetables las verduras
  baird**oo**rass

vegetarian (*male/female*) el
  vegetariano be**He**tar-y**a**no/la
  vegetari**a**na

vending machine la máquina
  mak**ee**na

very muy mwee

  very little for me un poquito
  para mí pok**ee**to

  I like it very much me gusta
  mucho may g**oo**sta m**oo**cho

vest (*under shirt*) la camiseta
  kamees**ay**ta

via por

video el video be**e**day-o

view la vista b**ee**sta

villa el chalet chal**ay**

village el pueblo pw**e**blo

vinegar el vinagre been**a**gray

vineyard el viñedo been-y**ay**do

visa la visa

visit (*verb*) visitar beese**e**tar

  I'd like to visit Valencia...
  me gustaría ir a Valencia may

vital: it's vital that... es de vital
  importancia que... day be**e**tal
  eemport**a**nth-ya kay

vodka el vodka b**o**dka

voice la voz both

voltage el voltaje bolta**H**ay

vomit vomitar bome**e**tar

W

waist la cintura theent**oo**ra

waistcoat el chaleco chal**ay**ko

wait esperar espa**i**rar

  wait for me espéreme
  espa**i**raymay

  don't wait for me no me
  esp**e**re may

  **can I wait until my wife/
  partner gets here?** ¿puedo
  esperar hasta que llegue mi
  mujer/compañero? pw**ay**do –
  asta kay y**ay**gay

  can you do it while I wait?
  ¿puede hacerlo mientras
  espero? pw**ay**day ath**ai**rlo
  m-y**e**ntrass

  **could you wait here for
  me?** ¿puede esperarme aquí?
  espa**i**rarmay ak**ee**

waiter el camarero kamar**ai**ro

  waiter! ¡camarero!

waitress la camarera kamar**ai**ra

  waitress! ¡señorita! sen-yor**ee**ta

**wake: can you wake me up at
  5.30?** ¿podría despertarme a
  las cinco y media? despert**a**rmay

wake-up call la llamada para
  despertar yam**a**da

Wales Gales g**a**less

walk: is it a long walk?
  ¿se tarda mucho en llegar
  andando? say – m**oo**cho en yeg**a**r

it's only a short walk está cerca th**ai**rka

I'll walk iré andando eer**ay**

I'm going for a walk voy a dar una vuelta boy – bw**e**lta

wall (inside) la pared par**ay**
(outside) la t**a**pia

wallet la billetera bee-yet**ai**ra

wander: I like just wandering around me gusta caminar por ahí may g**oo**sta – a-**ee**

want: I want a... quiero un/una... k-y**ai**ro

I don't want... no quiero...

I want to go home quiero irme a casa eerm**ay**

I don't want to no quiero

he wants to... quiere... k-y**ai**ray

what do you want? ¿qué quiere? kay

ward (in hospital) la habitación abeetath-y**o**n

warm caliente kal-y**e**ntay

I'm so warm tengo mucho calor m**oo**cho

was: it was... era... **ai**ra; estaba... (see note on p.8)

wash (verb) lavar lab**a**r

can you wash these? ¿puede lavarlos? pw**ay**day lab**a**rloss

washer (for bolt etc) la arandela arand**ay**la

washhand basin el lavabo lab**a**bo

washing (clothes) la ropa sucia s**oo**th-ya

washing machine la lavadora labad**o**ra

washing powder el detergente detairH**e**ntay

washing-up liquid el (detergente) lavavajillas daytairH**e**ntay lababaHee-yass

wasp la avispa ab**ee**spa

watch (wristwatch) el reloj rayl**o**H

will you watch my things for me? ¿puede cuidarme mis cosas? pw**ay**day kweed**a**rmay meess

watch out! ¡cuidado! kweed**a**do

watch strap la correa korr**ay**-a

water el agua **a**gwa

may I have some water? ¿me da un poco de agua? may – day

waterproof (adj) impermeable eempairm**ay**-ablay

waterskiing el esquí acuático esk**ee** akw**a**teeko

wave (in sea) la ola

way: it's this way es por aquí ak**ee**

it's that way es por allí a-y**ee**

is it a long way to...? ¿queda lejos...? k**ay**da l**ay**Hoss

no way! ¡de ninguna manera! day – man**ai**ra

DIALOGUE

could you tell me the way to...? podría indicarme el camino a...? eendeek**a**rmay

go straight on until you reach the traffic lights siga recto hasta llegar al semáforo asta yegar

turn left gire a la izquierda Heeray

take the first on the right tome la primera a la derecha tomay

see **where**

we nosotros, nosotras

weak (person, drink) débil daybeel

weather el tiempo t-yempo

what's the weather going to be like? ¿qué tiempo va a hacer? kay – ba a athair

it's going to be fine va a hacer bueno bwayno

it's going to rain va a llover yobair

it'll brighten up later despejará más tarde despayHara – tarday

website el sitio web seet-yo web

wedding la boda

wedding ring el anillo de casado anee-yo

Wednesday miércoles m-yairkoless

week la semana

a week (from) today dentro de una semana day

a week (from) tomorrow dentro de una semana a partir de mañana man-yana

weekend el fin de semana feen

at the weekend el fin de semana

weight el peso payso

weird extraño extran-yo

weirdo: he's a weirdo es un tipo raro

welcome: welcome to... bienvenido(s) a... b-yenbeneedo(ss)

you're welcome (don't mention it) de nada day

well: I don't feel well no me siento bien may s-yento b-yen

she's not well no se siente bien say

you speak English very well habla inglés muy bien abla – mwee

well done! ¡bravo! brabo

this one as well éste también estay tamb-yen

well well! (surprise) ¡vaya, vaya! ba-ya

how are you? ¿cómo está?

very well, thanks muy bien, gracias mwee b-yen

– and you? – ¿y usted? ee oostay

well-done (meat) muy hecho mwee aycho

Welsh galés galayss

I'm Welsh (*male/female*) soy galés/galesa

were: we were estábamos; éramos airamoss (*see note on p.8*)

you were estabais estaba-eess;
erais aira-eess

they were estaban; eran airan

west el oeste o-estay

in the west en el oeste

West Indian (*adj*) antillano
antee-yano

wet mojado moHado

what? ¿qué? kay

what's that? ¿qué es eso? ayso

what should I do? ¿qué
hago? a-go

what a view! ¡qué vista!
beesta

what number is it? ¿qué
numero es?

wheel la rueda rwayda

wheelchair la silla de ruedas
see-ya day rwaydass

when? ¿cuándo kwando

when we get back cuando
volvamos bolbamoss

when's the train/ferry?
¿cuándo es el tren/ferry?

where? ¿dónde? donday

I don't know where it is no
sé dónde está say

DIALOGUE

where is the cathedral?
¿dónde está la catedral?

it's over there está por ahí
a-ee

**could you show me where
it is on the map?** ¿puede
enseñarme en el mapa
dónde está? pwayday ensen-
yarmay

it's just here está justo ahí
Hoosto a-ee

see **way**

which: which bus? ¿qué
autobús? kay

DIALOGUE

which one? ¿cuál? kwal

that one ese aysay

this one? ¿éste? estay

no, that one no, aquél akel

while: while I'm here mientras
esté aquí m-yentrass estay akee

whisky el whisky

white blanco

white wine el vino blanco beeno

who? ¿quién? k-yen

who is it? ¿quién es?

the man who... el hombre
que... kay

whole: the whole week toda
la semana

the whole lot todo

whose: whose is this? ¿de
quién es esto? day k-yen

why? ¿por qué? kay

why not? ¿por qué no?

wide ancho

wife: my wife mi mujer mee
mooHair

Wi-Fi el wifi wee-fee

will: will you do it for me?
¿puede hacer esto por mí?
pwayday athair

wind el viento b-yento

window (of house) la ventana
bentana

(of ticket office, vehicle) la
ventanilla bentanee-ya

near the window cerca de la
ventana thairka day

in the window (of shop) en el
escaparate eskaparatay

window seat el asiento junto a
la ventana as-yento Hoonto

windscreen el parabrisas

windscreen wiper el
limpiaparabrisas leemp-ya-
parabreesass

windsurfing el windsurf

windy: it's so windy hace mucho
viento athay moocho b-yento

wine el vino beeno

**can we have some more
wine?** ¿podría traernos más
vino? tra-airnoss

wine list la lista de vinos leesta
day beenoss

winter el invierno eemb-yairno

in the winter en el invierno

winter holiday las vacaciones de
invierno bakath-yonayss day

wire el alambre alambray

(electric) el cable eléctrico kablay

wish: best wishes saludos
saloodoss

with con

I'm staying with... estoy en
casa de... day

without sin seen

witness el/la testigo testeego

**will you be a witness for
me?** ¿acepta ser mi testigo?

athepta sair

woman la mujer mooHair

wonderful estupendo estoopendo

won't: it won't start no arranca

wood (material) la madera madaira

woods (forest) el bosque boskay

wool la lana

word la palabra

work el trabajo trabaHo

it's not working no funciona
foonth-yona

I work in... trabajo en...

world el mundo moondo

worry: I'm worried estoy
preocupado/preocupada pray-
okoopado

worse: it's worse es peor pay-or

worst el peor

worth: is it worth a visit? ¿vale
la pena visitarlo? balay la payna
beeseetarlo

**would: would you give this
to...?** ¿le puede dar esto a...?
lay pwayday

**wrap: could you wrap it
up?** ¿me lo envuelve? may lo
embwelbay

wrapping paper el papel de
envolver day embolbair

wrist la muñeca moon-yayka

write escribir eskreebeer

could you write it down?
¿puede escribírmelo? pwayday

how do you write it? ¿cómo
se escribe? say eskreebay

writing paper el papel de
escribir

wrong: it's the wrong key no es ésa la llave *ays*a la ya*bay*

this is the wrong train éste no es el tren e*stay*

the bill's wrong la cuenta está equivocada *kwen*ta – ekeebo*ka*da

sorry, wrong number perdone, me he equivocado de número pair*do*nay, may ay – day *noo*mairo

there's something wrong with... le pasa algo a... lay

what's wrong? ¿qué pasa? kay

X

X-ray la radiografía rad-yogra*fee*-a

Y

yacht el yate ya*tay*

yard (courtyard) el patio

year el año an-yo

yellow amarillo ama*ree*-yo

yes sí

yesterday ayer a-y*air*

yesterday morning ayer por la mañana man-*ya*na

the day before yesterday anteayer antay-ay*air*

yet

is it here yet? ¿está aquí ya? a*kee*

no, not yet no, todavía no toda*bee*-a

---

you'll have to wait a little longer yet todavía tendrá que esperar un poquito más kay espai*rar* oon po*kee*to

yobbo el gamberro gam*bai*rro

yoghurt el yogur yo*goor*

you (fam, sing) tú too

(pol, sing) usted oos*tay*

(fam, pl) vosotros bos*o*tross

(pol, pl) ustedes oos*tay*dess

this is for you esto es para tí/ usted

with you contigo/con usted

young joven Ho*ben*

your (fam, sing) tu; (pl) tus tooss

(fam, pl) vuestro b*west*ro, vu*est*ra; (pl) vu*est*ros, vu*est*ras

(pol, sing) su; (pl) sus sooss

yours (fam, sing) tuyo *too*-yo, *tu*ya

(fam, pl) vuestro b*west*ro, vu*est*ra

(pol, sing) suyo *soo*-yo, *su*ya; de usted day oos*tay*

youth hostel el albergue juvenil al*bair*gay Hoobay*neel*

Z

zero cero *thai*ro

zip la cremallera krema-*yai*ra

could you put a new zip in? ¿podría cambiar la cremallera? kamb-*yar*

zoo el zoo(lógico) tho(lo*Hee*ko)

SPANISH
→ **ENGLISH**

Colloquialisms

The following are words you might well hear. You shouldn't be tempted to use any of the stronger ones unless you are sure of your audience.

burro *m* boorro thickhead
cabrón! kabron bastard!
¡capullo! kapooyo dickhead!
cojones koHoness balls
es pan comido ess pan komeedo it's a piece of cake
estar borracho como una cuba estar borracho komo oona kooba to be drunk as a skunk
estar como una cabra estar komo oona kabra to be as mad as a hatter
estar de broma estar de broma to be joking
¡de puta madre! day poota madray fucking great!
¡Dios mío! dee-oss meeo my God!
gilipollas Heeleepo-yass dickhead
guay gwī cool
¡hijo de puta! eeHo de poota son of a bitch!
¡joder! Hodair fuck!
¡largo! largo beat it!
mamón mamon idiot
¡me cago en la puta! may kago en la poota fucking hell!
¡me importa un bledo! may

¡me importa un bledo! may eemporta oon blaydo I don't give a damn!
¡mierda! m-yairda shit!
¡ni hablar! nee ablar no way!
¡no digas tonterías! no deegass tontaireeass don't talk nonsense
¡no me digas! no may deegass you don't say!
¡no me jodas! no may Hodass you must be bloody joking!
¡qué coñazo! kay kon-yaTHo what a drag!
¡qué va! kay ba not at all!
tío *m* teeo bloke
tía *f* teea woman
tonto tonto silly
¡venga ya! baynga ya come on!
¡vete al carajo! baytay al karaHo sod off!
¡vete al infierno! baytay al eenfy-airno go to hell!
¡vete a tomar por culo! baytay a tomar por koolo fuck off!

A

a to; at; per; from
abajo abaHo downstairs
abierto ab-yairto open
abierto de... a... open from... to
abierto las 24 horas del día open 24 hours
abogado *m/f* lawyer
abonos *mpl* season tickets

aborrezco aborethko I hate

ábrase aquí open here

ábrase en caso de emergencia open in case of emergency

abrebotellas *m* abray-botay-yass bottle-opener

abrelatas *m* tin opener

abrigo *m* coat

abrigo de pieles p-yayless fur coat

abril *m* April

abrir to open

abróchense los cinturones fasten your seatbelts

abstenerse de fumar no smoking

abuela *f* abwayla grandmother

abuelo *m* grandfather

abuelos *mpl* grandparents

aburrido boring; bored

aburrirse aboorreersay to be bored; to get bored

acabar to finish

  acabo de... I have just...

acantilado *m* cliff

acceso a... access to...

acceso a los andenes to the trains

acceso playa to the beach

acceso prohibido no admittance

accidente *m* aktheedentay accident

  tener un accidente to have an accident

accidente de coche kochay car accident

accidente de montaña montan-ya mountaineering accident

accidente de tráfico road accident

accidente en cadena kadayna pile-up

acelerador *m* athelairador accelerator, gas pedal

acelerar athelairar to accelerate

acento *m* athento accent

aceptar atheptar to accept

acera *f* athaira pavement, sidewalk

acerca de athairka day about, concerning

acero *m* athairo steel

acetona *f* athaytona nail polish remover

ácido (*m*) atheedo sour; acid

acompañar akompan-yar to accompany

  le acompaño en el sentimiento condolences

acondicionador de pelo *m* akondeeth-yonador day paylo hair conditioner

aconsejar akonsay-Har to advise

acordarse akordarsay to remember

acostar: irse a acostar eersay to go to bed

acostarse akostarsay to lie down; to go to bed

  al acostarse when you go to bed

actriz *f* aktreeth actress

acuerdo *m* akwairdo agreement

estoy de acuerdo I agree

de acuerdo OK

adaptador *m* adaptor

> Travel tip The current in
> most of Spain is 220 or
> 225 volts AC (just occasion-
> ally, it's still 110 or 125V);
> most European appliances
> should work as long as
> you have an adaptor for
> European-style two-pin
> plugs. North Americans
> will need this plus a trans-
> former.

adelantado: por adelantado
adelantado in advance

adelantar to overtake

adelante adelantay come in

además de ademass day besides,
as well as

adentro inside

adiós ad-yoss goodbye

admitir to admit, to confess

adolescente *m/f* adolesthentay
teenager

aduana *f* ad-wana customs

aduanero *m* adwanairo customs
officer

aerobús *m* a-airobooss local train

aerodeslizador *m* a-airo-
desleethadór hovercraft

aerolínea *f* a-airoleenay-a airline

aeropuerto *m* a-airopwairto
airport

afeitarse afay-eetarsay to shave

aficionado a afeeth-yonado
keen on

afortunadamente -mentay
fortunately

afueras *fpl* afwairass suburbs

agarrar un colocón to get
drunk

agárrese aquí hold on here

agencia *f* a-Henth-ya agency

agencia de viajes b-yaHess
travel agency

agenda *f* a-Henda diary

agítese antes de usar(se)
shake before use

agosto *m* August

agradable agradablay pleasant

agradar to please

agradecer agradethair to thank

agradecido agradetheedo
grateful

agradezco agradethko I thank

agresivo aggressive

agricultor *m* farmer

agua *f* agwa water

agua de colonia kolon-ya eau
de toilette

aguantar: no aguanto...
agwanto I can't stand...

aguja *f* agooHa needle

agujero *m* agooHairo hole

ahora a-ora now

aire *m* a-eeray air

aire acondicionado akondeeth-
yonado air-conditioning

ajedrez *m* a-Hedreth chess

ajustado a-Hoostado tight

ala *f* wing

alambre *m* alam**b**ray wire

alarma *f* alarm

dar la señal de alarma
sen-ya**l** to raise the alarm

albergue *m* albair**g**ay country
hotel; hostel

albergue juvenil Hoobene**el**
youth hostel

albornoz *m* albor**n**oth bathrobe

alcohómetro *m* Breathalyzer

alegre ale**g**ray happy

alegro: ¡me alegro de verte!
bair**t**ay nice to see you!

alemán alay-ma**n** German

Alemania *f* aleman-ya Germany

alérgico a alair-**H**eeko allergic to

aletas *fpl* alay-tass flippers

alfarería *f* alfarair**ee**-a pottery

alfiler *m* alfeela**ir** pin

alfombra *f* rug, carpet

algo something

algo más something else

algodón *m* cotton; cotton wool,
absorbent cotton

alguien al**g**-yen somebody;
anybody

algún some; any

alguno some; any

alianza *f* al-ya**nth**a wedding ring

alicates *mpl* pliers

alimentación *f* aleementath-y**on**
groceries, foodstuffs

allá: más allá a-**y**a further

allí a-**y**ee there

almacén *m* alma**th**en department
store; warehouse

almohada *f* almo-**a**da pillow

almuerzo *m* almwa**ir**tho lunch

alojamiento *m* aloHam-y**en**to
accommodation

alojamiento y desayuno
desa-y**oo**no bed and breakfast

alpinismo *m* mountaineering

alquilar alkeela**r** to rent; to hire

alquiler *m* alkeela**ir** rental

alquiler de barcos boat hire

alquiler de bicicletas
beetheeklay**t**ass bike hire

alquiler de coches k**o**chess
car rental

alquiler de esquís eske**ess**
(water-)ski hire

alquiler de sombrillas sombree-
y**a**ss sunshade hire

alquiler de tablas surfboard
hire

alquiler de tumbonas
deckchair hire

alquileres rentals

alrededor (de) alray-day-d**o**r
around

alta costura *f* haute couture,
high fashion

alto high; tall

¡alto! stop!

en lo alto at the top

altura *f* altitude; height

altura máxima maximum
headroom

aluminio *m* aluminium

amable amab**l**ay kind

amamantar to breastfeed

amanecer *m* amaneth**ai**r sunrise,
daybreak

amargo bitter

amarillo amaree-yo yellow

ambos both

ambulancia f amboolanth-ya ambulance

ambulatorio national health clinic

América del Norte f nortay North America

América del Sur soor South America

americano American

amiga f friend

amigo m friend

aminorar la marcha to slow down

amor m love

hacer el amor to make love

amortiguador m amorteegwador shock-absorber

amperio m ampair-yo amp

ampliación f amplee-ath-yon enlargement

amplio loose-fitting

ampolla f ampo-ya blister

analgésico m anal-Hayseeko painkiller

análisis clínicos mpl clinical tests

anaranjado anaran-Hado orange

ancho wide

ancho m width, breadth

anchura f width, breadth

¡anda ya! get away!, come off it!

andaluz andalooth Andalusian

andar to walk

andén m platform, track

a los andenes to the trains

anduve andoobay I walked

anémico anaemic

anestesia f anestays-ya anaesthetic

anfiteatro m anfeetay-atro amphitheatre

angina (de pecho) f an-Heena angina

anginas fpl tonsillitis

anillo m anee-yo ring

anoche last night

anochecer m anochethair nightfall, dusk

ante m suede

anteayer antay-a-yair the day before yesterday

antepasado m ancestor

antes de before

antes de que before

antes de ayer a-yair the day before yesterday

antes de entrar dejen salir let passengers off first

anticonceptivo m anteekonthepteebo contraceptive

anticongelante m anteekon-Helantay antifreeze

anticuado anteekwado out of date

anticuario m antiques dealer

antigüedad: una tienda de antigüedades t-yenda day anteegway-dadess antique shop

antiguo anteegwo ancient

antihistamínico m antee-eestameeneeko antihistamine

anulado cancelled

anular to cancel

añadir an-yadeer to add

año *m* an-yo year

Año Nuevo *m* nwaybo New Year

  día de Año Nuevo *m* dee-a New Year's Day

  ¡feliz Año Nuevo! feleeth Happy New Year!

apagar to switch off

apagar los faros to switch off one's lights

apagar luces de cruce headlights off

apagón *m* power cut

apague el motor switch off your engine

apague las luces switch off your lights

aparato *m* device

aparatos electrodomésticos electrical appliances

aparcamiento *m* aparkam-yento car park, parking lot

aparcamiento privado private parking

aparcamiento reservado this parking place reserved

aparcamiento subterráneo underground parking

aparcamiento vigilado supervised parking

aparcar to park

aparecer aparethair to appear

aparezco aparethko I appear

apartamento *m* apartment

apasionante apass-yonantay thrilling

apearse de apay-arsay to get off

apellido *m* apay-yeedo surname

apenado distressed, sorry

apenas apaynass scarcely

  apenas… (cuando) kwando hardly… when

apetecer: me apetece may apetaythay I feel like

apetito *m* appetite

apodo *m* nickname

apoplejía *f* apoplay-Hee-a stroke

aprender aprendair to learn

aprensivo fearful, apprehensive

apresurarse -arsay to rush

aproveche: ¡que aproveche! aprobay-chay enjoy your meal!

aproximadamente -mentay about

aquel akel that

aquél that (one)

aquella akay-ya that

aquélla that (one)

aquellas akay-yass those

aquéllas those (ones)

aquellos akay-yoss those

aquéllos those (ones)

aquí akee here

  aquí tiene t-yaynay here you are

árabe arabay Arabic

aragonés Aragonese

araña f aran-ya spider

arañazo m aran-yatho scratch

árbol m tree

arcén m arthen lay-by

archivo m archeebo file

ardor de estómago m heartburn

área de servicios m service area, motorway services

arena f arayna sand

Argelia f arHaylee-a Algeria

armario m cupboard

armería f armairee-a gunsmith's

arqueología f arkay-oloHee-a archaeology

arrancar to start up

arreglar to mend; to sort out, to arrange

arrepentido sorry

arriba up; upstairs; on top

arroba f at sign, @

arroyo m stream

arte m artay art

artesanía f crafts

artículos de artesanía mpl arts and crafts

artículos de baño ban-yo swimwear

artículos de boda wedding presents

artículos de deporte sports goods

artículos de limpieza household cleaning products

artículos de ocasión bargains; second hand goods

artículos de piel leather goods

artículos de playa beachwear

artículos de regalo gifts

artículos de viaje travel goods

artículos para el bebé babywear

artículos para el colegio schoolwear

artista m/f artist

artritis f -treeteess arthritis

asador m restaurant specializing in roast meats and/or fish

ascensor m asthensor lift, elevator

asegurar to insure

aseos mpl asay-oss toilets, rest room

así like this; like that

así que so (that)

asiático Asian

asiento m ass-yento seat

asma m asthma

aspiradora *f* Hoover

asqueroso askair*o*so disgusting

astigmático long-sighted

asturiano astoor-y*a*no Asturian

asustado afraid

asustar to frighten

atacar to attack

atajo *m* ata*H*o shortcut

ataque *m* at*a*kay attack

ataque al corazón kora*th*on heart attack

atascado stuck

atasco (de tráfico) *m* traffic jam

atención atenth-y*o*n please note

¡atención! take care!, caution!

atención al tren beware of trains

ateo at*a*y-o atheist

aterrizaje *m* atairreetha*H*ay landing

aterrizaje forzoso forth*o*so emergency landing

aterrizar atairreeth*a*r to land

atestado *m* report

atletismo *m* athletics

atracar to assault, to hold up

atracciones turísticas *fpl* atrakth-y*o*ness tourist attractions

atraco a mano armada *m* hold-up

atractivo attractive

atrás at the back; behind

¡atrás! get back!

la parte de atrás p*a*rtay the back

está más atrás it's further back

años atrás years ago

atravesar to go through

atravieso atrab-y*a*yso I go through

atreverse atrebair*sa*y to dare

atropellar atropay-y*a*r to knock over

atroz atr*o*th dreadful

audífono *m* owd*ee*fono hearing aid

aun even

aún a-*oo*n still; yet

aunque a-*oo*nkay although

autobús *m* owtob*oo*ss bus

autobús sólamente buses only

autocar *m* coach, bus

auto-estopista *m/f* -estop*ee*sta hitch-hiker

automotor *m* local short-distance train

automóvil *m* car

automovilista *m/f* car driver

autopista *f* motorway, highway

autopista (de peaje) pay-a*H*ay (toll) motorway/highway

auto-servicio *m* owto-sairb*ee*th-yo self-service

autorizada para mayores de 18 años for adults only

autorizada para mayores de 14 años y menores acompañados authorized for those over 14 and young people accompanied by an adult

autorizada para todos los públicos suitable for all

autostop *m* hitchhiking

hacer autostop to hitchhike

autovía *f* -bee-a dual carriageway, divided highway

AVE *m* high-speed train on the Madrid-Seville line

avenida *f* avenue

avergonzado abairgonthado embarrassed

avería *f* abairee-a breakdown

averiado out of order

averiarse abairee-arsay to break down

avión *m* ab-yon aeroplane

por avión by air

avisar to inform

aviso *m* information

aviso a los señores pasajeros passenger information

avispa *f* wasp

ayer a-yair yesterday

ayer por la mañana man-yana yesterday morning

ayer por la tarde tarday yesterday afternoon

ayuda *f* a-yooda help

ayudar to help

ayuntamiento *m* ayoontam-yento town hall

azafata *f* athafata air hostess

azul (*m*) athool blue

azul claro light blue

azul marino navy blue

B

baca *f* roof rack

bahía *f* ba-ee-a bay

bailar ba-eelar to dance

ir a bailar to go dancing

baile *m* ba-eelay dance; dancing

bajar baHar to go down

bajar de to get off

bajarse baHarsay to get off

bajo baHo low; short; under(neath)

balcón *m* balcony

Baleares balay-aress Balearics

balón *m* ball

balón volea bolay-a volleyball

baloncesto *m* balonthesto basketball

balonmano *m* handball

banco *m* bank; bench

> **Travel tip** Banking hours are usually Mon–Fri 8.30am–2pm, with some city branches open Sat 8.30am–1pm (except June–Sept when all banks close on Sat), although times can vary from bank to bank. Outside these times, it's usually possible to change cash at larger hotels or with travel agents – useful for small amounts in a hurry.

---

bandeja *f* bandayHa tray

bandera *f* bandaira flag

bañador *m* ban-yador swimming costume

bañarse ban-yarsay to go swimming; to have a bath

bañera f ban-yaira bathtub

baño m ban-yo bathroom; bath

baraja f baraнa pack of cards

barato cheap, inexpensive

barba f beard

barbacoa f barbako-a barbecue

barbería f barbairee-a barber's

barbero m barber

barbilla f barbee-ya chin

barca de remos f rowing boat

barcas para alquilar boats to rent

barco m boat

barco de vela sailing boat

barra de labios f lab-yoss lipstick

barrio m barr-yo district, area

bastante bastantay enough

   bastante más quite a lot more

   bastante menos maynoss quite a lot less

basura f litter

bata f dressing gown

bate m batay bat

batería f batairee-a battery

batería de cocina kotheena pots and pans

batín m dressing gown

bautismo m bowteesmo christening

bebé m baby

beber bebair to drink

bello bay-yo beautiful

benvengut (Catalan) benvengoot welcome

besar to kiss

beso m kiss

betún m betoon shoe polish

biblioteca f beebl-yotayka library; bookcase

bici: ir a dar una vuelta en bici bwelta en beethee to go for a cycle

bicicleta f beetheeklayta bicycle

bien b-yen well

   ¡bien! good!

   bien... bien either... or...

   o bien... o bien either... or...

bienes mpl b-yayness possessions

¡bienvenido! welcome!

bifurcación f beefoorkath-yon fork

bigote m beegotay moustache

billete m bee-yaytay ticket

billete de andén platform ticket

billete de banco banknote, bill

billete de ida single ticket, one-way ticket

billete de ida y vuelta bwelta return ticket, round trip ticket

blanco (m) white

blusa f blouse

boca f mouth

bocina f botheena horn

boda f wedding

bodega f bodayga wine cellar; wine bar

boite f bwat night club

bolígrafo m Biro

bolsa f bag; stock exchange

bolsa de plástico plastic bag

bolsa de viaje b-ya**H**ay travel bag

bolsillo m bols**ee**-yo pocket

bolso m handbag, purse

bomba f bomb

bomberos mpl bomb**ai**ross fire
brigade

bombilla f bomb**ee**-ya light bulb

bombona de gas f camping gas
cylinder

bonito (m) nice; tuna fish

bonobús book of 10 reduced-
price bus tickets

bordado embroidered

borracho drunk

bosque m b**o**skay forest

bota f boot

botas de agua **a**gwa wellingtons

botas de esquiar eskee-**a**r ski
boots

botella f bot**ay**-ya bottle

botiquín m boteek**ee**n first aid kit

botón m button

botón desatascador coin
return button

boxeo m boks**ay**-o boxing

boya f buoy

bragas fpl panties

brazo m br**a**tho arm

bricolaje m breekol**a**Hay DIY

brillar bree-y**a**r to shine

brisa f breeze

británico British

brocha de afeitar f afay-**ee**tar
shaving brush

broche m br**o**chay brooch

bronce m br**o**nthay bronze

bronceado m br**o**nthay-**a**do
suntan

bronceador m bronthay-ad**o**r
suntan oil/lotion

bronquitis f bronk**ee**teess
bronchitis

brújula f broo**H**oola compass

Bruselas Brussels

bucear boothay-**a**r to (skin-)dive

buceo m boothay-o skin-diving

¡buenas! bw**a**ynass hello!

bueno bw**ay**no good; good-
natured

buenas noches goodnight

buenas tardes good evening

buenos días dee-**a**ss good
morning

bufanda f scarf

bujía f boo**H**ee-a spark plug

bulto m piece of luggage

burro m donkey

buscar to look for

busqué boosk**ay** I looked for

butacas stalls

buzón booth**o**n letter box, mail
box

C

c/ (calle) street

c/c (cuenta corriente) current
account

caballeros mpl kaba-ya**i**ross
gents, men's rest room

caballo m kaba-yo horse

cabello *m* kabay-yo hair

cabeza *f* kabaytha head

cabida... personas capacity... people

cabina telefónica *f* telephone booth, phone box

cable alargador *m* kablay extension lead

cabra *f* goat

cabrón *m* bastard

cacahuetes kakawaytess peanuts

cachondeo *m* kachonday-o laugh

lo digo de cachondeo I'm only joking

cada every

cadena *f* kadayna chain

cadera *f* kadaira hip

caduca... expires...

caer ka-air to fall

caerse ka-airsay to fall

cafetera *f* kafetaira coffee pot

cafetería *f* cafe, bar-type restaurant

caída *f* ka-eeda fall

cago: ¡me cago en diez! d-yayth for heaven's sake!

caja *f* kaHa cash desk; cashier

caja de ahorros a-orross savings bank

caja de cambios *f* kaHa gearbox

cajera *f* kaHaira, **cajero** *m* cashier

cajero automático owtomateeko cash dispenser, ATM

calambre *m* kalambray cramp

calcetines *mpl* kaltheteeness socks

calcetines de algodón cotton socks

calcetines de lana woollen socks

calculadora *f* calculator

calefacción *f* kalefakth-yon heating

calefacción central thentral central heating

calendario *m* -dar-yo calendar

calidad *f* quality

caliente kal-yentay hot

calle *f* ka-yay street

calle comercial komairth-yal shopping street

calle de dirección única deerekth-yon one-way street

calle peatonal pay-atonal pedestrianized street

calle principal preentheepal main street

callejón sin salida *m* cul-de-sac, dead end

callo *m* ka-yo corn (on foot)

calmante *m* tranquillizer

calor *m* heat

hace calor it's warm/hot

calvo bald

calzada deteriorada poor road surface

calzada irregular uneven surface

calzados shoe shop

calzoncillos *mpl* kalthonthee-yoss underpants

cama *f* bed

cama de campaña kampan-ya campbed

cama de matrimonio double bed

cama individual single bed

cámara *f* camera; inner tube

cámara fotográfica camera

camarera *f* kamaraira waitress; chambermaid

camarero *m* waiter

camarote *m* kamarotay cabin

cambiar kamb-yar to change

cambiarse (de ropa) kamb-yarsay to get changed

cambio *m* change; exchange; exchange rate

cambio de divisas currency exchange

cambio de moneda currency exchange

cambio de sentido junction, take filter lane to exit and cross flow of traffic

caminar to walk

camino *m* path

camino cerrado (al tráfico) road closed to (traffic)

camino privado private road

camión *m* lorry, truck

camioneta *f* van

camisa *f* shirt

camiseta *f* T-shirt; vest

camisón *m* nightdress

campana *f* bell

camping *m* camping; campsite; caravan site, trailer park

campo *m* countryside; pitch; court; field

campo de deportes sports field

campo de futból football ground

campo de golf golf course

Campsa State-owned oil company

canadiense kanad-yensay Canadian

Canal de la Mancha *m* English Channel

Canarias *fpl* kanar-yass Canaries

cancelado kanthelado cancelled

cancelar kanthelar to cancel

cancha *f* court; pitch

canción *f* kanth-yon song

canguro *m/f* kangooro baby-sitter

canoso greying; grey

cansado tired

cantar to sing

cantina *f* buffet

canto *m* singing

caña *f* kan-ya small glass of beer

caña de pescar fishing rod

capaz: ser capaz (de) sair kapath to be able (to)

capazo *m* kapatho carry-cot

capilla *f* kapee-ya chapel

capitán *m* captain

capó(t) *m* car bonnet, hood

cara *f* face

caramelos *mpl* karamayloss sweets, candies

caravana *f* caravan

carburador *m* carburettor

cárcel *f* karthel prison

cardenal *m* bruise

cargador *m* (phone) charger

carne *f* karnay flesh

carné de conducir *m* karnay day kondootheer driving licence

carnet de identidad *m* identity card

carnicería *f* karneethairee-a butcher's

caro expensive

carpintería *f* karpeentairee-a joiner's, carpenter's

carrera *f* karraira race

carrete *m* karraytay film (for camera)

carretera *f* karretaira road

carretera comarcal district highway

carretera cortada road blocked, road closed

carretera de circunvalación by-pass

carretera de doble calzada two-lane road

carretera nacional national highway

carretera principal main highway

carril *m* lane

carrito *m* trolley, cart

carrito portaequipajes porta-aykeepaHess baggage trolley

carta *f* letter; menu

cartel *m* poster

cartelera de espectáculos *f* kartelaira entertainments guide

cartera *f* kartaira briefcase; wallet

carterista *m* pickpocket

cartero *m* postman, mailman

cartón *m* cardboard; carton

casa *f* house

  en casa at home

  en casa de Juan at Juan's

casa de huéspedes wespedess guesthouse

casa de socorro emergency first-aid centre

casado married

casarse kasarsay to get married

cascada *f* waterfall

casi almost

casino *m* leisure club; casino

caso *m* case

  en caso de que in case

caso urgente oorнentay emergency

casete *f*, **cassette** *f* kaset cassette

casete *m*, **cassette** *m* cassette player

caspa *f* dandruff

castaño (*m*) kastan-yo sweet chestnut; brown

castañuelas *fpl* kastan-waylass castanets

castellano kastay-yano Castilian; another word for the Spanish language

Castilla kastee-ya Castile

castillo *m* castle

casualidad: por casualidad kaswaleeda by chance

Cataluña kataloon-ya Catalonia

catarro: tengo catarro I've got a cold

católico (*m*) Catholic

catorce katorthay fourteen

caucho *m* kowcho rubber

causa *f* kowsa cause

  a causa de because of

cayó ka-yo he fell

caza *f* katha hunting

cazadora *f* kathadora bomber jacket, blouson

cazar kathar to hunt

cazo *m* katho saucepan

ceda el paso give way, yield

ceder el paso thedair to give way

ceja *f* thayнa eyebrow

celoso theloso jealous

cementerio *m* thementair-yo cemetery

cena *f* thayna dinner

cenar to have dinner

cenicero *m* thayneethairo ashtray

central telefónica *f* thentral telephone exchange

centro comercial *m* thentro komairthee-al shopping centre

centro urbano/ciudad *m* th-yooda city/town centre

ceñido then-yeedo tight-fitting

cepillo *m* thepee-yo brush

cepillo de dientes d-yentess toothbrush

cepillo del pelo hairbrush

cera *f* thaira wax

cerámica *f* thairameeka ceramics

cerca de thairka near

cercanías *m* thairkanee-ass local short-distance train

cerilla f thair**ee**-ya match

cero th**ai**ro zero

cerrado thairr**a**do closed

> Travel tip August is
> traditionally Spain's own
> holiday month, when the big
> cities – especially Madrid
> and Barcelona – are semi-
> deserted, with many of
> the shops and restaurants
> closed for the duration. It
> can be difficult to find a
> room in the more popular
> coastal and mountain
> resorts – be sure to book
> in advance.

cerrado por defunción closed
due to bereavement

**cerrado por descanso del
personal** closed for staff
holidays

**cerrado por obras/reforma/
vacaciones** closed for
alteration/renovation/
holidays

cerradura f thairrad**oo**ra lock

cerramos los... we close
on...

cerrar thairr**a**r to close

cerrar con llave ya**b**ay to lock

cerrojo m thairr**o**Ho bolt

certificado m thairteefeek**a**do
certificate; registered letter

cervecería f thairbethair-**ee**-a bar
specializing in beer

cerveza f thairb**ay**tha beer

césped m th**e**sped lawn

cesta f th**e**sta basket

cesto de la compra m
shopping basket

CH (casa de huespedes) f
w**e**spedess boarding house,
low-price hostel

chaleco m waistcoat

chalecos salvavidas life-
jackets

chalet m chal**ay** villa

champú m shampoo

chandal m tracksuit

chaparrón m shower;
downpour

chaqueta f chak**ay**ta cardigan;
jacket

chaquetón m chaket**o**n jacket;
three-quarter length jacket

charcutería f delicatessen

charlar to chat

cheque m ch**ay**kay cheque,
check

cheque de viaje m day b-ya**H**ay
travellers' cheque

chica f girl

chicle m ch**ee**klay chewing gum

chico m boy

chillar chee-y**a**r to shout

chino Chinese

chiringuito m cheereeng**ee**to
open-air bar

chiste m ch**ee**stay joke

chocar con to run into

chocolate con leche m
chokol**a**tay kon l**e**chay milk
chocolate

chocolate de hacer ath**a**ir plain
chocolate

chubasco *m* sudden short shower

chubasquero *m* choobaskairo cagoule

Chupa-Chups *m* lollipop

Cía. (compañía) company

cicatriz *f* theekatreeth scar

ciclismo *m* theekleesmo cycling

ciclista *m/f* theekleesta cyclist

ciego th-yaygo blind

cielo *m* th-yaylo sky

cien th-yen hundred

ciencia *f* th-yenth-ya science

ciento… th-yento a hundred and…

cierren las puertas close the doors

cierro th-yairro I close

cigarrillo *m* theegarree-yo cigarette

cinco theenko five

cincuenta theen-kwenta fifty

cine *m* theenay cinema

cinta *f* theenta tape; ribbon

cintura *f* theentoora waist

cinturón *m* theentooron belt

cinturón de seguridad seat belt

circo *m* theerko circus

circulación *f* theerkoolath-yon traffic; circulation

circulación en ambas direcciones two-way traffic

circule despacio drive slowly

circule por la derecha keep to your right

circunvalación *f* theerkoonbalath-yon ring road

cistitis *f* theesteeteess cystitis

cita *f* theeta appointment

ciudad *f* thee-oo-da town, city

claro clear

¡claro! of course!

clase *f* klasay class

clavo *m* nail

claxon *m* klakson horn

clima *m* climate

climatizado -thado air-conditioned

clínica *f* hospital; clinic

cobrador *m* conductor

cobre *m* kobray copper

cocer kothair to cook; to boil

coche *m* kochay car

en coche by car

coche-cama *m* sleeper, sleeping car

cochecito *m* kochetheeto pram

coche comedor dining car

coche de línea leenay-a long-distance bus

coche de niño neen-yo pram; pushchair, baby buggy

coche-restaurante *m* -restowrantay restaurant car

cocina *f* kotheena kitchen; cooker

cocinar kotheenar to cook

cocinera *f* kotheenaira, **cocinero** *m* cook

código de la circulación *m* theerkoolath-yon highway code

código postal postcode, zip code

codo *m* elbow

coger koH**air** to catch; to take

cojo (*m*) ko**HO** I catch; I take; person with a limp

cola *f* tail; queue

　hacer cola to queue

colchas *fpl* bedspreads

colchón *m* mattress

colchoneta inflable *f* eenflab**lay** air mattress

colección *f* kolekth-**yon** collection

colegio *m* kolay**H**-yo school

colgante *m* kolg**antay** pendant

colina *f* hill

collar *m* ko-**yar** necklace

colocar to place, to put

color *m* colour

columna vertebral *f* spine

combinación *f* kombeenath-**yon** combination; petticoat

combustible *m* kombooste**eblay** fuel

comedor *m* dining room

comenzar komenth**ar** to begin

comer kom**air** to eat

comerciante *m* komairth-**yantay** shopkeeper; dealer

comida *f* lunch; food; meal

comidas para llevar take-away meals

comienzo kom-y**entho** I begin

comisaría *f* police station

comisaría de policía polee-**thee**-a police station

como as; like

¿cómo? pardon?; how?

　¿cómo dice? dee**thay** pardon?

¿cómo está? how are you?

¿cómo le va? lay how are things?

como quieras k-ya**irass** it's up to you

compañera *f* kompan-ya**ira** girlfriend

compañero *m* mate; boyfriend

compañía *f* kompan-**yee**-a company

compañía aérea a-a**iray**-a airline

comparar to compare

compartir to share

completamente -m**entay** completely

completo full, no vacancies

complicado complicated

compra: hacer la compra ath**air** to do the shopping

compramos a... buying rate

comprar to buy

comprender komprend**air** to understand

　no comprendo I don't understand

compras: ir de compras to go shopping

compresa *m* kompray**sa** sanitary towel, sanitary napkin

comprimido efervescente *m* soluble tablet

comprimidos tablets

computadora *f* computer

comunicando engaged; busy

con with

concha *f* shell

concierne konth-**yair**nay it concerns

concierto *m* konth-**yair**to concert

condición: a condición de que kondeeth-**yon** on condition that

condón *m* condom

conducir kondooth**eer** to drive

conductor *m*, **conductora** *f* driver

conduzca con cuidado drive with care

conduzco kond**oo**thko I drive

conejo *m* kon**ay**-Ho rabbit

confección *f* konfekth-**yon** clothing industry

confección de caballero kaba-**yair**o menswear

confección de señoras ladies' fashions

confecciones *fpl* ready-to-wear clothes

conferencia internacional *f* konfair**enth**-ya eentairnath-**yon**al international call

conferencia interurbana long-distance call

confesar to admit, to confess

confirmar to confirm

confitería *f* konfeetair**ee**-a sweetshop, candy store

conforme kon**for**may as

estar conforme to agree

conformidad *f* agreement

congelado konHay**la**do frozen

congelador *m* konHay**la**dor freezer

congelados *mpl* konHay**la**doss frozen foods

conjunto *m* konH**oon**to group; band

conmigo with me

conmoción cerebral *f* konmoth-**yon** thair**ebra**l concussion

conocer konoth**air** to know

conozco kon**oth**ko I know

conque kon**kay** so, so then

conserje *m* kons**air**Hay janitor, porter

conservas *fpl* jams; preserves

consérvese en sitio fresco store in a cool place

consigna *f* kons**eeg**-na left luggage (office), baggage check

consigna automática left luggage lockers

consigo with himself; with herself; with yourself; with themselves; with yourselves

consulado *m* consulate

consulta médica surgery, doctor's office

consúmase antes de... best before...

contable *m/f* kon**tab**lay accountant

contacto: ponerse en contacto con to contact

contado: pagar al contado to pay cash

contagioso kontaH-**yos**o contagious

contaminado polluted

contar to count; to tell

contener kontenair to contain

contenido *m* contents

contento happy

contestar to reply, to answer

contigo with you

continuación: a continuación konteen-wath-yon then, next

continuar konteen-war to continue

contorno de cadera *m* hip measurement

contorno de cintura theentoora waist measurement

contorno de pecho bust/chest measurement

contra against

contradecir kontradetheer to contradict

contraindicaciones *fpl* contra-indications

contraseña *f* kontrasen-ya password

contraventanas *fpl* shutters

control de pasaportes *m* passport control

convalecencia *f* konbalethenth-ya convalescence

¡coño! kon-yo fuck!

copa *f* glass

coquetear koketay-ar to flirt

corazón *m* korathon heart

corbata *f* tie, necktie

cordero *m* kordairo lamb

cordones *mpl* kordoness (shoe) laces

correa del ventilador *f* korray-a fan belt

correo *m* korray-o mail

correo aéreo a-airay-o airmail

correo urgente oorнentay express

correos *m* post office

Correos y Telégrafos Post Office

correr korrair to run

corrida de toros *f* bullfight

corriente peligrosa dangerous current

corrimiento de tierras danger: landslides

cortadura *f* cut

cortar to cut

cortarse kortarsay to cut oneself

cortauñas *m* korta-oon-yass nail clippers

corte de pelo *m* kortay haircut

corte y confección konfekth-yon dressmaking

cortina *f* curtain

corto short

cosa *f* thing

coser kosair to sew

costa *f* coast

costar to cost

costilla *f* kostee-ya rib

costumbre *f* kostoombray custom

cráneo *m* kranay-o skull

crédito *m* credit; unit(s)

creer kray-air to believe

crema *f* krayma cream

crema base basay foundation cream

crema de belleza bay-yaytha cold cream

crema hidratante eedratantay
moisturizer

crema limpiadora leemp-yadora
cleansing cream

cremallera f krema-yaira zip,
zipper

creyó kray-yo he/she believed

crisis hipotecaria f kreeseess
eepotekar-ya credit crunch

crisis nerviosa f nairb-yosa
nervous breakdown

cristal m kreestal crystal; glass

cristalería f glassware

crítica f criticism

criticar to criticize

cruce m kroothay junction,
intersection; crossing;
crossroads

cruce de ciclistas danger:
cyclists crossing

cruce de ganado danger: cattle
crossing

crucero m kroothairo cruise

Cruz Roja f krooth roнa Red
Cross

cruzar kroothar to cross

CTNE f Spanish national
telephone company

cuaderno m kwadairno
notebook

cuadrado kwadrado square

cuadro m kwadro painting
de cuadros checked

cual kwal which; who

¿cuándo? kwando when?

¿cuánto? kwanto how much?
en cuanto... as soon as...
¡cuánto lo siento! s-yento I'm
so sorry!

¿cuántos? how many?

cuarenta kwarenta forty

cuartel de la guardia civil m
civil guard barracks

cuartilla *f* kwartee-ya writing paper

cuarto (*m*) kwarto quarter; fourth; room

cuarto de hora ora quarter of an hour

cuarto de baño ban-yo bathroom

cuarto de estar sitting room

cuarto piso fourth floor, (US) fifth floor

cuatro kwatro four

cuatrocientos kwatro-th-yentoss four hundred

cubierta *f* koob-yairta deck

cubierto (*m*) covered; overcast; meal

cubiertos *mpl* cutlery

cubo *m* bucket; cube

cubo de la basura dustbin, trashcan

cucaracha *f* cockroach

cuchara *f* spoon

cucharilla *f* koocharee-ya teaspoon

cuchilla de afeitar *f* koochee-ya day afay-eetar razor blade

cuchillería *f* koochee-yairee-a cutlery

cuchillo *m* koochee-yo knife

cuelgue, espere y retire la tarjeta hang up, wait and remove card

cuello *m* kway-yo neck; collar

cuenco *m* kwenko bowl

cuenta *f* kwenta bill; account

cuentas corrientes current accounts

cuento *m* kwento tale

cuerda *f* kwairda rope; string

cuero *m* kwairo leather

cuerpo *m* kwairpo body

cuesta (*f*) kwesta it costs; slope

cueva *f* kweba cave

cuidado (*m*) kweedado take care; look out; care

cuidado con... caution...

cuidado con el escalón mind the step

cuidado con el perro beware of the dog

cuidar to look after; to nurse

culebra *f* snake

culpa *f* fault, blame; guilt

es culpa mía it's my fault

culturismo *m* body building

cumplas: ¡que cumplas muchos más! many happy returns!

cumpleaños *m* koomplay-an-yoss birthday

cuna *f* cot, crib

cuneta *f* koonayta gutter

cuñada *f* koon-yada sister-in-law

cuñado *m* brother-in-law

cura *m* priest

curado cured; smoked

curar to cure; to dress

curarse koorarsay to heal up

curva *f* bend; curve

curva peligrosa dangerous bend

cuyo koo-yo whose; of which

D

D. (Don) Mr

damas *fpl* ladies' toilet, ladies' restroom

danés Danish

danza *f* dantha dancing; dance

daños *mpl* dan-yoss damage

dar to give

dar el visto bueno a bwayno to approve

dcha. (derecha) right

de of; from

de 2 metros de alto two metres high

debajo de debaHo under

deber (*m*) debair to have to; to owe; duty

deberes *mpl* debairess homework

débil weak

decepción *f* dethepth-yon disappointment

decepcionado dethepth-yonado disappointed

decidir detheedeer to decide

décimo detheemo tenth

decir detheer to say; to tell

declaración *f* deklarath-yon declaration; statement

declarar to declare, to state

dedo *m* daydo finger

dedo del pie p-yay toe

defectuoso defekt-woso faulty

degustación *f* degoostath-yon café specializing in coffee

dejar dayHar to leave; to let

dejar de beber to stop drinking

delante de delantay in front of

delantera *f* delantaira front (part)

delantero front

la parte delantera partay the front (part)

delgado thin

delicioso deleeth-yoso delicious

demás: los demás the others

demasiado demass-yado too

demasiados too many

demora *f* delay

dentadura postiza *f* posteetha dentures

dentista *m/f* dentist

dentro (de) inside

dentro de dos semanas in two weeks' time

depende dependay it depends

dependiente *m/f* depend-yentay shop assistant

deporte *m* deportay sport

deportes de invierno *mpl* eemb-yairno winter sports

deportivo deporteebo sports

deportivos *mpl* trainers

depósito *m* tank; deposit

deprimido depressed

derecha *f* right

a la derecha (de) on the right (of)

derecho: todo derecho straight ahead

derribar to wreck, to demolish

desacuerdo *m* desakwairdo disagreement

desafortunadamente -amentay unfortunately

desagradable -dablay unpleasant

desagradar to displease

desaparecer desaparaythair to disappear

desastre *m* desastray disaster

desayunar desa-yoonar to have breakfast

desayuno *m* desa-yoono breakfast

descansar to rest

descarado cheeky

descargar to download

descarrilar to be derailed

descolgar el aparato lift receiver

descubierto deskoob-yairto discovered

descubrir to discover

descuelgue el auricular lift the receiver

descuentos deskwentoss discounts

descuidado deskweedado careless

desde (que) desday since

desde luego lwaygo of course

desear desay-ar to want; to wish

    ¿qué desea? kay desay-a what can I do for you?

desembarcadero *m* desembarkadairo quay

desfile de modelos *m* desfeelay fashion show

desgracia: por desgracia desgrath-ya unfortunately

deshacer las maletas dess-athair to unpack

desinfectante *m* -tantay disinfectant

desmaquillarse desmakee-yarsay to remove one's makeup

desmayarse desmayarsay to faint

desnudo naked

desobediente desobayd-yentay disobedient

desodorante *m* -rantay deodorant

desordenado untidy

desorientarse desor-yentarsay to lose one's way

despachador automático *m* ticket machine

despacho de billetes *m* bee-yaytess ticket office

despacio despath-yo slowly

despedirse despedeersay to say goodbye

despegar to take off

despegue *m* despay-gay take-off

despejado despayнado clear

despertador *m* despairtador alarm clock

despertar to wake

despertarse -tarsay to wake up

despierto desp-yairto awake

desprendimiento de terreno danger: landslides

despreocupado despray-okoopado thoughtless

después despwess afterwards

después de after

destinatario m addressee

destino m destination

destornillador m destornee-yador screwdriver

destruir destr-weer to destroy

desvestirse desbesteersay to undress

desviación f desb-yath-yon diversion

desvío m desbee-o detour, diversion

desvío provisional temporary diversion

detener detenair to arrest; to stop

detergente en polvo m detairHentay washing powder

detergente lavavajillas lababaHee-yass washing-up liquid

detestar to detest

detrás (de) behind

devolver debolbair to give back; to vomit

di I gave; tell me

día m dee-a day

día festivo public holiday

diamante m d-yamantay diamond

diapositiva f d-yaposeeteeba slide

diario m d-yar-yo diary; daily newspaper

diarrea f d-yarray-a diarrhoea

días azules athooless cheap travel days

días festivos public holidays

días laborables weekdays

dibujar deebooHar to draw

dibujos animados mpl deebooHoss cartoons

diccionario m deekth-yonar-yo dictionary

dice deethay he/she says; you say

dicho said

　¿qué ha dicho? what did you say?; what did he/she say?

diciembre m deeth-yembray December

diecinueve d-yetheenwaybay nineteen

dieciocho d-yethee-ocho eighteen

dieciséis d-yetheesay-eess sixteen

diecisiete d-yethees-yaytay seventeen

diente m d-yentay tooth

dieron d-yairon they gave; you gave

dieta f d-yayta diet

diez d-yeth ten

difícil deefeetheel difficult

diga tell me

dígame deegamay hello, yes

digo I say

dije deeHay I said

dijeron deeHairon they said; you said

dijiste deeHeestay you said

dijo deeHo he/she said; you say

diminuto tiny

Dinamarca f Denmark

dinero m deenairo money

dinero suelto *swelto* small change

Dios *m* *dee-oss* God

¡Dios mío! *mee-o* my God!

dirección *f* *deerekth-yon* direction; address; steering; management

dirección prohibida no entry

dirección única one-way traffic

director *m*, **directora** *f* manager; director; headteacher

dirigir *deereeHeer* to direct; to lead

disco *m* record

disco compacto compact disc

disco obligatorio parking disk must be displayed

disconformidad *f* disagreement

discoteca *f* disco, discotheque

disculparse *deeskoolparsay* to apologize

disculpe *deeskoolpay* excuse me

disculpen las molestias we apologize for any inconvenience

discurso *m* speech

discusión *f* *deeskoos-yon* discussion; argument

discutir to argue

diseñador de modas *m* *deesen-yador* fashion designer

distancia *f* *deestanth-ya* distance

distinto different

distraído *deestra-eedo* absent-minded

distribuidor *m* *deestreebweedor* distributor

distrito postal *m* postcode, zip code

disuélvase en agua dissolve in water

divertido entertaining; funny

divertirse *deebairteersay* to have a good time

divisas *fpl* foreign currency

divorciado *deeborth-yado* divorced

divorciarse *deeborth-yarsay* to divorce

divorcio *m* *deeborth-yo* divorce

doble *doblay* double

doce *dothay* twelve

docena (de) *f* *dothayna* dozen

dólar *m* dollar

doler *dolair* to hurt

dolor *m* pain

dolor de cabeza *kabaytha* headache

dolor de garganta sore throat

dolor de muelas toothache

dolor de oídos *o-eedoss* earache

doloroso painful

domicilio *m* *domeetheel-yo* place of residence; commercial headquarters

domingo *m* Sunday

domingos y festivos Sundays and public holidays

¡dominguero! *domeengairo* learn to drive!

don Mr

donaciones donations

donde *donday* where

doña *don-ya* Miss; Mrs

dorado gold, golden

dormido asleep

dormir to sleep

dormitorio *m* dormee**to**r-yo bedroom; dormitory

dos two

doscientos doss-thy**en**toss two hundred

doy I give

droga *f* drug

droguería *f* droga**ree**-a drugstore; household cleaning materials

ducha *f* shower

ducharse doocharsay to have a shower

dudar to doubt; to hesitate

duele dway**lay** it hurts

dulce dool**thay** sweet; gentle

dunas *fpl* sand dunes

durante doorantay during

duro (*m*) hard; tough guy

E

e and

ebanistería *f* ebaneestairee-a cabinetmaker's

echar to throw

echo de menos a mi... dee may**noss** I miss my...

echar al buzón booth**on** to post, to mail

echar el cerrojo thairro**Ho** to bolt

echar el correo korr**ay**-o to post, to mail

echarse la siesta echarsay to have a nap

edad *f* age

edificio *m* edee**feeth**-yo building

edredón *m* quilt, eiderdown; duvet

educado polite

EE.UU. (Estados Unidos) USA

efectivo: en efectivo in cash

eje *m* ay**Hay** axle

eje del cigüeñal theegwen-**yal** crankshaft

ejemplo *m* eHemplo example

por ejemplo for example

el the

él he; him

elástico elastic

electricidad *f* elektreetheeda electricity

electricista *m* elektreetheesta electrician

eléctrico electric

electrodomésticos *mpl* electrical appliances

elegir elayHeer to choose

ella ay-ya she; her

ellas they; them

ellos they; them

embajada *f* embaHada embassy

embarazada embarath**a**da pregnant

embarque *m* embarkay embarcation

embotellado en... bottled in...

embotellamiento *m* embotay-yam-**yento** traffic jam

embrague *m* embragay clutch

embudo *m* funnel

emergencia *f* emairḪenth-ya emergency

emergencias casualty; emergencies

emisión *f* emeess-yon programme; emission; distribution date; issue

emocionante emoth-yonantay exciting

empalme *m* empalmay junction

empaquetado *m* empaketado packing

empaste *m* empastay filling

empeorar empay-orar to get worse

empezar empethar to begin

empinado steep

empleada *f* emplay-ada, **empleado** *m* shop assistant, employee

empujar empooḪar to push

en in; at; on; by

enagua de medio cuerpo *f* enagwa day mayd-yo kwairpo underskirt

enamorados: día de los enamorados *m* St Valentine's Day

encantado delighted

¡encantado! pleased to meet you!

encantador lovely

encantar to please

encendedor *m* enthendedor lighter

encender enthendair to light; to switch on

encender luces de cruce switch headlights on

encendido *m* enthendeedo ignition

enchufe *m* enchoofay plug; socket

encienda las luces switch on your lights

encierro enth-yairro bull-running in Pamplona, the bulls loose in the streets

encima entheema above

encima de on (top of)

encontrar to find

encontrarse (con/a) -trarsay to meet

encuentro *(m)* enkwentro meeting, encounter; I find

enero *m* enairo January

enfadado angry

enfadarse -darsay to get angry

enfermedad *f* enfairmeda disease

enfermedad venérea benairay-a sexually transmitted disease

enfermera *f* enfairmaira nurse

enfermero *m* male nurse

enfermo enfairmo ill

enfrente de enfrentay opposite

enhorabuena: ¡enhorabuena! enorabwayna congratulations!

dar la enhorabuena a to congratulate

enlace *m* enlathay connection; wedding

enlatados *mpl* canned food

enorme enormay enormous

enseñar ensen-yar to teach

entender entendair to understand

entero entairo whole

entiendo ent-yendo I understand

entierro m ent-yairro funeral

entonces entonthess then;
therefore

entrada f entrance, way in; ticket

entrada gratis admission free

entrada libre admission free

entrada por delante entry at
the front

entrar to go in

entre entray among; between

entre sin llamar enter without
knocking

entreacto m entray-akto
intermission

entretanto meanwhile

enviar emb-yar to send

envolver embolbair to wrap up;
to involve

equipaje m ekeepahay luggage,
baggage

equipaje de mano hand
baggage

equipajes mpl left-luggage office,
baggage check

equipo m ekeepo team

equitación f ekeetath-yon horse
riding

equivocado ekeebokado wrong

equivocarse ekeebokarsay to
make a mistake

equivocarse de número to dial
the wrong number

era aira I/he/she/it was; you were

erais aira-eess you were

éramos we were

eran they were; you were

eras you were

eres you are

erupción f airoopth-yon rash;
eruption

es he/she/it is; you are

ésa aysa that one

esa that

ésas those ones

esas those

escala f intermediate stop; scale;
ladder

escalera automática f escalator

escaleras fpl stairs

escalón lateral ramp; uneven
road surface; no hard shoulder

escandaloso shocking

Escandinavia f Scandinavia

escarcha f frost

escayola f eska-yola plaster cast

escocés eskothayss Scottish

Escocia f eskoth-ya Scotland

escoger eskoHair to choose

esconder eskondair to hide

escribir to write

escrito written

escuchar to listen; to listen to

escuela f eskwayla school

escuela de párvulos
kindergarten

escurrir a mano to wring by
hand

ése aysay that one

ese that

esencial esenth-yal essential

esfuerzo m esfwairtho effort

esmalte de uñas *m* esmaltay day **oo**n-yass nail polish

esmeralda *f* emerald

eso ayso that

  eso es that's it, that's right

ésos those ones

esos those

espalda *f* back

espantoso dreadful; frightening

España *f* espan-ya Spain

español (*m*) espan-yol Spanish; Spaniard

española *f* Spaniard, Spanish woman/girl

especialista *m/f* specialist

especialmente espeth-yalmentay especially

espejo *m* espay**H**o mirror

esperar espairar to wait; to hope

espere espai**ray** please wait

¡espéreme! espai**ray**may wait for me!

espere tono más agudo wait for higher pitched tone

espeso espay**so** thick

esponja *f* espon**Ha** sponge

esposa *f* wife

esposo *m* husband

espuma de afeitar *f* afay-eetar shaving foam

esquí *m* eskee ski; skiing

esquí acuático akwateeko waterski; waterskiing

esquiar eskee-**ar** to ski

esquina *f* eskeena corner

esta this

está he/she/it is; you are

ésta this one

estación *f* estath-yon station; season

estación de autobuses owtoboo**sess** bus station

estación de servicio sairbeeth-yo service station

estación de trenes train station

estación principal central station

estacionamiento limitado restricted parking

estacionamiento vigilado supervised parking

estacionarse estath-yon*ar*say to park

estadio de fútbol *m* estad-yo football stadium

Estados Unidos *mpl* United States

estáis you are

estamos we are

estampado *m* pattern; printed

están they are; you are

estanco *m* tobacconist's

estanque *m* estankay pond

estaño *m* estan-yo tin; pewter

estar to be

estárter *m* estartair choke

estas these

estás you are

éstas these ones

estatua *f* estatwa statue

este *m* estay east

este this

éste this one

esterilizado estaireeleethado sterilized

esto this

estómago *m* stomach

estornudar to sneeze

estos these

éstos these ones

estoy I am

estrecho narrow; tight

Estrecho de Gibraltar *m* Heebraltar Strait of Gibraltar

estrella *f* estray-ya star

estrellarse contra estray-yarsay to run into

estreno *m* estrayno new film release

estreñido estren-yeedo constipated

estreñimiento *m* estren-yeem-yento constipation

estropear estropay-ar to damage

estudiante *m/f* estood-yantay student

estudiar estood-yar to study

estupendo wonderful, great

estúpido stupid

etiqueta *f* eteekayta label

... de etiqueta formal...

europeo ay-ooropay-o European

evidente ebeedentay obvious

exactamente -mentay exactly

¡exacto! exactly!

excelente esthelentay excellent

excepto... except...

excepto domingos y festivos except Sundays and holidays

excepto sábados except Saturdays

exceso de equipaje *m* esthayso day ekeepaHay excess baggage

exceso de velocidad belotheeda speeding

excursión *f* eskoors-yon trip

expedir espede**er** to dispatch

explicación f espleekath-y**o**n explanation

explicar explain

explorar to explore

exportación f esportath-y**o**n export

exposición f esposeeth-y**o**n exhibition

exprés m slow night train stopping at all stations

expreso m fast train; special delivery

exterior (m) estairee-**o**r exterior, outer; foreign; overseas

extintor (de incendios) m eenth**e**nd-yoss fire extinguisher

extra premium petrol/gas

extranjera f estranH**ai**ra foreigner

extranjero (m) estranH**ai**ro foreign; abroad; overseas; foreigner

en el extranjero abroad

extraño estran-yo strange

F

fábrica f factory

fabricado por... made by...

fácil fa**t**heel easy

factura f bill; invoice

facturación f faktoorath-y**o**n check-in

facturar el equipaje ekeepa**H**ay to check in

falda f skirt; hillside

falda pantalón culottes

falso false

falta f lack; mistake; defect; fault

no hace falta que... a**t**hay it's not necessary to...

falta de visibilidad poor visibility

familia f fam**ee**l-ya family

famoso famous

farmacia f farm**a**th-ya pharmacy

farmacia de guardia gw**a**rd-ya emergency pharmacy

faro m light; headlight; lighthouse

faro antiniebla anteen-y**e**bla fog lamp

favor: a favor de fab**o**r in favour of

por favor please; please do; excuse me

febrero m febr**a**iro February

fecha f date

fecha de caducación kadookath-y**o**n expiry date

fecha de caducidad kadooth**ee**da expiry date

fecha de nacimiento natheem-y**e**nto date of birth

fecha límite de venta sell-by date

¡felices Pascuas y próspero Año Nuevo! feleeth**e**ss p**a**skwass ee pr**o**spairo **a**n-yo nw**ay**bo Merry Christmas and a Happy New Year!

felicidad f feleeth**ee**da happiness

¡felicidades! feleeth**ee**da**d**ess happy birthday!; congratulations!

felicitar feleetheetar to congratulate

feliz feleeth happy

¡feliz cumpleaños! koomplay-an-yoss happy birthday!

feo fay-o ugly

feria de... ... fair

ferias *fpl* fair-yass fair

ferretería *f* fairraytairee-a hardware store

ferrobús *m* local short-distance train

ferrocarril *m* railway, railroad

festividad *f* celebration

festivos bank holidays, public holidays

fibras naturales natooraless natural fibres

fiebre *f* f-yebray fever

fiebre del heno ayno hay fever

fiesta *f* public holiday; party

fiesta de... feast of...

fiesta nacional nath-yonal bullfighting

Travel tip Even the smallest village or most modern suburb devotes at least a couple of days a year to partying, and coinciding with a fiesta can propel you into the heart of Spanish culture. Some major events are worth planning a trip around – the Fiesta de San Fermín at Pamplona (July), Las Fallas in Valencia (March), Seville's Feria de Abril, the pre-Lenten Carnival festivities and Semana Santa, leading up to Easter.

fila *f* row

filtro *m* filter

fin *m* feen end; purpose

a fin de que day kay so that

fin de semana weekend

fin de serie sair-yay discontinued articles

final *m* feenal end

final de autopista end of motorway/highway

fingir feenHeer to pretend

fino fine; delicate

firma *f* signature; company

firmar to sign

firme deslizante slippery surface

firme en mal estado bad surface

flaco skinny

flequillo *m* flekee-yo fringe

flor *f* flower

floristería *f* florist

flotador *m* rubber ring

flotadores *mpl* flotadoress lifebelts

folleto *m* fo-yayto leaflet

fonda *f* (simple) restaurant; boarding house

fondo *m* bottom; background

en el fondo (de) at the bottom (of)

fontanero *m* fontanairo plumber

footing *m* jogging

forma *f* form

en forma fit

formato MP3 *m* formato emay pay tress MP3 format

foto *f* photograph

hacer fotos to take photographs

fotografía *f* photograph; photography

fotografiar fotograf-*yar* to photograph

fotógrafo *m* photographer

fotómetro *m* light meter

francamente -men*tay* frankly

francés fran*thayss* French

Francia *f* franth-*ya* France

franqueo *m* fran*kay*-o postage

fregadero *m* sink

fregar los platos to do the washing up

freír fray-*eer* to fry

frenar fre*nar* to brake

freno *m* fray*no* brake

freno de mano handbrake

frente *f* fren*tay* forehead

fresco fresh

frigorífico *m* fridge

frío free-o cold

hace frío a*thay* it's cold

frontera *f* fron*taira* border

frutería *f* fruit shop/store; greengrocer

fue fway he/she/it went; he/she/it was; you went; you were

fuego *m* fway*go* fire

¿tiene fuego? have you got a light?

fuegos artificiales arteefeeth-*yaless* fireworks

fuente *f* fwen*tay* fountain; source; font

fuera fwai*ra* outside; he/she/it was; he/she/it went; you were; you went

fuera de apart from

fuera de horas punta off-peak hours

fuera de servicio out of order

fuerais fwai*ra*-eess you were; you went

fuéramos fwai*ra*moss we were; we went

fueran fwai*ran* they were; they went; you were; you went

fueras fwai*rass* you were; you went

fueron fwai*ron* they were; they went; you were; you went

fuerte fwai*rtay* strong; loud

fuerza *f* fwai*rtha* force; strength

fui fwee I was; I went

fuimos fwee*moss* we were; we went

fuiste fwee*stay* you were; you went

fuisteis fwee*stay*-eess you were; you went

fumadores smoking

fumar to smoke

funcionar foonkth-yo*nar* to work

funcionario *m* foonkth-yo*nar*-yo civil servant

funeraria *f* undertaker's

furgón *m* van

furgoneta *f* van

furioso foor-yo*so* furious

furúnculo *m* abscess; boil

fusible *m* fooseeblay fuse

fútbol *m* football

futuro *m* footooro future

Travel tip The football
season runs from late
August until May or June,
and most games kick off
at 5 or 7pm on Sundays,
though live TV demands
that one key game kicks off
at 9 or 10pm on Saturday
and Sunday. With the
exception of a few big
games, tickets are not
too hard to get, starting
around €30 for La Liga
matches.

G

gabardina *f* raincoat

gafas *fpl* glasses, eyeglasses

gafas de bucear boothay-ar
goggles

gafas de sol sunglasses

galería *f* galairee-a gallery

galería de arte day artay art
gallery

galerías *fpl* store

Gales *m* galess Wales

galés Welsh

gallego ga-yay-go Galician

ganar to win; to earn

ganga *f* bargain

ganso *m* goose

garaje *m* garaHay garage

garantía *f* guarantee

garganta *f* throat

gas-oil *m* diesel

gasóleo *m* gasolay-o diesel

gasolina *f* petrol, fuel

gasolina normal regular petrol/
gas

gasolina super premium
petrol/gas

gasolinera *f* gasoleenaira petrol/
gas station, filling station

gastar to spend

gato *m* cat; jack

gemelos *mpl* Haymayloss twins;
cufflinks

generalmente Henairalmentay
generally; usually

¡genial! Hayn-yal great!, fantastic!

genio: tener mal genio Hayn-yo
to be bad-tempered

gente *f* Hentay people

gerente *m* Hairentay manager

¡gilipollas! Heeleepo-yass stupid
idiot!

gimnasia *f* Heemnas-ya
gymnastics

gimnasio *m* gymnasium

ginecólogo *m* Heenekologo
gynaecologist

girar Heerar to turn

giro *m* Heero money order; turn

gitano *m* Heetano gypsy

glorieta *f* glor-yayta roundabout

gobierno *m* gob-yairno
government

gol *m* goal

Golfo de Vizcaya *m* beethka-ya
Bay of Biscay

golpe *m* golpay blow

de golpe all of a sudden

golpear golpay-ar to hit

goma *f* rubber; glue

goma elástica rubber band

gordo fat

gorra *f* cap

gorro *m* bonnet, cap

gorro de baño ban-yo bathing cap

gorro de ducha shower cap

gota *f* drop

gotera *f* gotaira leak

gracias grath-yass thank you

gracias, igualmente eegwalmentay thank you, the same to you

gracioso grath-yoso funny

grados *mpl* degrees

gramática *f* grammar

gramo *m* gramme

Gran Bretaña *f* bretan-ya Great Britain

grande granday big, large

grandes almacenes *mpl* almathaynayss large department store

grandes rebajas rebaHass sales

granizo *m* graneetho hail

granja *f* granHa farm

granjero *m* granHairo farmer

grano *m* spot

grasa *f* fat

grasiento grass-yento greasy

graso greasy

gratificación *f* grateefeekath-yon reward; tip

gratis free

grave grabay serious

gravilla *f* grabee-ya loose chippings

Grecia *f* greth-ya Greece

grifo *m* tap, faucet

gripe *f* greepay flu

gris grey

gritar to shout

grosero grosairo rude

grúa *f* groo-a tow truck, breakdown lorry; crane

grueso grwayso thick

grupo *m* group

grupo sanguíneo sangeenay-o blood group

guante *m* gwantay glove

guapo gwapo handsome

guardacostas *m/f* gwardakostass coastguard

guardar gwardar to keep; to put away

guardarropa *m* gwardarropa cloakroom, checkroom

guardería (infantil) *f* gwardairee-a (infanteel) crèche; nursery school

guárdese en sitio fresco keep in a cool place

guardia civil *m/f* gward-ya theebeel police; policeman/ policewoman

guateque *m* gwatay-kay party

guerra *f* gairra war

guerra civil civil war

guía *m/f* gee-a guide

guía telefónica *f* phone book, telephone directory

guía turística tourist guide

guisar *geesar* to cook

guitarra *f geetarra* guitar

gustar to please

me gusta… I like…

gusto: mucho gusto pleased to meet you!

con mucho gusto certainly, with great pleasure

el gusto es mío how do you do, it is a pleasure

H

H is not pronounced in Spanish

ha *he/she/it has; you have

habéis *abay-eess* you have

habilidoso skilful

habitación *f abeetath-yon* room

habitación con dos camas twin room

habitación doble *doblay* double room

Travel tip In most towns you'll be able to get a no-frills double room in a pensión or small hotel for as little as €40. Outside of Madrid, Barcelona and the biggest resorts, expect to pay upwards of €90 for a three-star hotel, from around €120 for four-star and boutique places, and €150–200 for five-star hotels and historic paradores

---

habitación individual *eendeebeedwal* single room

habitar to live

hablador talkative

hablar to speak

hable aquí speak here

habrá there will be; he/she/it will have; you will have

habrán they will have; you will have

habrás you will have

habré *abray* I will have

habréis *abray-eess* you will have

habremos we will have

habría *abree-a* I would have; he/she/it would have; you would have

habríais *abree-a-eess* you would have

habríamos *abree-amoss* we would have

habrían *abree-an* they would have; you would have

habrías *abree-ass* you would have

hace *athay:* **hace… días**… days ago

hace calor it is hot

hacer *athair* to make; to do

hacerse *athairsay* to become

hacia *ath-ya* towards

hago I do; I make

hambre: tengo hambre *ambray* I'm hungry

hamburguesería *f amboorgaysairee-a* restaurant selling hamburgers, hot dogs

han an they have; you have

haré aray I will do

harto: estar harto (de) arto to be fed up (with)

has ass you have

hasta asta even; until

  hasta que kay until

¡hasta la vista! see you!

¡hasta luego! lwaygo cheerio!; see you later!

¡hasta mañana! man-yana see you tomorrow!

¡hasta pronto! see you soon!

hay ī there is; there are

  hay... we sell...

haya ī-a I have; he/she/it has; you have

haz ath do; make

he ay I have

hecho m ay-cho fact

hecho made; done

hecho a la medida made-to-measure

helada f frost

heladería f eladairee-a ice-cream parlour

helado f elado ice-cream

helar to freeze

hembra female

hemos we have

herida f aireeda wound

herido injured

hermana f airmano sister

hermano m brother

hermoso airmoso beautiful

herramientas fpl airram-yentass tools

hervir airbeer to boil

hice eethay I made; I did

hidratante: crema hidratante f eedratantay moisturizer

hidropedales *mpl* eedropedaless pedalos

hielo *m* yaylo ice

hierba *f* yairba grass

hierro *m* yairro iron

hija *f* eeHa daughter

hijo *m* son

hilo *m* thread

hipermercado eepairmairkado hypermarket

hipo *m* hiccups

hipódromo *m* horse-racing track

historia *f* eestor-ya history; story

hizo eetho he/she made; he/she did; you made; you did

hogar *m* home; household goods

hoja *f* oHa leaf; sheet of paper

hoja de afeitar day afay-eetar razor blade

¡hola! hello!, hi!

hombre *m* ombray man

¡hombre! hey there!; you bet; oh come on!

hombre de negocios negoth-yoss businessman

hombro *m* shoulder

hondo deep

honrado honest

hora *f* ora hour

¿qué hora es? what time is it?

hora local local time

horario *m* orar-yo timetable, schedule

horario de autobuses owtoboosess bus timetable/ schedule

horario de invierno eemb-yairno winter timetable/schedule

horario de recogidas rekoHeedass collection times

horario de trenes train timetable/schedule

horario de verano summer timetable/schedule

horas de consulta surgery hours, office hours (of doctor)

horas de oficina ofeetheena opening hours

horas de visita visiting hours

horas punta rush hour

hormiga *f* ant

horno *m* oven

horquilla *f* orkee-ya hairpin

hospedarse ospedarsay to stay

hostal *m* ostal restaurant specializing in regional dishes; boarding house

hostal-residencia *m* reseedenth-ya long-stay boarding house

hostería *f* ostairee-a restaurant specializing in regional dishes

hotel-residencia *m* residential hotel

hoy oy today

HR (hostal-residencia) *m* boarding house where no meals are served, often lower-priced, residential hotel

hube oobay I had

hubieron oob-yairon they had; you had

hubimos oobeemoss we had

hubiste oobeestay you had

hubisteis oobeestay-ess you had

hubo oobo he/she/it had; you had; there was/were

huelga *f* welga strike

hueso *m* wayso bone

huésped *m/f* wesped guest

huevo *m* waybo egg

humedad *m* humidity, dampness

húmedo damp

humo *m* smoke

humor *m* humour

hundirse oondeersay to sink

hurto *m* theft

idéntico (a/que) identical (to)

idioma *m* eed-yoma language

idiota *m/f* eed-yota idiot

iglesia *f* eeglays-ya church

igual eegwal equal; like

> Travel tip Churches are often kept locked, opening only for worship in the early morning and/or the evening (between around 6 and 9pm), so you'll either have to visit at these times, or find a sacristan or custodian, who almost always live nearby, to let you in. You're expected to give a small donation.

me da igual it's all the same to me

imbécil *m* eembaytheel nutter; stupid

impaciente eempath-yentay impatient

imperdible *m* eempairdeeblay safety pin

impermeable *m* eempairmay-**a**blay waterproof; raincoat

importación *f* eemportath-yon imported goods

importante eemportantay important

importar: no importa it doesn't matter

¿le importa si…? do you mind if…?

importe *m* eemportay amount

importe del billete bee-yaytay fare

importe total total due

imposible eemposeeblay impossible

impreso *m* eemprayso form

impuesto *m* eempwesto tax

incendiar eenthend-yar to set fire to

incendio *m* eenthend-yo fire (blaze)

incluido eenkl-weedo included

incluso even

increíble eenkray-eeblay incredible

indemnizar eendemneethar to compensate

independiente eendepend-yentay independent

indicaciones *fpl* instructions for use

indicador *m* indicator

indicador de nivel gauge

indicar to indicate

indicativos de paises country codes

indicativos provinciales area codes

indignado indignant

indispuesto eendeespwesto unwell

infantil children's

infarto m heart attack

infectarse eenfektarsay to become infected

inflamado swollen

inflamarse eenflamarsay to swell

influenciar eenflwenth-yar to influence

información f eenformath-yon information

información de vuelos bwayloss flight information

información turística tourist information

información y turismo tourist information office

informar to inform

informarse (de/sobre) -marsay (day/sobray) to get information (on/about)

infracción f eenfrakth-yon offence

Inglaterra f eenglatairra England

inglés m een-glayss English; Englishman

inglesa f Englishwoman

ingresos mpl deposits; income

iniciales fpl eeneeth-yaless initials

inmediatamente eenmed-yatamentay immediately

inocente eenothentay innocent

insertar monedas insert coins

inserte moneda insert coin

insistir to insist

insolación f eensolath-yon sunstroke

instituto de belleza m bay-yaytha beauty salon

instrucciones de lavado mpl washing instructions

inteligente eenteleeHentay intelligent

intentar to try

interés m eentairayss interest

interesante eentairesantay interesting

interior m eentairee-or interior, inner; domestic, home

intermedio m eentairmayd-yo intermediate; intermission, interval

intermitente m eentairmeetentay indicator

interruptor m switch

interurbana long-distance

intoxicación alimenticia f eentokseekath-yon aleementeeth-ya food poisoning

introduzca el dinero exacto insert exact amount

introduzca moneda insert coin

introduzca la tarjeta y marque insert card and dial

inútil useless, pointless

invierno m eemb-yairno winter

invitada *f*, **invitado** *m* guest

invitar to invite

inyección *f* eenyekth-yon injection

ir to go

ir de paseo pasay-o to go for a walk

Irlanda *f* eerlanda Ireland

Irlanda del Norte nortay Northern Ireland

irlandés *m* eerlandayss Irish; Irishman

irlandesa *f* Irishwoman

irse eersay to go away

isla *f* island

Islas Canarias *fpl* kanar-yass Canary Islands

itinerario *m* eeteenairar-yo itinerary

IVA (impuesto sobre el valor añadido) eeba VAT

Travel tip Non-EU residents are able to claim back the sales tax on purchases that come to over €90. To do this, make sure the shop you're buying from fills out the correct paperwork, and present this to customs before you check in at the airport for your return flight.

---

izq. (izquierda) left

izquierda *f* eethk-ya**i**rda left

  a la izquierda (de) on the left (of)

J

jabón *m* Habon soap

jabón de afeitar afay-eetar shaving soap

jamonería *f* Hamonairee-a ham shop

jarabe *m* Harabay syrup

jardín *m* Hardeen garden

jardines públicos Hardeeness park, public gardens

jarra *f* Harra jug

jarrón *m* Harron vase

jefe *m* Hayfay boss

jefe de tren guard

jersey *m* Hairsay-ee jumper

jersey de cuello alto kway-yo polo neck jumper

¡Jesús! Haysooss bless you!

¡joder! Hodair hell!

joven (*m/f*) Hoben young; young man; young woman

joyas *fpl* Hoyass jewellery

joyería *f* Hoyairee-a jewellery; jeweller's

judío Hoodee-o Jewish

juego *m* Hway-go game; I play

jueves *m* waybess Thursday

jugar Hoogar to play

juguete *m* Hoogaytay toy

juguetería *f* Hoogaytairee-a toy shop

juicio *m* Hweeth-yo judgement; opinion; reason

julio *m* Hool-yo July

junio *m* Hoon-yo June

junto (a) Hoonto next (to)

juntos together

justo Hoosto just

K

kiosko de periódicos m k-yosko day pairee-**o**deekoss newsagent's, newsstand

kiosko de prensa newsagent's, newsstand

L

la the; her; it

labio m lab-yo lip

laborables laborabless weekdays, working days

laca f hair spray

lado m side

al lado de beside, next to

ladrillo m ladree-yo brick

ladrón m thief

lagartija f lagarteeHa lizard

lago m lake

lámpara f lamp

lana f wool

lana pura pure wool

lanas al peso wool sold by weight

lápiz m lapeeth pencil

lápiz de memoria m memor-ya memory stick

lápiz de ojos oHoss eyeliner

largo (m) length; long

a lo largo de along

largura f length

las the; them; you

las que... the ones that...

lástima: es una lástima it's a pity

lastimarse la espalda lasteem**a**rsay to hurt one's back

lata f can; nuisance

latón m brass

lavabo m lababo washbasin

lavabos toilets, rest room

lavado m labado washing

lavadora f labadora washing machine

lavandería f labandairee-a laundry

lavandería automática owtomateeka launderette, laundromat

lavaplatos m labaplatoss dishwasher

lavar labar to wash

lavar a mano wash by hand

lavar en seco dry clean

lavar la ropa to do the washing

lavarse labarsay to wash

lavar separadamente wash separately

laxante m laksantay laxative

le lay him; her; you

lección f lekth-yon lesson

leche f lechay milk

leche limpiadora f leemp-yadora skin cleanser

lechería f lechairee-a dairy shop; dairy produce

leer lay-**air** to read

lejía f le**H**ee-a bleach

lejos lay**H**oss far away

lejos de far from

lencería f lenthairee-a drapery

lentillas fpl lentee-yass contact lenses

lentillas blandas soft lenses

lentillas duras hard lenses

lentillas porosas gas permeable lenses

lento slow

leotardos mpl lay-otardoss tights, pantyhose

les them; you

letra f letter; banker's draft

levantar lebantar to raise, to lift

levantarse lebantarsay to get up

ley f lay-ee law

libra f pound

libre leebray free; vacant

libre de impuestos duty-free

librería f leebrairee-a bookshop, bookstore

libreta de ahorros f leebra**y**ta day a-**o**rross savings account book

libreta de direcciones deerekth-y**o**ness address book

libro m book

libro de frases phrase book

libros de bolsillo bolsee-yo paperbacks

líder m leedair leader

ligero lee**H**airo light

lima de uñas f oon-yass nailfile

límite f leemeetay limit

límite de altura maximum height

límite de peso pay**s**o weight limit

límite de velocidad day belotheeda**d** speed limit

Travel tip The Spanish drive on the right, and speed limits are enforced throughout the country: 120kph on most *autopistas*, on the *autovía* 90kph, and 50kph in towns and villages. Police can fine drivers on the spot for speeding or other transgressions, and if you don't have any cash, they will escort you to the nearest ATM.

---

limpiaparabrisas m leemp-yaparabr**ee**sass windscreen wiper

limpiar leemp-yar to clean

limpieza f leemp-ya**y**tha cleanliness; cleaning

limpieza de coches car wash

limpieza en seco dry-cleaning

limpio leemp-yo clean

línea f leenay-a line

en línea online

linterna f leentairna torch

lío m lee-o mess

liquidación f leekeedath-yon sale

liquidación total clearance sale

liso flat; plain; straight

lista f list

lista de correos korray-oss poste restante, general delivery

lista de espera espaíra standby

listo clever; ready

litera f leetaíra couchette

litro m litre

llamada f yamada call

llamada a cobro revertido rebairteedo reverse charge call

llamar yamar to call; to name

llamar por teléfono telayfono to call, to phone

llamarse yamarsay to be called

llame a la puerta please knock

llame al timbre please ring

llame antes de entrar knock before entering

llamo: me llamo… may yamo my name is…

llave f yabay key; spanner

llave inglesa eenglaysa spanner

llegada f yaygada arrival

llegadas internacionales international arrivals

llegadas nacionales domestic arrivals

llegar yegar to arrive; to get to

llegué yegay I arrived

llenar yenar to fill

llenar el depósito to fill up

lleno yayno full

llevar yebar to carry; to take; to bring; to give a lift to

llevar a juicio Hweeth-yo to prosecute

llevarse yebarsay to take away

llorar yorar to cry

llover yobair to rain

lloviendo: está lloviendo yob-yendo it's raining

llovizna f yobeethna drizzle

llueve y-way-bay it is raining

lluvia f yoob-ya rain

lo it; the

localidad f place

localidades tickets

loción antimosquitos f loth-yon anteemoskeetoss insect repellent

loción bronceadora bronthay-adora suntan lotion

loción para después del afeitado despwess del afay-eetado after-shave

loco (m) mad; madman

locomotora f engine

locutorio telefónico m telephone booth

Londres londress London

longitud f lonHeetoo length

los the

los que… the ones that…

loza f lotha crockery

luces de posición fpl loothess day poseeth-yon sidelights

luces traseras trasaírass rear lights

luego lwaygo then

luego que after

lugar m place

en lugar de instead of

lugar de veraneo bairanay-o summer resort

lugares de interés places of interest

lujo *m* looно luxury

lujoso luxurious

luna *f* moon

lunes *m* looness Monday

luz *f* looth light

luz de carretera main beam

luz de cruce kroothay dipped
  headlights

M

machista *m* male chauvinist,
  sexist

madera *f* madaira wood

madre *f* madray mother

madrileño madreelayn-yo from
  Madrid, Madrid

madrugada *f* small hours

maduro ripe

maestra *f* ma-estra, **maestro** *m*
  primary school teacher

mal (*m*) badly; unwell, ill, sick;
  evil

¡maldita sea! say-a damn!

maleducado rude

malentendido *m*
  misunderstanding

maleta *f* suitcase

  hacer las maletas to pack

maletero *m* maletairo car boot,
  trunk

mal genio *m* нayn-yo bad temper

mal humor *m* bad mood; bad
  temper; anger

Mallorca ma-yorka Majorca

malo bad

mamá *f* mum

manantial *m* manant-yal spring

mancha f stain

mandar to send; to order

mandíbula f jaw

manera: de esta manera manaira in this way

    de manera que so (that)

mano f hand

manoplas fpl mittens

manta f blanket

mantel m tablecloth

mantelerías fpl mantelairee-ass table linen

mantenga limpia España keep Spain tidy

mantenga limpia la ciudad keep our city tidy

manténgase en sitio fresco store in a cool place

manténgase alejado de los niños keep out of the reach of children

manual de conversación m manwal day konbairsath-yon phrasebook

mañana f man-yana morning; tomorrow

    por la mañana in the morning

    ¡hasta mañana! see you tomorrow!

mañana por la mañana tomorrow morning

mañana por la tarde tarday tomorrow afternoon/evening

mapa m map

mapa de carreteras road map

mapa de recorrido network map

maquillaje m makee-yaHay make-up

maquillarse makee-yarsay to put one's make-up on

máquina de afeitar eléctrica f makeena day afay-eetar electric shaver

máquina de escribir typewriter

máquina de fotos camera

máquina tragaperras makeena slot machine

maquinaria f makeenar-ya machinery

maquinilla de afeitar f makeenee-ya razor

mar m sea

    la mar de... lots of...; very...

maravilloso marabee-yoso marvellous

marca registrada f reHeestrada registered trade mark

marcar to dial

marcar el número dial the number

marcha f gear

marcha atrás reverse gear

marcharse marcharsay to go away

marea f maray-a tide

mareado maray-ado sick; merry, drunk

mares: a mares loads

marido m husband

mariposa f butterfly

marisquería f mareeskairee-a shellfish restaurant

marque... dial...

marrón brown

marroquinería f marrokeen-airee-a fancy leather goods

Marruecos m marrway-koss Morocco

martes m martess Tuesday

martes de carnaval Shrove Tuesday

martillo m martee-yo hammer

marzo m martho March

más more

más de more than

más pequeño smaller

el más caro the most expensive

ya no más no more

más o menos maynoss more or less

matar to kill

matrícula f number plate; registration; registration fees

máximo personas maximum number of people

mayo m ma-yo May

mayor mayor adult; bigger; older; biggest; oldest

la mayor parte (de) partay most (of)

mayor de edad of age, adult

mayoría: la mayoría mayoree-a most

me me; myself

me duele aquí dwaylay I have a pain here

mecánico m mechanic

mechas fpl highlights

media docena (de) f dothayna half a dozen

media hora f half an hour

media pensión f pens-yon half board, European plan

mediano mayd-yano medium; average

medianoche f mayd-yanochay midnight

medias fpl mayd-yass stockings

ir/pagar a medias to go Dutch

medias panty tights, pantyhose

medicina f medeetheena medicine

médico m maydeeko doctor

médico general Hay-nairal GP

medida: a medida que as

medida del cuello f kway-yo collar size

medio m mayd-yo middle

por medio de by (means of)

medio: de tamaño medio medium-sized

medio billete m bee-yaytay half(-price ticket)

medio litro half a litre

mediodía m mayd-yodee-a midday

medir to measure

medusa f jellyfish

mejor mayHor best; better

mejorar mayHorar to improve

mejoría f mayHoree-a recovery

mencionar menth-yonar to mention

menor men**or** smaller; younger; smallest; youngest

menor de edad minor

menos may**noss** less; fewest; least

  a menos que unless

mensaje de texto *m* mensa**H**ay day tek**s**to text (message)

menudo tiny, minute

  a menudo often

menú turístico *m* set menu

mercadillo *m* mairka**dee**-yo street market

mercado *m* market

mercado cubierto koob-**yair**to indoor market

mercado de divisas exchange rates

mercería *f* mairthair**ee**-a haberdashery

merendar to have an afternoon snack

merendero *m* mairen**dair**o open-air café

merienda *f* mair-**yen**da tea, afternoon snack

mes *m* month

mesa *f* table

mesón *m* inn

meta **may**ta goal

metro *m* metre; underground, subway

mezquita *f* meth**kee**ta mosque

mi my

mí me

mía **mee**-a mine

microbús *m* minibus

miedo *m* m-**yay**do fear

tengo miedo (de/a) I'm afraid (of)

mientras m-**yen**trass while

mientras que whereas

mientras tanto meanwhile

miércoles *m* m-**yair**koless Wednesday

miércoles de ceniza then**ee**tha Ash Wednesday

¡mierda! m-**yair**da shit!

mil meel thousand

militar *m* serviceman

millón *m* mee-**yon** million

minifalda *f* mini-skirt

ministerio de… ministry of…

minúsculo tiny

minusválido (*m*) disabled; disabled person

minuto *m* minute

mío **mee**-o mine

miope m-**yo**pay short-sighted

mirador *m* scenic view, vantage point

mirar to look (at)

mis my

misa *f* mass

mismo same

mitad *f* half

mitad de precio pra**yth**-yo half price

mobilette *f* mobee**lettay** moped

mochila *f* rucksack

moda *f* fashion

  de moda fashionable

moda jóvenes **H**obayness young fashions

moda juvenil Hoobayneel young fashions

modas caballeros kaba-yaiross men's fashions

modas niños/niñas neen-yoss children's fashions

modas pre-mamá maternity fashions

modas señora ladies' fashions

modelo *m* model; design; style

moderno modairno modern

modista *f* dressmaker; fashion designer

modisto *m* fashion designer

modo: de modo que so (that)

modo de empleo instructions for use

mojado moHado wet

moldeado con secador de mano molday-ado blow-dry

molestar to disturb; to bother

molesto annoying

monedas *fpl* coins

monedero *m* monedairo purse

montacargas *m* service lift, service elevator

montaña *f* montan-ya mountain

montañismo *m* montan-yeesmo climbing

montar to get in; to ride; to assemble

montar a caballo kaba-yo to go horse-riding

montar en bici beethee to cycle

moquetas *fpl* mokaytass carpets

morado purple

mordedura *f* bite

moreno morayno dark-haired

morir to die

moros *mpl* Moors

morriña: tengo morriña morreen-ya I'm homesick

mosca *f* fly

mostrador *m* counter

mostrador (de equipajes) day ekeepaHess check-in

mostrar to show

moto *f* motorbike

motora *f* motorboat

mover mobair to move

mozo *m* motho porter

muchacha *f* girl

muchacho *m* boy

muchas gracias grath-yass thank you very much

muchísimas gracias thank you very much indeed

muchísimo enormously, a great deal

mucho much; a lot; a lot of
  mucho más a lot more
  mucho menos maynoss a lot less
  muchos/muchas a lot; a lot of; many

muebles *mpl* mwaybless furniture

muela *f* mwayla back tooth

muela del juicio Hweeth-yo wisdom tooth

muelle *m* mway-yay spring; quay

muerte *f* mwairtay death

muerto mwairto dead

mujer *f* mooHair woman; wife

muletas *fpl* crutches

multa *f* fine; parking ticket

multa por uso indebido
penalty for misuse

mundo *m* world

muñeca *f* moon-yeka wrist; doll

muro *m* wall

músculo *m* muscle

museo *m* moosay-o museum

museo de arte artay art gallery

música *f* music

muslo *m* thigh

musulmán Muslim

muy mwee very

muy bien b-yen very well

N

N (carretera nacional) national
highway

nacido natheedo born

nacimiento *m* natheem-yento
birth

nacional nath-yonal domestic

nacionalidad *f* nath-yonaleeda
nationality

nada nothing

de nada you're welcome, don't
mention it

nada que declarar nothing to
declare

nadar to swim

nadie nad-yay nobody

naranja *f* naranHa orange

nariz *f* nareeth nose

natación *f* natath-yon swimming

naturaleza *f* natooralaytha nature

naturalmente -mentay naturally;
of course

náusea: siento náuseas
s-yento nowsay-ass I feel sick

navaja *f* nabaHa penknife

Navidad *f* Christmas

¡feliz Navidad! feleeth merry
Christmas!

neblina *f* mist

necesario nethesar-yo necessary

necesitar: necesito…
netheseeto I need…

negar to deny

negativo (*m*) negative

negocio *m* negoth-yo business

negro *m* black; furious

nena *f* nayna baby girl; little girl

nene *m* naynay baby boy; little
boy

nervioso nairb-yoso nervous

neumático *m* nay-oomateeko
tyre

**neumáticos - se reparan, se
arreglan** tyres repaired

neurótico nay-ooroteeko
neurotic

nevar to snow

ni neither, nor

ni… ni… neither… nor…

niebla *f* n-yebla fog

nieta *f* n-yayta grand-daughter

nieto *m* grandson

nieva n-yayba it is snowing

nieve *f* n-yaybay snow

ningún neengoon nobody; none;
not one; no…

en ningún sitio seet-yo nowhere

ninguno nobody; none; not one; no…

niña f neen-ya child

niñera f neen-yaira nanny

niño m neen-yo child

nivel del aceite m athay-eetay oil level

no no; not

no admite plancha do not iron

no aparcar no parking

no aparcar, llamamos grúa illegally parked vehicles will be towed away

no contiene alcohol does not contain alcohol

no entrada por detrás no entry at the rear

no exceda la dosis indicada do not exceed the stated dose

no fumadores no smoking

no funciona out of order

no hay de qué no ī day kay you are welcome

no hay localidades sold out

no molestar do not disturb

no para en… does not stop in…

no… pero sí not… but

no pisar el césped keep off the grass

no recomendada para menores de 18 años not recommended for those under 18 years of age

no se admiten caravanas no caravans allowed

no se admiten devoluciones no refunds given

no se admiten perros no dogs allowed

no tocar please do not touch

no utilizar lejía do not bleach

noche f nochay night

esta noche tonight

por la noche at night

nochebuena f nochay-bwayna Christmas Eve

nochevieja f nochay-b-yayнa New Year's Eve

nombre m nombray name

nombre de pila first name

nombre de soltera soltaira maiden name

nordeste m nordestay north-east

normal (m) normal normal; regular petrol/gas

normalmente -mentay usually

noroeste m noro-estay north-west

norte m nortay north

al norte de la ciudad north of the town

Noruega f norwayga Norway

nos us; ourselves

nosotras, nosotros we; us

noticias fpl noteeth-yass news

novecientos nobay-th-yentoss nine hundred

novela f novel

noveno nobayno ninth

noventa ninety

novia f nob-ya girlfriend; fiancée; bride

noviembre *m* nob-yembray
November

novillada *f* nobee-yada bullfight
featuring young bulls

novio *m* nob-yo boyfriend; fiancé;
groom

nube *f* noobay cloud

nublado cloudy

nuboso cloudy

nuera *f* nwaira daughter-in-law

nuestra nwestra, **nuestras,
nuestro, nuestros** our

Nueva York nwayba New York

nueve nwaybay nine

nuevo new

número *m* noomairo number

número (de calzado) day
kalthado (shoe) size

número de teléfono phone
number

nunca never

O

o or

o... o... either... or...

objeción *f* ob-Heth-yon objection

objetar obHaytar to object

objetivo *m* obHayteebo lens;
objective

objetos de escritorio
obHaytoss day eskreetor-yo
office supplies

objetos perdidos lost property,
lost and found

obra *f* work; play

obras *fpl* roadworks

obstruido obstr-weedo blocked

obturador *m* shutter

ocasión *f* okass-yon occasion;
opportunity; bargain

  de ocasión second hand

occidental oktheedental
Western

ochenta eighty

ocho eight

ochocientos ochoth-yentoss eight
hundred

ocho días *mpl* dee-ass week

octavo eighth

octubre *m* oktoobray October

oculista okooleesta optician

ocupado engaged; occupied;
busy

ocupantes del coche *mpl*
okoopantess del kochay
passengers

odiar od-yar to hate

oeste *m* o-estay west

  al oeste de la ciudad west of
the town

ofender ofendair to offend

oferta (especial) *f* ofairta
(espeth-yal) (special) offer

oficina *f* ofeetheena office

oficina de correos korray-oss
post office

**oficina de correos y
telégrafos** post office and
telegrams

**oficina de información y
turismo** eenformath-yon tourist
information office

oficina de objetos perdidos

obH**ay**toss lost property office, lost and found

oficina de reclamaciones reklamath-**yo**ness complaints department

oficina de registros re**Hee**stross registrar's office

oficina de turismo tourist information office

oficinista *m/f* ofeetheen**ee**sta office worker

oficio *m* ofeeth-yo job

ofrecer ofreth**air** to offer

oído (*m*) o-**ee**do ear; hearing; heard

¡oiga! oyga listen here!; excuse me!

oigo I hear

oír o-**eer** to hear

ojo *m* o**Ho** eye

ojo al tren beware of the train

ola *f* wave; fashion

ola de calor heatwave

oler ol**air** to smell

olor *m* smell

olvidar to forget

omnibús *m* local short-distance train

once onthay eleven

operadora *f* operator

operarse opair**ar**say to have an operation; to come about

oportunidad *f* chance, opportunity

oportunidades bargains

óptica *f* optician's

óptico *m* optician

optimista optimistic

orden *m* order

ordenador *m* computer

ordenador portátil portat**eel** laptop

oreja *f* or**ay**-Ha ear

organizar organeeth**ar** to organize

orgulloso orgoo-**yo**so proud

orilla *f* or**ee**-ya shore

oro *m* gold

orquesta *f* ork**es**ta orchestra

os you; to you

oscuro dark

otoño *m* ot**on**-yo autumn, fall

otorrinolaringólogo ear, nose and throat specialist

otra vez beth again

otro another (one); other

oveja *f* ob**ay**Ha sheep

oye o-yay he/she hears; you hear; listen

P

p (paseo) street; parking

paciente path-**yen**tay patient

pacotilla: de pacotilla pakot**ee**-ya rubbishy; second-rate

padecer de padeth**air** to suffer from

padecer del corazón korath**on** to have a heart condition

padre *m* p**a**dray father

padres *mpl* parents

pagadero payable

pagar to pay

página *f* paнeena page

páginas amarillas amaree-yass yellow pages

pagos *mpl* deposits

pague el importe exacto (please tender) exact money

país *m* pa-eess country

País Vasco Basque Country

País de Gales: el País de Gales galess Wales

paisaje *m* pa-eesaнay scenery

pájaro *m* paнaro bird

pala *f* spade

palabra *f* word

palacio *m* palath-yo palace

palacio de congresos conference hall

Palacio de Justicia Hoosteeth-ya Law Courts

Palacio de la Opera opera house

palacio real ray-al royal palace

palanca de velocidades *f* belotheedadess gear lever

palco *m* box (at theatre)

palomitas de maíz *fpl* ma-eeth popcorn

palos de golf *mpl* golf clubs

pan *m* bread

panadería *f* panadairee-a baker's

pantalla *f* panta-ya screen

pantalón corto *m* shorts

pantalones *mpl* pantaloness trousers, pants

pantalones cortos *mpl* shorts

pantalones vaqueros bakaiross jeans

panties *mpl* tights

pantorrilla *f* pantorree-ya calf

pañal *m* pan-yal nappy, diaper

pañería *f* pan-yairee-a drapery

pañuelo *m* panwaylo handkerchief; scarf

pañuelo (de cabeza) day kabaytha (head)scarf

papá *m* dad

papel *m* papel paper; rôle

papel celo thaylo Sellotape, Scotch tape

papel de envolver embolbair wrapping paper

papel de escribir writing paper

papel de plata silver foil

papel higiénico eeн-yayneeko toilet paper

papelera *f* litter; litter bin

papelería *f* papelai**ree**-a stationery, stationer's

papeles pintados *mpl* wallpaper

paquete *m* pak**ay**tay packet

par *m* pair

para for; in order to

para automáticas for automatic washing machines

para que kay in order that

para uso del personal staff only

para uso externo not to be taken internally

parabrisas *m* windscreen

paracaidismo *m* paraka-ee**dee**smo parachuting

parachoques *m* parach**o**kess car bumper, fender

parada *f* stop

parada de autobuses bus stop

parada de taxis taxi rank

parador *m* hotel restaurant; luxury hotel

parador nacional nath-y**o**nal state-owned hotel, often a historic building which has been restored

paraguas *m* par**a**gwass umbrella

parar to stop

parecer paret**hair** to seem; to resemble

parecido paret**hee**do similar

pared *f* par**ay**d wall

pareja *f* par**ay**-нa pair; couple

parezco paret**h**ko I seem

pariente *m/f* par-y**e**ntay relative

parking *m* car park, parking lot

paro: en paro unemployed

parque *m* par**kay** park

parque de atracciones atrakth-y**o**ness amusement park

parque de bomberos bomb**ai**ross fire station

parque de recreo rekr**ay**-o amusement park

parque infantil children's park; playpen

parrilla *f* parree-ya grill

parte *f* par**tay** part

en todas partes everywhere

en otra parte elsewhere

en alguna parte somewhere

¿de parte de quién? day k-yen who's calling?

parte antigua anteegwa old town

parte meteorológico *m* maytay-orol**o**Heeko weather forecast

particular private

partida *f* game

partido *m* match

pasado last

la semana pasada last week

pasado mañana the day after tomorrow

pasado de moda out of fashion

poco pasado rare

pasador *m* hairslide

pasaje *m* pasa**Hay** plane ticket

pasajero *m* pasa**Hai**ro passenger

pasajeros de tránsito transit passengers

pasaporte *m* pasaportay passport

pasaportes passport control

pasar to pass; to overtake; to happen

pasar la aduana ad-wana to go through customs

pasarlo bien b-yen to enjoy oneself

pasarlo bomba to have a great time

pasatiempo *m* pasat-yempo hobby

Pascua pask-wa Easter

pasear pasay-ar to go for a walk

pasen enter; cross, walk

paseo *m* pasay-o walk; drive; ride

paseo de... ... avenue

pasillo *m* pasee-yo corridor

paso *m* passage; pass; step

    estar de paso to be passing through

paso a nivel level crossing, grade crossing

paso de cebra thaybra zebra crossing

paso de contador unit

paso de peatones pay-atoness pedestrian crossing

paso subterráneo pedestrian underpass

pasta de dientes *f* d-yentess toothpaste

pastelería *f* pastelairee-a cake shop

pastilla *f* pastee-ya tablet

pastillas para la garganta throat pastilles

patatas fritas chips, French fries; crisps, potato chips

patinaje *m* pateenaнay skating

patinar to skid; to skate

patio de butacas *m* stalls

peaje *m* pay-aнay toll

peatón *m* pay-aton pedestrian

peatón, camine por la izquierda pedestrians keep to the left

peatón, circula por tu izquierda pedestrians keep to the left

peatonal pedestrian

peatones pedestrians

peatones, caminen por la izquierda pedestrians keep to the left

pecho *m* chest; breast

pedazo *m* pedatho piece

pediatra *m/f* pedee-atra pediatrician

pedir to order; to ask for

pedir disculpas to apologize

pedir hora ora to make an appointment

peinar pay-eenar to comb

peinarse pay-eenarsay to comb one's hair

peine *m* pay-eenay comb

pelea *f* pelay-a fight

peletería *f* peletairee-a furs, furrier

película *f* film, movie

película en versión original bairs-yon oreeнeenal film in the original language

peligro *m* danger

peligro de incendio danger:
fire hazard

peligro deslizamientos
slippery road surface

peligroso dangerous

   es peligroso bañarse
   danger: no swimming

   es peligroso asomarse al
   exterior do not lean out

pelirrojo peleerroнo redheaded

pelo *m* paylo hair

   me está tomando el pelo
   you're pulling my leg

pelón bald

pelota *f* ball

peluca *f* wig

peluquería *f* pelookairee-a
hairdresser's

peluquería de caballeros
kaba-yaiross men's
hairdresser's

peluquería de señoras ladies'
salon

peluquera *f* pelookaira,
peluquero *m* hairdresser

pena *f* payna grief, sorrow

   ¡qué pena! kay what a pity!

pendiente de pago
outstanding

pendientes *mpl* pend-yentess
earrings

pene *m* paynay penis

penicilina *f* peneetheeleena
penicillin

pensar to think

pensión *f* pens-yon guesthouse,
boarding house; pension

pensión completa komplayta
full board, American
plan

pensionista *m* pens-yoneesta
old-age pensioner

peor pay-or worse; worst

pequeño (*m*) pekayn-yo small;
child

percha *f* paircha coathanger

perder pairdair to lose; to miss

perderse pairdairsay to get lost

pérdida *f* loss

perdón sorry, excuse me;
pardon, pardon me

perezoso pairethoso lazy

perfecto pairfekto perfect

perfumería *f* pairfoomairee-a
perfume shop

periódico *m* pairee-odeeko
newspaper

periodista *m* pair-yodeesta
journalist

Travel tip Of the Spanish
national newspapers, the
best are the Madrid-based
centre-left *El País* and the
centre-right *El Mundo*, both
of which have good arts
and foreign news coverage,
including comprehensive
regional "what's on" list-
ings and supplements every
weekend. Other national
papers include the solidly
elitist *ABC* and Barcelona's
La Vanguardia.

período *m* pairee-odo period

perla *f* pairla pearl

permanente *f* pairmanentay perm

permiso *m* pairmeeso licence

permitido allowed

permitir to allow

pero pairo but

perra: no tengo una perra I'm broke

perro *m* pairro dog

persona *f* pairsona person

persuadir pairswadeer to persuade

pesadilla *f* pesadee-ya nightmare

pesado heavy

pésame: dar el pésame paysamay to offer one's condolences

pesar weight

a pesar de que despite the fact that

a pesar de in spite of

pesca *f* fishing

ir de pesca to go fishing

pescadería *f* peskadairee-a fishmonger's

pescar to fish; to catch out

peso *m* payso weight

peso máximo maximum weight

peso neto net weight

pestañas *fpl* pestan-yass eyelashes

petición de mano *f* peteeth-yon engagement

pez *m* peth fish

picadura *f* bite

picante peekantay hot

picar to sting; to itch

picor *m* itch

pidió peed-yo he/she asked for; you asked for

pie *m* p-yay foot

a pie on foot

piedra *f* p-yedra stone

piedra preciosa preth-yosa precious stone

piel *f* p-yayl skin

pienso p-yenso I think

pierna *f* p-yairna leg

pieza de repuesto *f* p-yaytha day repwesto spare part

piezas de recambio rekamb-yo spares

pijama *m* peeнama pyjamas

pila *f* battery; pile

píldora *f* pill

piloto *m* pilot

pilotos *mpl* rear lights

pincel *m* peenthayl paint brush

pinchazo *m* peenchatho puncture

pintar to paint

pintura *f* painting; paint

pinza de la ropa *f* clothes peg

pinzas *fpl* peenthass tweezers

piña *f* peen-ya pineapple

pipa *f* pipe

piragua *f* peeragwa canoe

piragüismo *m* peeragweesmo canoeing

Pirineos *mpl* peereenay-oss Pyrenees

piscina *f* peestheena swimming pool

piscina cubierta koob-ya**i**rta indoor swimming pool

piso *m* floor; flat, apartment

piso amueblado amweb**la**do furnished apartment

piso bajo ba**H**o ground floor, US first floor

piso sin amueblar amweb**la**r unfurnished apartment

pista *f* track; clue

pista de baile ba-**ee**lay dance floor

pista de patinaje pateena**H**ay skating rink

pista de tenis tennis court

pistas de esquí es**kee** ski runs

pistola *f* gun

plancha *f* iron

planchar to iron

plano (*m*) flat; map

planta *f* plant; floor

planta baja ba**H**a ground floor, (US) first floor

planta primera pree**mai**ra first floor, (US) second floor

planta sótano lower floor; basement

planta superior soopair-y**o**r upper floor

plástico (*m*) plastic

plata *f* silver

plateado platay-**a**do silver

platillo *m* pla**tee**-yo saucer

plato *m* plate; dish, course

playa *f* pla-ya beach

playeras *fpl* pla-**ya**irass trainers

plaza *f* pla**tha** square; seat

en plaza current prices

plaza de abastos marketplace

plaza de toros bullring

plazas libres lee**b**ress seats available

pluma *f* pen; feather

población *f* poblath-y**o**n village; town; population

pobre po**b**ray poor

poco little

poco profundo shallow

pocos few

unos pocos a few

poder (*m*) pod**ai**r to be able to; power

podrido rotten

policía *f* poleethee-a police

policía *m/f* policeman; policewoman

policía municipal *f* mooneetheepal municipal police

polideportivo *m* sports centre

polígono industrial *m* industrial estate

política *f* politics

político political

póliza de seguros *f* insurance policy

polo *m* ice lolly

polvos *mpl* powder

pomada *f* ointment

pon put

poner pon**ai**r to put

ponerse en marcha pon**ai**rsay to set off

ponerse en pie p-yay to stand up

poney *m* pony

pongo I put

poquito: un poquito pok**ee**to a little bit

por by; through; for

  por allí a-y**ee** over there

  por fin at last

  por lo que kay for which reason

  por lo menos mayn**oss** at least

  por qué kay why

  por semana per week

  por si in case

por ciento th-y**ento** per cent

por favor please

por favor, use un carrito please take a trolley

por favor, use una cesta please take a basket

porcelana f porth**ela**na porcelain

porque p**or**kay because

portaequipajes m porta-ekeepa**hess** luggage rack

portátil porta**teel** portable

portero m porta**ir**o porter; doorman; goalkeeper

portugués portoog**ayss** Portuguese

posada f inn

posible pos**ee**blay possible

postal f postcard

precaución f prekowth-y**on** caution

precio m pr**eth**-yo price

precioso pr**eth**-y**o**so beautiful; precious

precio unidad unit price

precios fijos fee**Hoss** fixed prices

preferencia f prefaire**nth**-ya right of way; preference

preferir prefaire**er** to prefer

prefijo m prefee**Ho** dialling code, area code

pregunta f question

preguntar to ask

prendas f pl clothing

prensa f press; newspapers

preocupado pray-okoop**a**do worried

preocupes: ¡no te preocupes! no tay pray-ok**oo**pess don't worry

preparar to prepare

prepararse prepararsay to get ready

presentar to introduce

preservativo m presairbat**ee**bo condom

presión f press-y**on** pressure

presión de los neumáticos nay-oomat**ee**koss tyre pressure

prestado: pedir prestado to borrow

prestar to lend

prima f cousin

primavera f preemab**ai**ra spring

primer preem**air** first

primer piso m first floor, (US) second floor

primer plato m first course

primera (clase) f kl**a**say first class

primero first

primeros auxilios owk-s**ee**l-yoss first-aid post

primo *m* cousin

princesa *f* preenth**ay**sa princess

principal preenth**ee**pal main

príncipe *m* preenth**ee**pay prince

principiante *m/f* preenth**ee**p-yantay beginner

principio *m* preenth**ee**p-yo beginning

principio de autopista start of motorway/highway

prioridad a la derecha give way/yield to vehicles coming from your right

prioridad de paso priority

prisa: darse prisa d**a**rsay to hurry

¡dese prisa! d**ay**say hurry up!

privado private

probablemente probablem**e**ntay probably

probador *m* fitting room

probar to try

probarse to try on

problema *m* problem

procesiones de Semana Santa *fpl* prothess-y**o**ness Holy Week processions

producido en... produce of...

producto preparado con ingredientes naturales product prepared using natural ingredients

productos alimenticios aleement**ee**th-yoss foodstuffs

productos de belleza bay-y**ay**tha beauty products

profesor *m*, **profesora** *f* teacher; lecturer

profundidad *f* depth

profundo deep

programa infantil *m* children's programme

prohibida la entrada no entry, no admission

prohibida la entrada a menores de... no admission for those under... years of age

prohibida su reproducción copyright reserved

prohibida su venta not for sale

prohibido pro-eeb**ee**do prohibited, forbidden; no

prohibido acampar no camping

prohibido adelantar no overtaking, no passing

prohibido aparcar no parking

prohibido aparcar excepto carga y descarga no parking except for loading and unloading

prohibido asomarse do not lean out

prohibido asomarse a la ventana do not lean out of the window

prohibido asomarse a la ventanilla do not lean out of the window

prohibido bañarse no swimming

prohibido cambiar de sentido no U-turns

prohibido cantar no singing

prohibido el paso no entry; no trespassing

prohibido encender fuego no campfires

prohibido escupir no spitting

prohibido estacionar no parking

prohibido fijar carteles stick no bills

prohibido fumar no smoking

prohibido girar a la izquierda no left turn

prohibido hablar con el conductor do not speak to the driver

prohibido hacer auto-stop no hitch-hiking

prohibido hacer sonar el claxon/la bocina do not sound your horn

prohibido pescar no fishing

prohibido pisar el césped keep off the grass

prohibido pisar la hierba keep off the grass

prohibido tirar basura no litter

prohibido tirar escombros no dumping

prohibido tocar la bocina/el claxon do not sound your horn

prohibido tomar fotografías no photographs

prometer prometair to promise

prometida f fiancée

prometido (m) engaged; fiancé

pronóstico del tiempo m t-yempo weather forecast

pronto soon

¡hasta pronto! asta see you soon!

llegar pronto yegar to be early

pronunciar pronoonth-yar to pronounce

propiedad privada private property

propietario m prop-yetar-yo owner

propina f tip

propósito: a propósito deliberately

proteger protay-Hair to protect

provecho: ¡buen provecho! bwen probay-cho enjoy your meal!

provincia f probeenth-ya district

provocar to cause

próximo next

la semana próxima next week

prudente proodentay careful

prueba de alcoholemia f pr-wayba day alko-olaym-ya breath test

pts (pesetas) pesetas

pub bar in which no meals are served, often higher priced and disco music played

público (m) public; audience

pueblo m pweblo village; people

puede pwayday he/she can; you can

puede ser sair maybe

puedo pwaydo I can

puente m pwentay bridge

puente aéreo a-airay-o shuttle plane

puente de fuerte pendiente humpbacked bridge

puente de peaje pay-a**H**ay toll bridge

puente romano Roman bridge

puerta *f* p**wai**rta door; gate

  por la otra puerta use other door

puerta de embarque emb**ar**kay gate

puerta nº. gate no.

puerto *m* harbour; pass; port

puerto deportivo marina

puerto de montaña montan-ya (mountain) pass

pues p**way**ss since; so

puesta de sol *f* p**we**sta sunset

puesto de periódicos pairee-**o**deeko**ss** newspaper kiosk

puesto de socorro *m* first-aid post

puesto que kay since

pulga *f* flea

pulmones *mpl* lungs

pulmonía *f* poolmon**ee**-a pneumonia

pulse botón para cruzar press button to cross

pulsera *f* pools**ai**ra bracelet

pulso *m* pulse

puntual: llegar puntual poont-**wal** to arrive on time

punto de vista *m* point of view

punto: hacer punto ath**ai**r to knit

¡puñeta! poon-y**ay**ta hell!

  ¡vete a hacer puñetas!

ba**y**tay a ath**ai**r bugger off!

pura lana virgen beer**H**en pure new wool

puro *m* cigar

puse p**oo**say I put

Q

que kay who; that; which; than

  que... o que whether... or

¿qué? what?

¿qué hay? ī how's things?

¿qué tal?, mucho gusto how do you do?, nice to meet you

¡qué va! no way!

quedarse ked**ar**say to stay

quedarse con to keep

quedarse sin gasolina to run out of petrol/gas

quejarse kay**Har**say to complain

quemadura *f* kemad**oo**ra burn

quemadura de sol sunburn

quemar kemar to burn

quemarse kem**ar**say to burn oneself

querer ker**ai**r to love; to want

querido kair**ee**do dear

¿quién? k-yen who?

quiero k-y**ai**ro I want; I love

  no quiero I don't want to

quince k**een**thay fifteen

quince días dee-a**ss** fortnight

quinientos keen-y**en**to**ss** five hundred

quinto k**een**to fifth

quiosco *m* k-y**o**sko kiosk

quisiera keess-yaira I would like; he/she would like; you would like

quiso keeso he/she wanted; you wanted

quitaesmalte m keeta-esmaltay nail polish remover

quitar keetar to remove

quizá(s) keetha(ss) maybe

R

rabioso rab-yoso furious

R.A.C.E (Real Automóvil Club de España) Spanish Royal Automobile Club

ración f rath-yon portion

radiador m rad-yador radiator

radio m rad-yo spoke

radio f radio

radiografía f rad-yografee-a X-ray

rápidamente -mentay quickly

rápido fast

rápido m train stopping at many stations

raqueta de tenis f rakayta tennis racket

raro rare; strange

rata f rat

ratón m mouse

rayas: a rayas ra-yass striped

razón f rathon reason; rate
    razón aquí apply within
    tiene razón you're right

razonable rathonablay reasonable

rea sale

realmente ray-almentay really

rebajado rebaHado reduced

rebajas fpl rebaHass reductions, sale

rebajas de verano bairano summer sale

rebanada f slice

recado m message

recepción f rethepth-yon reception

recepcionista m/f rethepth-yoneesta receptionist

receta f rethayta recipe; prescription
    con receta médica only available on prescription

recetar rethaytar to prescribe

recibir retheebeer to receive

recibo m retheebo receipt

recién reth-yen recently

recién pintado wet paint

reclamación de equipajes f reklamath-yon day ekeepaHess baggage claim

reclamaciones fpl reklamath-yoness complaints

recoger rekoHair to collect; to pick up

recogida de equipajes f rekoHeeda baggage claim

recoja su ticket take your ticket

recomendar to recommend

reconocer rekonothair to recognize; to examine

recordar to remember

recorrido m journey

recto straight

recuerdo (*m*) rekwairdo souvenir; I remember

red *f* network; net

redondo round

reduzca la velocidad reduce speed now

reembolsar ray-embolsar to refund

reembolsos refunds

reestreno ray-estrayno re-release (of a classic movie)

regalo *m* present

regatear regatay-ar to haggle

régimen *m* ray-Heemen diet

registrar reHeestrar to search

regla *f* rule; period

registro de equipajes *m* reHeestro day ekeepaHess check-in

registros sanitarios government health certificate

regresar to return

reina *f* ray-eena queen

Reino Unido *m* United Kingdom

reír ray-eer to laugh

rejoneador *m* reHonay-ador bullfighter on horseback

relajarse relaHarsay to relax

rellenar ray-yaynar to fill in

reloj *m* rayloH watch; clock

reloj de pulsera poolsaira (wrist) watch

relojería *f* ray-loHairee-a watches and clocks

remar to row

remite *m* remeetay sender's name

and address

remitente *m/f* remeetentay sender

remo *m* raymo oar

remolque *m* remolkay trailer

remonte *m* remontay ski tow

Renacimiento *m* renatheem-yento Renaissance

RENFE (Red Nacional de Ferrocarriles Españoles) Spanish Railways/Railroad

reparación *f* reparath-yon repair(s)

reparación de calzado shoe repairs

reparaciones faults service

reparar to repair

repente: de repente repentay suddenly

repetir to repeat

replicar to reply

reponerse reponairsay to recover

reposar to rest

representante *m/f* repraysentantay representative, agent

repuestos *mpl* repwestoss spare parts

repugnante repoognantay disgusting

resaca *f* hangover

resbaladizo resbaladeetho slippery

resbalar to slip

rescatar to rescue

reserva *f* resairba reservation

reserva de asientos seat reservation

reservado reserved

reservado el derecho de admisión the management reserve the right to refuse admission

reservado socios members only

reservar to reserve; to book

reservas *fpl* reservations

resfriado *m* resfree-**a**do cold

respirar to breathe

responder respond**air** to answer

responsable responsa**blay** responsible

respuesta *f* resp**we**sta answer

resto *m* rest

retales *mpl* re**tal**ess remnants

retrasado late

retrasado mental mentally handicapped

retraso *m* delay

retrete *m* retray**tay** toilets, rest rooms

reumatismo *m* ray-oomat**ee**smo rheumatism

reunión *f* ray-oon-**yon** meeting

revelado *m* film processing

revelar to develop; to reveal

revisar to check

revisor *m* ticket collector

revista *m* magazine

rey *m* ray king

Reyes: día de los Reyes *m* **dee**-a day loss **ray**-ess 6th of January, Epiphany

rico rich

ridículo ridiculous

rímel *m* mascara

rincón *m* corner

riñón *m* reen-**yon** kidney

río *m* ree-o river

rizado reeth**a**do curly

robar to steal

robo *m* theft

roca *f* rock

rodilla *f* rodee-ya knee

rojo ro**Ho** red

románico romanesque

rómpase en caso de emergencia break in case of emergency

romper to break

ropa *f* clothes

ropa confeccionada ready-to-wear clothes

ropa de caballeros kaba-yai**ross** men's clothes

ropa de cama bed linen

ropa de señoras ladies' clothes

ropa infantil children's clothes

ropa interior *f* eentair-**yor** underwear

ropa sucia sooth-ya laundry

rosa (*f*) pink; rose

roto broken

rotulador *m* felt-tip pen

rubéola *f* roobay-ola German measles

rubí *m* roo**bee** ruby

rubio roo**b**-yo blond

rueda *f* rw**ay**da wheel

rueda de repuesto *f* repwesto
  spare wheel

ruedo *m* bullring

ruego rwaygo I request

ruido *m* rweedo noise

ruidoso rweedoso noisy

ruinas *fpl* rweenass ruins

rulo *m* roller, curler

rulot(a) *f* caravan, trailer

ruta *f* route

S

S.A. (Sociedad Anónima)
  plc, Inc

sábado *m* Saturday

sábana *f* sheet

saber sabair to know

  saber a to taste of

sabor *m* taste

sabroso tasty

sacacorchos *m* sakakorchoss
  corkscrew

sacar to take out; to get out

sacar un billete bee-yaytay to
  buy a ticket

saco de dormir *m* sleeping bag

sal (f) salt; leave

sala *f* room; hall

sala climatizada air
  conditioned

sala de baile ba-eelay dance hall

sala de cine theenay cinema,
  movie theater

sala de conciertos konth-
  yairtoss concert hall

sala de embarque embarkay
  departure lounge

sala de espera espaira waiting
  room

sala de exposiciones
  esposeeth-yoness exhibition hall

sala de tránsito transit lounge

sala X X-rated cinema

salado salty

saldar to sell at a reduced price

saldo *m* clearance; balance

saldos sales

sales de baño *fpl* saless day
  ban-yo bath salts

salgo I leave

salida *f* exit; departure

salida ciudad take this direction
  to leave the city

salida de ambulancias
  ambulance exit

salida de autopista end of
  motorway/highway; motorway
  exit

salida de camiones heavy
  goods vehicle exit, works exit

salida de emergencia
  aymairHenth-ya emergency exit

salida de fábrica factory exit

salida de incendios fire exit

salida de socorro *f* emergency
  exit

salidas *fpl* departures

salidas de noche night life

salidas internacionales
  international departures

salidas nacionales domestic
  departures

salir to go out; to leave

salón *m* lounge

salón de belleza bay-**yay**tha beauty salon

salón de demostraciones exhibition hall

salón de peluquería pelookair**ee**-a hairdressing salon

saltar to jump

salud *f* sal**oo** health

  ¡salud! cheers!

saludar to greet

saludos best wishes

salvo que kay except that

sandalias *fpl* sand**al**-yass sandals

San Fermín fairm**ee**n July 7th, when the 'encierro' happens

sangrar to bleed

sangre *f* s**a**ngray blood

sano healthy

Santiago sant-y**a**go July 25th, a national holiday

sarampión *m* saramp-y**o**n measles

sartén *f* frying pan

sastre *m* s**a**stray tailor

se say himself; herself; itself; yourself; themselves; yourselves; oneself

sé say I know

  no sé I don't know

se aceptan tarjetas de crédito we accept credit cards

se alquila for hire, to rent

se alquila piso flat/apartment for rent

se alquilan habitaciones rooms to rent

se alquilan hidropedales pedalos for hire

se alquilan sombrillas parasols for hire

se alquilan tumbonas deckchairs for hire

se habla inglés English spoken

se hacen fotocopias photocopying service

se necesita... ... needed

se precisa... ... needed

se prohibe... ... forbidden

se prohibe fumar no smoking

se prohibe hablar con el conductor do not speak to the driver

se prohibe la entrada no entry, no admittance

se prohibe tirar basura no litter

se ruega... please...

se ruega desalojen su habitación antes de las doce please vacate your room by 12 noon

se ruega no... please do not...

se ruega no aparcar no parking please

se ruega no molestar please do not disturb

se ruega pagar en caja please pay at the desk

se vende for sale

secador de pelo *m* paylo hair
   dryer
secadores *mpl* dryers
secar to dry
secarse el pelo sekarsay to dry
   one's hair; to have a blow-dry
sección *f* sekth-yon department
seco dry
secretaria *f*, **secretario** *m*
   secretary
secreto secret
sed: tengo sed seth I'm thirsty
seda *f* silk
seda natural pure silk
seguida: en seguida segeeda
   immediately, right away
seguir segeer to follow
según according to
segunda clase *f* klasay second
   class

segundo (*m*) second
   de segunda mano secondhand
segundo piso *m* second floor,
   (US) third floor
segundo plato *m* main course
seguridad *f* segooreeda safety;
   security
seguro (*m*) safe; sure; insurance
seguro de viaje *m* b-yaHay travel
   insurance
seis say-eess six
seiscientos say-eess-th-yentoss
   six hundred
sello *m* say-yo stamp
semáforos *mpl* traffic lights
semana *f* week
Semana Santa Holy Week
semanarios *mpl* weeklies
sencillo senthee-yo simple

sensible sens*ee*blay sensitive

sentar: sentar bien (a) b-yen to suit

sentarse sentar*say* to sit down

sentido *m* direction; sense; meaning

sentir to feel

señal de tráfico *f* sen-yal day trafeeko roadsign

señas *fpl* sen-yass address

señor sen-yor gentleman, man; sir

  el señor Brown Mr Brown

señora *f* sen-yora lady, woman; madam

  la señora Brown Mrs Brown

señoras *fpl* ladies' toilet, ladies' room; ladies' department

señores *mpl* sen-yoress gents' toilet, men's room

señorita *f* sen-yoreeta young lady, young woman; miss

  la señorita Brown Miss Brown

separado separate; separated

  por separado separately

septiembre *m* sept-yembray September

séptimo seventh

sequía *f* sekee-a drought

ser sair to be

  a no ser que unless

serio sair-yo serious

servicio *m* sairbeeth-yo service; toilet

servicio a través de operadora operator-connected calls

servicio automático direct dialling

servicio de habitaciones room service

servicio de fotocopias photocopying service

servicio (no) incluido service charge (not) included

servicios *mpl* sairbeeth-yoss toilets, rest rooms

servicios de rescate mountain rescue

servicios de socorro emergency services

servilleta *f* sairbee-yayta serviette

servir sairbeer to serve

sesenta saysenta sixty

sesión continua continuous showing

sesión de noche late showing

sesión de tarde early showing

setecientos saytay-th-yentoss seven hundred

setenta setenta seventy

sexto sesto sixth

si see if

sí see yes; oneself; herself; itself; yourself; themselves; yourselves; each other

si no otherwise

SIDA *m* AIDS

sido been

siempre s-yempray always

siempre que kay whenever; so long as

siento s-yento I sit down; I feel; I regret

lo siento I'm sorry

siete s-yaytay seven

siga adelante straight ahead

siglo *m* century

siglo de oro XVI–XVII century

significar to mean

siguiente seeg-yentay next

  el día siguiente dee-a the day
  after

silencio *m* seelenth-yo silence

silla *f* see-ya chair

silla de ruedas rwaydass
  wheelchair

sillita de ruedas see-yeeta
  pushchair, buggy

sillón *m* see-yon armchair

similar (a) similar (to)

simpático nice

sin seen without

sin duda undoubtedly

sin embargo however

sin plomo unleaded

sinagoga *f* synagogue

sincero seenthairo sincere

sino but

sino que kay but

siquiera seek-yaira even if

sírvase seerbasay please

sírvase coger una cesta please
  take a basket

sírvase frío serve cold

sírvase usted mismo help
  yourself

sitio *m* seet-yo place

  en ningún sitio neen-goon
  nowhere

sitio web *m* website

smoking *m* dinner jacket

sobrar to be left over; to be too
  many

sobre (*m*) sobray envelope; on;
  above

sobrecarga sobraykarga excess
  weight; extra charge

sobrina *f* niece

sobrino *m* nephew

sobrio sobr-yo sober

sociedad *f* soth-yayda society;
  company

socio *m* soth-yo associate;
  member

socorrer sokorair to help

socorrista mf lifeguard

¡socorro! help!

sois soyss you are

sol *m* sun

  al sol in the sun

solamente solamentay only

soleado solay-ado sunny

solo alone

sólo only

  no sólo… sino también
  tamb-yen not only… but also

sólo carga y descarga loading
  and offloading only

sólo laborables weekdays only

**sólo monedas de nueva
  emisión** only new coins

sólo motos motorcycles only

**solo para residentes (del
  hotel)** hotel patrons only

soltero (*m*) soltairo single;
  bachelor

solterón *m* bachelor

solterona *f* spinster

solución… gotas solution…
drops

sombra *f* shade; shadow

sombra de ojos oHoss eye
shadow

sombrero *m* sombrairo hat

sombrilla *f* sombree-ya parasol

somnífero *m* somneefairo
sleeping pill

somos we are

son they are; you are

sonreír sonray-eer to smile

sordo deaf

sorprendente sorprendentay
surprising

sorpresa *f* surprise

sortija *f* sorteeHa ring

sótano *m* basement

soy soy I am

sport: de sport casual

Sr (Señor) Mr

Sra (Señora) Mrs

Sres (Señores) Messrs

Srta (Señorita) Miss

starter *m* choke

stop *m* stop sign

su soo his; her; its; their; your

suave swabay soft

subir to go up; to get on; to get
in; to put up

subtitulada subtitled

subtítulos *mpl* subtitles

suburbios *mpl* sooboorb-yoss
suburbs

suceder soothedair to happen

sucio sooth-yo dirty

sucursal *f* branch

sudar to sweat

Suecia *f* swayth-ya Sweden

sueco swayko Swedish

suegra *f* swaygra mother-in-law

suegro *m* father-in-law

suela *f* swayla sole

suelo (*m*) floor; I am used to

suelto *m* swelto change

sueño *m* swayn-yo dream; I
dream

tener sueño to be sleepy

suerte *f* swairtay luck

por suerte luckily, fortunately

¡buena suerte! bwayna good
luck!

suéter *m* swaytair sweater

suficiente: es suficiente
soofeeth-yentay that's enough

sugerencias de presentación
serving suggestions

Suiza *f* sweetha Switzerland

sujetador *m* sooHay-tador bra

sumar to add

supe soopay I knew

súper *m* soopair premium gas/
petrol; supermarket

supermercado *m*
soopairmairkado supermarket

supuesto: por supuesto
soopwesto of course

sur *m* south

al sur de south of

sureste *m* soorestay south-east

suroeste *m* sooro-estay south-west

surtido *m* assortment

sus sooss his; her; its; their; your

susto *m* shock

susurrar to whisper

sutil subtle

suyo soo-yo his; hers; its; theirs; yours

T

T.V.E. (Television Española) Spanish Television

Tabacalera SA Spanish tobacco monopoly

tabaco *m* tobacco

tabla de surf *f* surfboard

tabla de windsurf sailboard

tablero de instrumentos *m* dashboard

tablón de anuncios *m* notice board, bulletin board

tablón de información tablon day eenformath-yon indicator board

tacón *m* heel

tacones altos takoness high heels

tacones planos flat heels

TAF *m* slow diesel train

Tajo *m* taHo Tagus

tal such

  con tal (de) que provided that

tal vez beth maybe

talco *m* talcum powder

TALGO *m* fast diesel train, luxury train (supplement required)

talla *f* ta-ya size

tallas sueltas odd sizes

tallas grandes large sizes

taller (de reparaciones) *m* ta-yair (day reparath-yoness) garage

talón *m* heel

talón de equipajes ekeepaHess baggage slip

talonario de cheques *m* talonar-yo day chekess cheque book

tamaño *m* taman-yo size

también tamb-yen also

  yo también me too

tampoco neither, nor

  yo tampoco me neither

tan: tan bonito so beautiful

  tan pronto como as soon as

tancat (Catalan) closed

tanto (*m*) so much; point

tanto... como... both... and...

tantos so many

tapa *f* lid

tapas *fpl* savoury snacks, tapas

tapón *m* plug

taquilla *f* takee-ya ticket office

tarde *f* tarday afternoon; evening; late

  a las tres de la tarde at 3 p.m.

  esta tarde this afternoon, this evening

  por la tarde in the evening

  llegar tarde yegar to be late

tarifa *f* charge, charges

tarifa especial estudiante espeth-yal estood-yantay student reduced rate

tarifa normal standard rate

tarifa reducida redootheeda reduced rate

tarifas de servicio fares

tarjeta f tarHayta card

tarjeta bancaria cheque card

tarjeta de crédito credit card

tarjeta de embarque embarkay boarding pass

tarjeta de transporte público transportay travel card

tarjeta postal postcard

tarjeta telefónica phonecard

tauromaquia f towromak-ya bullfighting

taxista m/f taxi driver

taza f tatha cup

te tay you; yourself

teatro m tay-atro theatre

techo m ceiling

teclado m keyboard

tejado m teHado roof

tejanos mpl teHanoss jeans

tejidos mpl teHeedoss materials, fabrics

tela f tayla material; dosh

tele f taylay TV

telecabina f cable car

teleférico m cable car

telefonear telefonay-ar to telephone

teléfono m telephone

teléfono interurbano long-distance phone

teléfono móvil m mobeel mobile phone, cell phone

teléfonos para casos urgentes emergency telephone numbers

telesilla m telesee-ya chairlift

telesquí m teleskee ski lift

televisor m television (set)

temer temair to fear

temor m fear

tempestad f storm

temporada f season

temprano early

ten hold

tenedor m fork

tener tenair to have

tener derecho to have the right

tener prisa to be in a hurry

tener prioridad pree-oreeda to have right of way

tener que kay to have to

tengo que I have to, I must

¡tenga cuidado! kweedado be careful!

tenis m tennis

tensión f tens-yon blood pressure

teñirse el pelo ten-yeersay el paylo to dye one's hair; to have one's hair dyed

TER m fast luxury diesel trains, a supplement is required

tercer piso m tairthair third floor, (US) fourth floor

tercero tairthairo third

tercio m tairth-yo third

terciopelo m tairth-yopaylo velvet

terco stubborn

terminal *f* tairmeenal terminus; terminal

terminal nacional domestic terminal

terminar to finish

termo *m* vacuum flask

termómetro *m* thermometer

test del embarazo embaratho pregnancy test

testigo *m* witness

tetera *f* tetaira teapot

tfno (teléfono) telephone

ti tee you

tía *f* tee-a aunt; bird, woman

tibio teeb-yo lukewarm

tiburón *m* shark

tiempo *m* t-yempo time; weather

a tiempo on time

tiempo de recreo rekray-o leisure

tiempo libre leebray free time

tienda *f* t-yenda shop, store; tent

esta tienda se translada a… business is transferred to…

tienda de artículos de piel p-yayl leather goods shop

tienda de artículos de regalo gift shop

tienda de comestibles komesteebless grocer's

tienda de deportes deportess sports shop

tienda de discos record shop

tienda de electrodomésticos electrical goods shop

tienda de lanas woollen goods shop

tienda de muebles mwaybless furniture shop

tienda de regalos gift shop

tienda de ultramarinos grocer's

tienda de vinos y licores off-licence, liquor store

tienda libre de impuestos leebray day eempwestoss duty-free shop

tiendas: ir de tiendas to go shopping

tiene que t-yaynay kay he/she must

¿tiene…? have you got…?

tierra *f* t-yairra earth

tijeras *fpl* teeHairass scissors

timbre *m* teembray bell

timbre de alarma alarm bell

tímido shy

tintorería *f* teentorairee-a dry-cleaner's

tío *m* tee-o uncle; bloke, guy

tipo de cambio *m* kamb-yo exchange rate

tirar to pull; to throw; to throw away

tirita *f* Elastoplast, Bandaid

toalla *f* to-a-ya towel

toalla de baño ban-yo bath towel

tobillo *m* tobee-yo ankle

tocadiscos *m* record player

tocar to touch; to play

todavía todabee-a still; yet

todavía no not yet

todo all, every; everything
   todos los días every day
todo derecho straight on
todo seguido segeedo straight ahead
todos everyone
tomamos la tensión we take your blood pressure
tomar to take
tomar el sol to sunbathe
tomavistas *m* cine-camera
tome usted take
tómese antes de las comidas to be taken before meals
tómese después de las comidas to be taken after meals
tómese... veces al día to be taken... times per day
tonelada *f* tonne
tono *m* dialling tone; shade
tonto silly
torcer torthair to twist; to sprain

torcerse un tobillo oon tobee-yo to twist one's ankle
torero *m* torairo bullfighter
tormenta *f* storm
tormentoso stormy
tornillo *m* tornee-yo screw
toro *m* bull
toros *mpl* bullfighting

> **Travel tip** The bullfight is a classic image of Spain, and an integral part of many fiestas. In the south, especially, any village that can afford it will put on a bullfight for an afternoon, while in big cities such as Madrid or Seville, the main festival times are accompanied by a season of prestige fights.

torpe torpay clumsy
torre *f* torray tower
tos *f* cough
toser tosair to cough

tosferina f tosfair**ee**na whooping cough

total: en total altogether

totalmente -**men**tay absolutely

tóxico t**o**kseeko poisonous

trabajador traba**Ha**dor industrious

trabajar traba**Har** to work

trabajo (*m*) traba**Ho** work; I work

traducir tradoot**heer** to translate

traer tra-**air** to bring

tragar to swallow

traigo tra-**ee**go I bring

traje tra**Hay** I brought

traje *m* suit; dress

traje de baño ban-yo swimming costume

traje de noche n**o**chay evening dress

traje de señora lady's suit

traje típico traditional regional costume

tranquilizante trankeeleeth**an**tay tranquillizer

tranquilizarse trankeeleeth**ar**say to calm down

tranquilo trank**ee**lo quiet

transbordo *m* transfer; change

   hacer transbordo en... change at...

transferencia f transfair**enth**-ya transfer

tras after

trasero (*m*) tras**ai**ro bottom; back; rear

tratar to treat

través: a través de across, through

travieso trab-**yay**so mischievous

trece tray**thay** thirteen

treinta tray-**een**ta thirty

tren *m* train

tren de carga goods train

trenes de cercanías tren**ess** day thairkan**ee**-ass local trains, suburban trains

tren de lavado automático car wash

tren de pasajeros pasa**Hai**ross passenger train

tren directo through train

tren tranvía tranbee-a stopping train

tres tress three

tres cuartos de hora *mpl* three quarters of an hour

trescientos tress-th-y**ent**oss three hundred

tripulación f treepoolath-y**on** crew

triste tr**ee**stay sad

tristeza f treest**ay**tha sadness

tronco *m* body; buddy

tropezar tropet**har** to trip

trozo (de) *m* tr**o**tho (day) piece (of)

trueno *m* trw**ay**no thunder

tu too your

tú too you

tú mismo yourself

tubería f toobair**ee**-a pipe

tubo de escape *m* esk**a**pay exhaust

tubo de respirar snorkel

tuerza tw**air**tha turn

tumbona *f* deck chair

túnel *m* tunnel

Túnez *m* too*neth* Tunisia

turista *m/f* tourist

turno *m* turn; round

    es mi turno it's my turn/
    round

turrón *m* toor*ron* nougat

tus tooss your

tuyo too*yo* yours

U

u oo or

Ud (usted) oostay you (*sing*)

Uds (ustedes) oostaydess you (*pl*)

úlcera (de estómago) *f* ool*thaira*
    (stomach) ulcer

últimamente oolteemamentay
    recently, lately

último last; latest

últimos días dee-ass last days

ultramarinos *m* grocer's

un oon a

una oona a

unas some

uno one; someone

unos some; a few

uña *f* oon-ya fingernail

urbana local

urbanización *f* oorbaneethath-yon
    housing estate

urgencias oorHenth-yass
    casualty department,
    emergencies

usado used; secondhand

usar to use

uso use

    **el uso del tabaco es
    perjudicial para su salud**
    smoking can damage your
    health

uso externo not to be taken
    internally

**uso obligatorio cinturón de
    seguridad** seatbelts must be
    worn

Usted oostay you

Ustedes oostaydess you

útil useful

**utilice sólo moneda
    fraccionaria** small change
    only

V

*v is pronounced more like a b than
an English v*

va he/she/it goes; you go

vaca *f* cow

vacaciones *fpl* bakath-yoness
    holiday, vacation

vacío bathee-o empty

vacuna *f* vaccination

vacunarse bakoonarsay to be
    vaccinated

vado permanente no parking
    at any time

vagón *m* carriage

vagón restaurante restowrantay
    restaurant car

vagón de literas leetairass sleeping car

vainilla f ba-eenee-ya vanilla

vais ba-eess you go

vajilla f baHee-ya crockery

vale balay OK

valer balair to be worth

valiente bal-yentay brave

valla f ba-ya fence

valle m ba-yay valley

valores mpl baloress securities

válvula f valve

vamos we go

van they go; you go

vapor m steamer

vaqueros mpl bakaiross jeans; cowboys

varicela f bareethay-la chickenpox

varios bar-yoss several

varón m male

varonil manly

vas you go

vasco Basque

Vascongadas fpl the Basque country

vaso m glass

vaya ba-ya go; I go; he/she goes; you go

¡vaya por Dios! dee-oss oh Christ!

¡váyase! ba-yasay go away!

¡váyase a paseo! pasay-o get lost!

Vd (usted) oostay you (sing)

Vds (ustedes) you (pl)

ve bay go; he/she sees; you see

veces: a veces baythess sometimes

vecino m betheeno neighbour

vehículos pesados heavy vehicles

veinte bay-eentay twenty

vejiga f beHeega bladder

vela f bayla candle; sail

velero m belairo sailing boat

velocidad f belotheeda speed

velocidad controlada por radar radar speed checks

velocidad limitada speed limits apply

velocidades fpl belotheedadess gears

velocímetro m belotheemetro speedometer

ven ben come; they see; you see

vena f bayna vein

venda f bandage

vendar to dress (wound)

vendemos a... selling rate

vender bendair to sell

veneno m benayno poison

vengo I come

venir to come

venta f sale

de venta aquí on sale here

venta de localidades tickets (on sale)

venta de sellos stamps sold here

ventana f window

ventanilla f bentanee-ya window; ticket office

ventas a crédito credit terms available

ventas a plazos hire purchase, installment plan

ventas al contado cash sales

ventilador *m* fan

ver bair to see; to watch

veraneante *m* bairanay-antay holidaymaker, vacationer

veranear bairanay-ar to holiday

verano *m* bairano summer

verbena *f* bairbayna open-air dance

verdad *f* bairda truth

  ¿de verdad? is that so?

  ¿verdad? don't you?; do you?; isn't he?; is he? etc

verdadero bairdadairo true

verde (*m*) bairday green

versión *f* bairs-yon version

  en versión original in the original language

vestido *m* dress

vestir to dress

  de vestir formal

vestirse besteeersay to get dressed

vestuarios *mpl* bestwar-yoss fitting rooms

vez *f* beth time

  una vez once

  en vez de instead of

vi bee I saw

vía aérea: por vía aérea by air mail

vía oral orally

vía rectal per rectum

viajar b-yaHar to travel

viaje *m* b-yaHay journey

  ¡buen viaje! bwen have a good trip!

viaje de negocios negoth-yoss business trip

viaje de novios nob-yoss honeymoon

viaje organizado organeethado package tour

viajero *m* b-yaHairo passenger

vida *f* life

vidrio *m* beedr-yo glass

viejo b-yayHo old

viene: la semana que viene b-yaynay next week

viento *m* b-yento wind

vientre *m* b-yentray stomach

viernes b-yairness Friday

Viernes Santo *m* Good Friday

vine beenay I came

vinos y licores wines and spirits

viñedo been-yaydo vineyard

violación *f* b-yolath-yon rape

violar b-yolar to rape

violento b-yolento violent; embarrassing, awkward

  sentirse violento to feel awkward

visado *m* visa

visita *f* visit

visita con guía gee-a guided tour

visitante *m/f* beeseetantay visitor

visitar to visit

visor *m* viewfinder

víspera *f* beespaira the day before

vista *f* view

¡hasta la vista! see you!

vista turística scenic view

visto seen

viuda *f* b-**yoo**da widow

viudo *m* widower

vivir to live

vivo alive; I live

VO (versión original) original language

volante *m* bola**n**tay steering wheel

volar to fly

voltaje bolta**Hay** voltage

volver bol**bair** to come back

volver a hacer algo to do something again

volver a casa to go home

vomitar to vomit

vosotras, **vosotros** you

v.o. subtitulada version in the original language with subtitles

voy I go

voz *f* both voice

vuelo *m* b**way**lo flight

vuelo nacional nath-**yon**al domestic flight

vuelo regular scheduled flight

vuelta *f* b**wel**ta change

la vuelta al colegio kolay-**Hyo** back to school

vuelvo b**wel**bo I return

vuestra b**wes**tra, **vuestras**, **vuestro**, **vuestros** your; yours

W

wáter ba**tair** toilet, restroom

Y

y ee and

ya already

ya está there you are

ya... ya sometimes… sometimes

ya que kay since

yerno *m* **yair**no son-in-law

yo I; me

yo mismo myself

Z

zapatería *f* thapatai**ree**-a shoe shop/store

zapatero *m* thapat**ai**ro cobbler; shoe repairer

zapatillas *fpl* thapat**ee**-yass slippers

zapatos *mpl* thapat**oss** shoes

zona *f* **tho**na area

zona azul a**thool** restricted parking area, permit holders only

zona de avalanchas frequent avalanches

zona de servicios sairb**eeth**-yoss service area

zona monumental historic monuments

zona (reservada) para peatones pedestrian precinct

zurdo th**oor**do left-handed

MENU READER

Food

Essential terms

bread el pan
butter la mantequilla mantekee-ya
cup la taza tatha
dessert el postre postray
fish el pescado
fork el tenedor
glass (wine glass) la copa
knife el cuchillo koochee-yo
main course el plato principal
meat la carne karnay
menu el menú menoo
pepper (spice) la pimienta peem-yenta

plate el plato
salad la ensalada
salt la sal
set menu el menu del día menoo
soup la sopa
spoon la cuchara
starter (food) la entrada
table la mesa maysa

another..., please otro/otra...,
  por favor fabor
excuse me! (to call waiter/
  waitress) ¡por favor! fabor
could I have the bill, please?
  la cuenta, por favor kwenta

A–Z

aceite athay-eetay oil

aceite de oliva day oleeba olive oil

aceitunas athay-eetoonass olives

aceitunas aliñadas aleen-yadass olives with salad dressing

aceitunas negras black olives

aceitunas rellenas ray-yaynass stuffed olives

aceitunas verdes bairdess green olives

acelgas athelgass chard, spinach beet

achicoria acheekor-ya chicory

aguacate agwakatay avocado

aguja de ternera agooHa day tairnaira veal for stewing

ahumados a-oomadoss smoked fish

ahumados variados baree-adoss smoked fish

ajillo aHee-yo garlic

ajo aHo garlic

alaju ala-Hoo nougat-type sweet made from walnuts or pine nuts, toasted breadcrumbs and honey

albahaca alba-aka basil

albaricoque albareekokay apricot

albóndigas meatballs

albóndigas de lomo day pork meatballs

alcachofas artichokes

alcachofas a la andaluza andalootha artichokes with ham and bacon

alcachofas a la romana artichokes in batter

alcachofas en vinagreta beenagrayta artichokes in vinaigrette dressing

alcaparras capers

aliñada aleen-yada with salad dressing

ali oli garlic mayonnaise

almejas almay-Hass clams

almejas a la buena mujer bwayna mooHair clams stewed with chillies, white wine, lemon and herbs

almejas a la marinera mareenaira clams stewed in white wine and parsley

almejas a la valenciana balenth-yana clams in a white wine sauce

almejas al natural natooral live clams

almejas en salsa verde bairday clams in parsley and white wine sauce

almejas naturales natooraless live clams

almendra almond

alubias aloob-yass beans

alubias blancas white kidney beans

alubias rojas roHass red kidney beans

ancas de rana frogs' legs

ancas de rana albuferena alboofairayna frogs' legs in a sauce made from chicken soup, mushrooms and paprika

anchoas ancho-ass anchovies

anchoas a la barquera barkaìrà marinated anchovies with capers

anguila angeela eel

anguila ahumada a-oomada smoked eel

angulas baby eels

angulas al all-i-pebre all-ee-pebray baby eels with garlic and black pepper

añojo an-yoнo veal

apio ap-yo celery

arenques frescos arenkess fresh herrings

arroz arroth rice

arroz a la cubana boiled rice with fried eggs and either bananas or tomato sauce

arroz a la emperatriz empairatreeth rice with milk, apricots, truffles, raisins, Cointreau and gelatine

arroz a la turca toorka boiled rice with curry sauce, onions and tomatoes

arroz a la valenciana balenth-yana paella

arroz blanco boiled white rice

arroz con leche lechay rice pudding

asado roast

asados roast meats

asadurilla asadooree-ya lambs' liver stew

atún atoon tuna

atún al horno orno baked tuna

avellana abay-yana hazelnut

aves abess poultry

azafrán athafran saffron

azúcar athookar sugar

bacalao a la catalana bakala-o cod with ham, almond, garlic and parsley

bacalao al ajo arriero aнo arr-yaìro cod with garlic, peppers and chillies

bacalao a la vizcaína beethka-eena cod served with ham, peppers and chillies

bacalao al pil pil peel cod cooked in olive oil

baveresa de coco babairaysa day cold coconut sweet

becadas snipe

becadas a la vizcaína beethka-eena snipe served with bacon, onion and sherry sauce

becadas asadas baked snipe

berenjena bairenнayna aubergine, eggplant

berenjenas a la mallorquina ma-yorkeena aubergines/ eggplants with garlic mayonnaise

berza bairtha cabbage

besugo bream

besugo al horno al orno baked sea bream

besugo asado baked sea bream

besugo mechado sea bream stuffed with ham and bacon

bien hecho b-yen echo well done

bistec a la riojana r-yoнana steak with fried red peppers

bistec de ternera tairnaira veal steak

bizcocho beethkocho sponge finger

bocadillo bokadee-yo sandwich, snack

bogavante bogabantay lobster

bollo bo-yo roll

bomba helada elada baked alaska

bonito tuna

bonito al horno orno baked tuna

boquerones en vinagre bokaironess en beenagray anchovies in vinaigrette

boquerones fritos fried fresh anchovies

brandada de bacalao bakala-o creamy cod purée

brazo de gitano bratho day Heetano swiss roll

brevas brebass figs

broqueta de riñones broketa day reen-yoness kidney kebabs

buey boo-ay beef

buñuelos boon-ywayloss light fried pastry

buñuelos de bacalao bakala-o fried pastry containing flaked, dried, salted cod

buñuelos de cuaresma rellenos day kwaresma ray-yaynoss light fried pastries with chocolate and cream

butifarra Catalan sausage – contains bacon

butifarra con rovellons robay-yons Catalan sausage with mushrooms

butifarra con setas Catalan sausage with mushrooms

buvangos rellenos boobangoss ray-yaynoss stuffed courgettes/zucchini

cabello de ángel kabay-yo day sweet pumpkin filling (used in cakes)

cabracho mullet

cabrito asado roast kid

cacahuetes kakawaytess peanuts

cachelada kachelada pork stew with eggs, tomato, onion and boiled potatoes

cachelos kachayloss boiled potatoes served with spicy sausage and bacon

calabacines kalabatheeness courgettes, zucchini; marrow

calabaza kalabatha pumpkin

calamares a la romana kalamaress squid rings fried in batter

calamares en su tinta teenta squid cooked in their ink

calamares fritos fried squid

caldeirada kalday-eerada fish soup

caldera de dátiles de mar kaldaira day dateeless seafood stew

caldereta de cordero a la pastora kaldairayta day kordairo lamb and vegetable stew

caldereta gallega ga-yayga vegetable stew

caldo clear soup

caldo de gallina ga-yeena chicken soup

caldo de perdiz pairdeeth partridge soup

caldo de pescado clear fish soup

caldo gallego ga-yaygo clear soup with green vegetables, beans and pork

caldo guanche gwanchay soup made from potatoes, onions, tomatoes and courgettes/zucchini

callos a la madrileña ka-yoss a la madreelen-ya tripe cooked with chillies

camarones kamaroness baby prawns

canela kanayla cinnamon

canelones kaneloness cannelloni

cangrejo kangray-Ho crab

cangrejos de río river crabs

caracoles karakoless snails

caracoles a la madrileña madreelen-ya snails cooked with chillies

carbonada de buey boo-ay beef cooked in beer

cardo type of thistle, eaten as a vegetable

carne karnay meat

carne de cerdo thairdo pork

carne de membrillo membree-yo quince jelly (dessert)

carne de vaca baka beef

carne picada minced meat

carnero karnairo mutton

carnes karness meat; meat dishes

carro de queso kayso cheese board

carta menu

castaña kastan-ya chestnut

caza katha game

cazuela kathwayla casserole

cazuela de chichas meat casserole

cazuela de hígado eegado liver casserole

cebolla thebo-ya onion

cebolletas thebo-yetass spring onions

cecina thetheena dry cured meat

centollo thento-yo spider crab

centollo relleno ray-yayno spider crab cooked in its shell

cerdo thairdo pork, pig

cereza thairaytha cherry

cesta de frutas thesta day frootass a selection of fresh fruit

champiñón a la crema champeen-yon – krayma mushrooms in cream sauce

champiñón al ajillo aHee-yo mushrooms fried with garlic

champiñón a la plancha grilled mushrooms

champiñones champeen-yoness mushrooms

chanfaina chanfa-eena rice and black pudding stew

chanfaina castellana kastay-yana rice and sheeps' liver stew

changurro spider crab cooked in its shell

chanquetes chankaytess fish (like whitebait)

chateaubrian chatobree-an thick
steak

chicharros horse mackerel

chipirones cheepeeroness baby
squid

chipirones en su tinta teenta
baby squid cooked in their ink

chipirones rellenos ray-yaynoss
stuffed baby squid

chirimoyas cheereemo-yass
custard apples

chocos squid

chocos con habas abass squid
with broad beans

chorizo choreetho spicy red
sausage

chuleta choolayta chop

chuleta de buey day boo-ay
beef chop

chuleta de cerdo thairdo pork
chop

chuleta de cerdo empanada
breaded pork chop

chuleta de cordero kordairo
lamb chop

chuleta de ternera tairnaira
veal chop

chuleta de ternera empanada
breaded veal chop

chuletas de gamo venison
chops

chuletas de lomo ahumado
a-oomado smoked pork chops

chuletas de venado benado
venison chops

chuletitas de cordero day
kordairo small lamb chops

chuletón large chop

**chuletón de ternera a la
diable roja** d-yablay roHa large,
grilled, breaded veal chop

churros fried pastry strips

cigala theegala crayfish

cigalas a la parrilla parree-ya
grilled crayfish

cigalas cocidas kotheedass
boiled crayfish

ciruela theerwayla plum,
greengage

ciruelas pasas prunes

civet de liebre theebet day
l-yaybray marinated hare

coca amb pinxes koka am
peensess sardine pie

cochinillo asado kocheenee-yo
roast sucking pig

cocido kotheedo stew made from
meat, chickpeas and vegetables

cocido castellano/madrileño
kastay-yano/madreelen-yo stew
made from meat, chickpeas,
vegetables etc

cocochas (de merluza)
mairlootha hakes' gills

cóctel de bogavante
bogabantay lobster cocktail

cóctel de gambas prawn
cocktail

cóctel de langostinos king
prawn cocktail

cóctel de mariscos seafood
cocktail

codillo de cerdo con chucrut
kodee-yo day thairdo kon
chookroot pigs' trotters with
sauerkraut

codoñate kodon-ya**tay** cake made with chestnuts, honey and quince

codoñate de nueces nway**thess** cake made with walnuts

codornices kodor**nee**thess quail

codornices con uvas oo**bass** quail stewed with grapes

codornices estofadas braised quail

col cabbage

coles de Bruselas ko**less** day broos**ay**lass Brussels sprouts

coliflor cauliflower

coliflor con bechamel cauliflower cheese

comino cumin

conejo konay-**HO** rabbit

conejo encebollado enthebo-**ya**do rabbit served with onions

conejo estofado braised rabbit

congrio ko**ngr**-yo conger eel

consomé al jerez konsoma**y** al Hair**eth** consommé with sherry

consomé con yema yay**ma** consommé with egg yolk

consomé de ave a**bay** chicken consommé

consomé de pollo po-**yo** chicken consommé

contra de ternera con guisantes tairna**ira** kon gees**a**ntess veal stew with peas

contrafilete de ternera kontrafeel**ay**tay day veal fillet

copa de helado el**a**do assorted ice cream served in a stemmed glass

cordero kord**a**iro lamb

cordero chilindrón lamb stew with onion, tomato, peppers and eggs

corvina korb**ee**na Mediterranean fish, similar to sea bass

costillas de cerdo kost**ee**-yass day th**ai**rdo pork ribs

costillas de cerdo con chucrut chookr**oo**t pork ribs with sauerkraut

crema catalana kray**ma** crème caramel

cremada dessert made from egg, sugar and milk

crema de cangrejos kray**ma** day kangray-**HOSS** cream of crab soup

crema de espárragos cream of asparagus soup

crema de espinacas cream of spinach soup

crema de legumbres/ verduras leg**oo**mbrays/ baird**oo**rass cream of vegetable soup

crep(e) pancake

crep(e)s imperiales eempair-**ya**less crêpe suzette

criadillas kree-ad**ee**-yass bulls' testicles; truffles (edible fungus); root vegetable

criadillas de ternera tairna**ira** calves' testicles

criadillas de tierra t-yai**rra** truffles (edible fungus)

criadillas en salsa verde b**ai**rday root vegetable in parsley sauce

crocante krokantay ice cream with chopped nuts

croquetas krokaytass croquettes

crudo raw

cuajada kwaнada junket, curds

dátiles dateeless dates

dátiles de mar shellfish

delicias de queso deleeth-yass day kayso cheese croquettes

dulce de membrillo doolthay day membree-yo quince jelly

embutidos cured pork sausages

embutidos de la tierra t-yaírra local sausages

empanada gallega ga-yayga pie with chicken, chorizo sausage, peppers, ham, onions and tuna

empanada santiaguesa sant-yagaysa fish pie

empanado in breadcrumbs

empanadillas empanadee-yass small pies

empanadillas de chorizo choreetho small pies filled with spicy sausage

endivias endeeb-yass endive

ensaimada mallorquina ensa-eemada ma-yorkeena large, spiral-shaped bun

ensalada salad

ensalada de frutas fruit salad

ensalada ilustrada mixed salad

ensalada mixta meesta mixed salad

ensalada simple seemplay green salad

ensaladilla ensaladee-ya Spanish salad

ensaladilla rusa roosa Russian salad

entrantes entrantess entrées, starters

entrecot a la parrilla entrekot – parree-ya grilled entrecôte steak

entrecot a la pimienta peem-yenta entrecôte in black pepper sauce

entremés entremayss hors d'oeuvre, starter

entremeses entremaysess hors d'oeuvres

entremeses de la casa hors d'oeuvres – house speciality

entremeses variados bar-yadoss assorted hors d'oeuvres

escabeche de... eskabechay marinated...

escalibada flaked cod and vegetable salad

escalope a la milanesa eskalopay breaded veal escalope with cheese

escalope a la parrilla parree-ya grilled veal

escalope a la plancha grilled veal

escalope Cordon Bleu veal escalope with ham and cheese

escalope de cerdo thaírdo pork escalope

escalope de lomo de cerdo escalope of fillet of pork

escalope de ternera taírnaíra veal escalope

escalopines al vino de Marsala eskalopeeness – beeno veal escalopes cooked in wine

escalopines de ternera tairnaira veal escalopes

escarola endive

espadín a la toledana kebab

espaguetis italiana espagayteess eetal-yana spaghetti

espárragos asparagus

espárragos calientes kal-yentess grilled asparagus with béchamel sauce

espárragos dos salsas asparagus with mayonnaise and vinagrette dressing

espárragos en vinagreta beenagrayta asparagus in vinaigrette dressing

espárragos trigueros treegayross green asparagus

especia espayth-ya spice

especialidad speciality

espina fishbone

espinacas spinach

espinazo de cerdo con patatas espeenatho day thairdo pork ribs with potatoes

espuma de jamón day Hamon boiled ham mousse

estofado stew; stewed

estofado de liebre l-yaybray hare stew

estofado de liebre con níscalos hare stew with wild mushrooms

estofados stews

estragón tarragon

fabada (asturiana) astoor-yana bean stew with red sausage, black pudding and pork

fabricación: de fabricación casera homemade

faisán fa-eesan pheasant

faisán trufado troofado pheasant with truffles

farinato fried sausage

fiambres f-yambress cold meats, cold cuts

fideos feeday-oss thin pasta; noodles; vermicelli

filete feelaytay steak; fillet

filete a la parrilla parree-ya grilled beef steak

filete a la plancha grilled beef steak

filete de cerdo thairdo pork steak

filete de ternera tairnaira veal steak

flan crème caramel

flan con nata crème caramel with whipped cream

flan de café day kafay coffee-flavoured crème caramel

flan de caramelo karamaylo crème caramel

flan (quemado) al ron kemado crème caramel with rum

frambuesa frambwaysa raspberry

fresa fraysa strawberry

fresas con nata strawberries and cream

fritanga al modo de Alicante day aleekantay dish of fried peppers, tuna and garlic

frito fried

fritos de la casa fried hors d'oeuvres – house speciality

fritos variados bar-yadoss fried hors d'oeuvres

fruta fruit

fruta variada bar-yada assorted fresh fruit

frutas en almíbar fruit in syrup

gachas manchegas type of sweet or savoury porridge

galleta ga-yayta biscuit

gallina a la cairatraca ga-yeena a la ka-eeratraka stewed chicken

gallina en pepitoria pepeetor-ya stewed chicken with peppers, onions and tomato

gamba prawn

gambas a la americana prawns with brandy and garlic

gambas al ajillo aHee-yo prawns with garlic

gambas a la plancha grilled prawns

gambas cocidas kotheedass boiled prawns

gambas en gabardina prawns in batter

gambas rebozadas rebothadass prawns in batter

garbanzos garbanthoss chickpeas

garbanzos a la catalana chickpeas with sausage, boiled eggs and pine nuts

gazpacho andaluz gathpacho andalooth cold soup made from tomatoes, onions, garlic, peppers and cucumber

gazpacho manchego rabbit stew with tomato and garlic, sometimes also with partridge meat

gelatina Helateena jelly

gratén de……. au gratin

grelo turnip

guisado de cordero geesado day kordairo stewed lamb

guisado de costillas de ternera kostee-yass day tairnaira rib of veal stew

guisado de ternera stewed veal

guisantes geesantess peas

habas abass broad beans

habas fritas fried young broad beans

habichuelas abeechwaylass haricot beans; white kidney beans

hamburguesa amboorgaysa hamburger

harina areena flour

helado elado ice cream

helado de caramelo karamaylo caramel ice cream

helado de mantecado dairy ice cream

helado de nata dairy ice cream

helado de vainilla ba-eenee-ya vanilla ice cream

hierbas yairbass herbs

hígado eegado liver

hígado de ternera estofado tairnaira braised calves' liver

hígado encebollado entheboyado liver in an onion sauce

hígado estofado braised liver

higos eegoss figs

higos secos dried figs

hornazo ornatho Easter cake

horno: al horno baked

huevo waybo egg

huevo duro dooro hard-boiled egg

huevo hilado eelado shredded boiled eggs used as a garnish

huevo pasado por agua ag-wa boiled egg

huevos a la española espanyola fried eggs

huevos a la flamenca baked eggs with sausage, tomato, peas, asparagus and peppers

huevos cocidos kotheedoss hard-boiled eggs

huevos con picadillo peekadeeyo eggs with minced sausage meat

huevos duros con mayonesa ma-yonaysa egg mayonnaise

huevos escalfados poached eggs

huevos fritos fried eggs

huevos fritos con chorizo choreetho fried eggs with Spanish sausage

huevos pasados por agua ag-wa boiled eggs

huevos rellenos ray-yaynoss stuffed eggs

huevos revueltos rebweltoss scrambled eggs

incluye pan, postre y vino includes bread, dessert and wine

IVA no incluido VAT not included

jamón Hamon ham

jamón con huevo hilado waybo eelado ham with shredded egg garnish

jamón de Jabugo day Haboogo Spanish ham from Jabugo, Huelva

jamón ibérico eebaireeko
Spanish ham

jamón serrano sairrano cured
ham, similar to Parma ham

jamón York boiled ham

jarrete de ternera Harraytay day
tairnaira veal hock

jeta Heta pigs' cheeks

jeta rebozada rebothada pigs'
cheek in batter

judías Hoodee-ass beans

judías verdes bairdess green
beans

judías verdes a la española
espan-yola French bean stew

judías verdes al natural
natooral plain green beans

judías verdes con jamón
Hamon French beans with ham

judiones Hood-yoness broad
beans

lacón con grelos bacon with
turnip tops

langosta lobster

langosta a la americana
lobster with brandy and
garlic

langosta a la catalana lobster
with mushrooms and ham in a
white sauce

langosta con mahonesa
ma-onaysa lobster with
mayonnaise

langosta fría con mayonesa
cold lobster with mayonnaise

langosta gratinada lobster au
gratin

langostinos a la plancha
grilled king prawns

langostinos dos salsas king
prawns cooked in two sauces

laurel lowrel bay leaves

lebrato hare

leche frita lechay freeta slices
of thick custard fried in
breadcrumbs

leche merengada cold
milk with meringues and
cinnamon

lechuga lechooga lettuce

lengua lengwa tongue

lengua de buey boo-ay ox
tongue

lenguado a la parrilla lengwado
a la parree-ya grilled sole

lenguado a la plancha grilled
sole

lenguado a la romana sole in
batter

**lenguado al chacolí con
hongos** ongoss sole with
mushrooms and white wine

lenguado frito fried sole

lenguado grillado gree-yado
grilled sole

lenguado menie/meuniere
men-yair sole meunière – sole
coated in flour, fried and
served with butter, lemon juice
and parsley

lenguado rebozado rebothado
sole in batter

lentejas lentay-Hass lentils

lentejas aliñadas aleen-yadass
lentils in vinaigrette dressing

lentejas onubenses
onoobensess lentils with spicy
sausage, onion and garlic

liba rebozada rebothada sea bass
fried in batter

liebre estofada l-yaybray stewed
hare

lima leema lime

limón lemon

lombarda red cabbage

lomo curado koorado cured pork
sausage

lomo de liebre l-yaybray loin
of hare

lonchas de jamón Hamon slices
of cured ham

longaniza longaneetha cooked
Spanish sausage

lubina a la cantábrica sea bass
with garlic, lemon juice and
white wine

lubina a la marinera mareenaira
sea bass in a parsley sauce

macarrones makarroness
macaroni

macarrones gratinados
macaroni cheese

macedonia de fruta mathedon-
ya fruit salad

maduro madooro ripe

magdalena magdalayna muffin

magras con tomate tomatay
slices of cured ham with
tomato

mahonesa ma-onaysa
mayonnaise

maíz ma-eeth sweetcorn

mandarinas tangerines

manises maneesess peanuts

manitas de cordero kordairo leg
of lamb

manos de cerdo thairdo pigs'
trotters

mantecadas small sponge cakes

mantecado vanilla ice cream

mantequilla mantekee-ya butter

manzana manthana apple

manzanas a la malvasía
malbassee-a apples in syrup

manzanas asadas baked apples

mariscada cold mixed shellfish

mariscos seafood

mariscos del día fresh shellfish

mariscos del tiempo t-yempo
seasonal shellfish

marmitako tuna and vegetable
stew

mayonesa ma-yonaysa
mayonnaise

mazapán mathapan marzipan

medallones de anguila meda-
yoness day angeela eel steaks

medallones de merluza
mairlootha hake steaks

mejillones may-Hee-yoness
mussels

mejillones a la marinera
mareenaira mussels in wine
sauce with garlic and parsley

mejillones con salsa mussels
with tomato and herb sauce

melocotón peach

melocotones en almíbar
melokotoness peaches in syrup

melón melon

melón al calisay kaleesī melon with a spirit or liqueur poured over it

melón con jamón Hamon melon with cured ham

membrillo membree-yo quince

menestra de legumbres legoombress vegetable stew made from pulses

menestra de verduras bairdoorass vegetable stew

menú menoo set menu

menú de la casa fixed price menu

menú del día today's set menu

merluza a la castellana mairlootha – kastay-yana hake with clams, prawns, linseeds, eggs and chilli

merluza a la cazuela kathwayla hake casserole

merluza al ajo arriero aHo arr-yairo hake with garlic and chillies

merluza a la riojana r-yoHana hake with chillies

merluza a la romana hake steaks in batter

merluza a la vasca baska hake in a garlic sauce

merluza caldo corto hake with vegetable sauce

merluza en salsa verde bairday hake in parsley and white wine sauce

merluza fría free-a cold hake

merluza frita fried hake

merluza koskera koskaira hake in a garlic sauce

merluza (lomos de) con angulas y almejas ee almay-Hass hake fillet with baby eels and clams

mermelada mairmelada jam; marmalade

mero mairo grouper

mero a la levantina lebanteena grouper with lemon juice and rosemary

mero en salsa verde bairday grouper with garlic, parsley and white wine sauce

miel m-yel honey

mojete moHay-tay 'dipping' sauce for bread, usually made from vegetables

mojojones moHoHoness mussels

mollejas con setas mo-yay-Hass lambs' gizzards with mushrooms

mollejas de ternera tairnaira calves' sweetbreads

mora blackberry

morcilla morthee-ya black pudding, blood sausage

morcilla de ternera tairnaira black pudding made from calves' blood

morros de cerdo thairdo pigs' cheeks

morros de vaca day baka cows' cheeks

morros de vaca pastora cows' cheeks with vegetables

mortadela salami-type sausage

morteruelo mortair-**way**lo
breaded minced liver

mostaza mos**ta**tha mustard

mousse de limón lemon
mousse

mújol guisado moo**Hol** geesado
red mullet

nabo turnip

naranja naran**Ha** orange

nata cream

nata batida whipped cream

natillas natee-yass cold custard
with cinnamon

natillas de chocolate chokolatay
cold custard with chocolate

níscalos wild mushrooms

nísperos neespaiross medlars –
fruit similar to crab apple

nueces nway**thess** walnuts

nuez nwayth nut

ñoquis n-yo**keess** potato gnocchi

oca en adobo marinaded goose

orejas de cerdo oray-**Has** day
thairdo pigs' ears

orejas y pie de cerdo ee p-yay
pigs' ears and trotters

ostra oyster

**otros mariscos según precios
en plaza** other shellfish,
depending on current prices

pa amb tomaquet bread spread
with olive oil and tomato sauce

paella pa-**ay**-ya fried rice with
seafood and chicken

paella castellana kastay-yana
meat paella

paella de marisco shellfish
paella

paella de pollo po-yo chicken
paella

paella especial espeth-yal paella
house speciality

paella mixta meesta shellfish
and chicken paella

paella valenciana balenth-yana
paella with assorted shellfish
and chicken

paleta de cordero lechal
kordairo shoulder of lamb

paloma pigeon

pan bread

panaché de verduras panachay
day bairdoorass vegetable stew

pan blanco white bread

panceta panthayta bacon

pan de higos eegoss dried fig
cake with cinnamon

pan integral wholemeal bread

parrilla: a la parrilla grilled

parrillada de caza parree-yada
day katha mixed grilled game

parrillada de mariscos mixed
grilled shellfish

pasas raisins

pasta biscuit; pastry; pasta

pastel cake; pie

pastel de hígado de cerdo
eegado day thairdo pigs' liver
pie

pastel de higos eegoss fig cake

pastel de ternera tairnaira
veal pie

pastel de verduras con salsa de champiñones silvestres bairdoorass – champeen-yoness seelbestress vegetable pie with wild mushroom sauce

pasteles pastayless cakes

patas de cordero kordairo stewed leg of lamb

patata potato

patatas a la pescadora potatoes with fish

patatas asadas roast potatoes

patatas bravas brabass potatoes in cayenne sauce

patatas con nabos potatoes with turnips

patatas estofadas boiled potatoes

patatas fritas chips, French fries; crisps, potato chips

patitos rellenos ray-yaynoss stuffed ducklings

pato duck

pato a la naranja naran-Ha duck à l'orange

pavipollo pabeepo-yo large chicken

pavo pabo turkey

pavo a la Asturiana astoor-yana turkey with red wine and paprika

pavo relleno a la catalana turkey stuffed with sausage, pork and plums

pavo trufado turkey stuffed with truffles

pecho de ternera tairnaira breast of veal

pechuga de pollo po-yo breast of chicken

peixo-palo a la marinera pesho – mareenaira stock-fish with potatoes and tomato

pepinillos pepeenee-yoss gherkins

pepinillos en vinagreta beenagrayta gherkins in vinaigrette dressing

pepino cucumber

pera pear

percebes pairthaybess barnacles

perdices pairdeethess partridges

perdices a la campesina partridges with vegetables

perdices a la manchega partridges cooked in red wine, garlic, herbs and pepper

perdiz encebollada pairdeeth enthebo-yada partridge with onion sauce

perejil pairay-Heel parsley

pescaditos fritos fried sprats

pescado fish

pestiños pesteen-yoss sugared pastries flavoured with aniseed

pestiños con miel m-yel fried sugared pastries flavoured with aniseed and honey

pez payth fish

pez espada ahumado a-oomado smoked swordfish

picadillo peekadee-yo salad of diced vegetables; stew of pork, bacon, garlic and eggs

picadillo de ternera tairnaira minced veal

pichones estofados peechoness stewed pigeon

pimentón paprika

pimienta (negra) peem-yenta black pepper

pimienta blanca white pepper

pimienta de cayena ka-yayna cayenne pepper

pimiento pepper

pimientos a la riojana r-yoHana baked red peppers fried in oil and garlic

pimientos fritos fried peppers

pimientos morrones morroness strong peppers

pimientos rellenos ray-yaynoss stuffed peppers

pimientos verdes bairdess green peppers

pinchitos snacks/appetizers served in bars; kebabs

pinchos snacks served in bars

pinchos morunos kebabs

pintada guinea fowl

piña peen-ya pineapple

piña al gratén pineapple au gratin

piña fresca fresh pineapple

piñones peen-yoness pine nuts

piparrada vasca basca pepper and tomato stew with ham and eggs

piriñaca peereen-yaka tuna and vegetable salad

pisto fried peppers, onions, tomatoes and courgettes/ zucchini

pisto manchego marrow, onion and tomato stew

plancha: a la plancha grilled

plátano banana

plátanos flameados flamay-adoss flambéed bananas

platos combinados meat and vegetables, hamburgers and eggs etc, mixture of various foods served as one dish; set menu

pochas con almejas almay-Hass white beans with clams

poco hecho echo rare

pollo po-yo chicken

pollo al ajillo aHee-yo fried chicken with garlic

pollo a la parrilla parree-ya grilled chicken

pollo a la riojana r-yoHana chicken with peppers and chillies

pollo asado roast chicken

pollo braseado brasay-ado braised chicken

pollo en cacerola kathairola chicken casserole

pollo en chanfaina chanfa-eena chicken with fried peppers, onions, tomatoes and courgettes/zucchini

pollo en pepitoria pepeetor-ya chicken in wine with saffron, garlic and almonds

pollo reina clamart ray-eena roast chicken with vegetables

pollos tomateros con zanahorias tomatairos kon thana-or-yass baby chickens with carrots

polvorones polboroness sugar-based dessert (eaten at Christmas)

pomelo grapefruit

postre postray dessert

postre sorpresa al DYC sorpraysa al deek whisky-flavoured dessert

potaje castellano potaHay kastay-yano thick broth

potaje de garbanzos garbanthoss chickpea stew

potaje de habichuelas habeechwaylass white bean stew

potaje de lentejas lentay-Hass lentil stew

primer plato starters

pucherete al estilo montañés poochairetay al esteelo montan-yess black pudding and spicy sausage stew

puchero canario poochairo kanar-yo casserole of meat, chickpeas and corn

puerro pwairro leek

pulpitos con cebolla thebo-ya baby octopuses with onions

pulpo octopus

puré de patata pooray day potato purée, mashed potatoes

purrusalda cod soup with leeks and potatoes

PVP price

> **Travel tip** Cheese is excellent throughout Spain: look out for Cabrales, a tangy blue cheese made in the Picos de Europa; Manchego, a sharp, nutty sheep's milk variety from La Mancha; Menorcan Mahon, often with paprika rubbed into its rind; Idiazábal, a Basque smoked cheese; and Zamorano, made from sheep's milk in Old Castille and León.

---

queso kayso cheese

queso con membrillo membree-yo cheese with quince jelly

queso de bola Edam

queso de Burgos soft white cheese

queso de cabrales kabraless Roquefort-type cheese

queso de cerdo thairdo similar to the pork in a pork pie, usually in slices

queso de Idiazábal eed-yathabal strong sheeps' cheese from the Basque country

queso del país pa-eess local cheese

queso de oveja obay-Ha sheep's cheese

queso de Roncal strong sheep's cheese from Navarra

queso gallego ga-yaygo creamy cheese from Galicia

queso manchego hard, strong cheese from La Mancha

quisquillas keeskee-yass shrimps

rábanos radishes

rabas squid rings fried in batter

rabo de buey boo-ay oxtail

ración rath-yon portion

ración pequeña para niños pekayn-ya – neen-yoss children's portion

ragout de ternera ragoot day tairnaira veal ragoût

rape a la americana rapay monkfish with brandy and herbs

rape a la cazuela kathwayla monkfish casserole

rape a la plancha grilled monkfish

ravioles rab-yoless ravioli

raya ra-ya skate

raya con manteca negra skate in butter and vinegar sauce

redondo al horno orno roast fillet of beef

redondo de ternera tairnaira fillet of veal

redondo en su jugo Hoogo fillet of beef cooked in its own sauce

relleno ray-yayno stuffed; stuffing

remolacha beetroot

repollo repo-yo cabbage

repostería de la casa cakes and desserts made on the premises

requesón rekay-son cream cheese, curd cheese

revuelto de ajos rebwelto day aHoss scrambled eggs with garlic

revuelto de ajos tiernos t-yairnoss scrambled eggs with spring garlic

revuelto de espárragos trigueros treegaiross scrambled eggs with asparagus

revuelto de sesos scrambled eggs with brains

revuelto de setas scrambled eggs with mushrooms

revuelto mixto meesto scrambled eggs with mixed vegetables

riñones a la plancha reen-yoness grilled kidneys

riñones al jerez Haireth kidneys in a sherry sauce

rodaballo rodaba-yo turbot

rodaballo al cava kaba turbot with champagne

romero romairo rosemary

romesco de pescado mixed fish

roscas sweet pastries

rosquillas roskee-yass small sweet pastries

rovellons robay-yons mushrooms

sal salt

salchicha sausage

salchichas blancas fried sausages with onions

salchichas de Frankfurt frankfurters

salchichón cured white sausage with pepper

salmón sal-mon salmon

salmón ahumado a-oomado smoked salmon

salmonetes sal-monaytess red mullet

salmonetes en papillote papee-yotay red mullet cooked in foil

salmón frío sal-mon free-o cold salmon

salmorejo salmoray-Ho thick sauce made from bread, tomatoes, olive oil, vinegar, green pepper and garlic, served cold with hard-boiled eggs and ham

salpicón de mariscos shellfish with vinaigrette dressing

salsa sauce

salsa ali oli/all-i-oli alee-olee garlic mayonnaise

salsa bechamel béchamel sauce, white sauce

salsa de tomate tomatay tomato sauce

salsa holandesa olandaysa hollandaise sauce – hot sauce made with eggs and butter

salsa mayonesa ma-yonaysa mayonnaise

salsa romesco sauce made from peppers, tomatoes and garlic

salsa tártara tartare sauce

salsa vinagreta beenagrayta vinaigrette dressing

salteado saltay-ado sautéed

sandía sandee-a water melon

sandwich mixto meesto cheese and ham sandwich

sangre de cerdo sangray day thaIrdo pigs' blood

sardina sardine

sardinas a la asturiana astoor-yana sardines in cider sauce

sardinas a la brasa barbecued sardines

sardinas a la parrilla parree-ya grilled sardines

sardinas fritas fried sardines

segundo plato main course

sesos brains

sesos a la romana brains in batter

sesos rebozados rebothadoss brains in batter

setas a la bordalesa bordalaysa mushrooms cooked in red wine and onions

setas a la plancha grilled mushrooms

setas rellenas ray-yaynass stuffed mushrooms

sobrasada soft red sausage with cayenne pepper

soldados de Pavia pabee-a fillets of cod, marinaded and fried

solomillo al vino solomee-yo al beeno fillet steak with red wine

solomillo con guisantes geesantess fillet steak with peas

solomillo con patatas fritas fillet steak with chips/French fries

solomillo de cerdo thairdo fillet of pork

solomillo de ternera tairnaira fillet of veal

solomillo de vaca baka fillet of beef

solomillo frío free-o cold roast beef

solomillo Roquefort rokayfor fillet steak with Roquefort cheese

sopa soup

sopa al cuarto de hora kwarto day ora soup made from ham, veal, chicken, almonds, vegetables and eggs

sopa castellana kastay-yana vegetable soup

sopa de ajo day aHo bread and garlic soup

sopa de almendras almond-based pudding

sopa de calducho clear soup

sopa de cola de buey boo-ay oxtail soup

sopa de fideos feeday-oss noodle soup

sopa de frutos de mar shellfish soup

sopa de gallina ga-yeena chicken soup

sopa del día soup of the day

sopa de legumbres legoombress vegetable soup

sopa de lentejas lentay-Hass lentil soup

sopa de marisco fish and shellfish soup

sopa de pescado fish soup

sopa de rabo oxtail soup

sopa de rabo de buey boo-ay oxtail soup

sopa de tortuga tortooga turtle soup

sopa mallorquina ma-yorkeena soup with tomatoes, meat and eggs

sopa sevillana sebee-yana fish and mayonnaise soup

sorbete sorbaytay sorbet

soufflé de fresones fresoness strawberry soufflé

suplemento de verduras extra vegetables

supremas de rodaballo soopraymass day rodaba-yo fish slices

tallarines ta-yareeness noodles

tallarines a la italiana eetal-yana tagliatelle

tapa de ternera rellena tairnaira ray-yayna stuffed veal hock

tapas appetizers

tarta cake

tarta Alaska baked alaska

tarta de almendra almond tart or gâteau

tarta de arroz arroth cake or tart containing rice

tarta de la casa tart or gâteau baked on the premises

tarta helada elada ice cream gâteau

tarta moca mocha tart

tartar crudo raw minced steak, steak tartare

tejos de queso tay-Hoss day kayso cheese pastries

tencas tench

tencas con jamón Hamon tench with ham

ternera tairnaira veal

ternera asada roast veal

tigres teegress mussels in cayenne sauce

tocinillo de cielo totheenee-yo day th-yaylo rich, thick crème caramel

todo incluido all inclusive

tomate tomatay tomato

tomates rellenos tomatess ray-yaynoss stuffed tomatoes

tomatics a es forn baked tomatoes

tomillo tomee-yo thyme

tordo thrush

tordos braseados brassay-adoss grilled thrushes

tordos estofados braised thrushes

torrijas torree-Hass sweet pastries

torta de chicharrones cheecharroness pie filled with assorted cooked and cured meats

torta de sardinas sardine pie

tortilla tortee-ya omelette

tortilla a la paisana pa-eesana omelette containing a variety of vegetables

tortilla aliada al-yada omelette with mixed vegetables

tortilla al ron omlette with rum

tortilla a su gusto omlette made as the customer wishes

tortilla de bonito tuna fish omlette

tortilla de champiñones champeen-yoness mushroom omelette

tortilla de chorizo choreetho spicy sausage omelette

tortilla de escabeche eskabechay fish omelette

tortilla de espárragos asparagus omelette

tortilla de gambas prawn omelette

tortilla de jamón Hamon ham omelette

tortilla de morcilla morthee-ya black pudding omelette

tortilla de patata potato omelette

tortilla de sesos brains omelette

tortilla de setas mushroom omelette

tortilla española espan-yola (cold slice of) Spanish omelette with potato, onion and garlic

tortilla francesa franthaysa plain omelette

tortilla granadina omelette with artichokes, asparagus, brains and peppers

tortilla sacromonte sakromontay vegetable, brains and sausage omelette

tortillas variadas bar-yadass assorted omelettes

tostada toast

tostón sucking pig

tostón asado roast sucking pig

tournedó fillet steak

tournedó a la salsa foie fwa fillet steak in pâté sauce

trucha troocha trout

trucha ahumada a-oomada smoked trout

trucha con jamón Hamon trout with ham

trucha escabechada marinated trout

truchas a la marinera mareenaira trout in white wine sauce

truchas molinera moleenaira trout meunière – trout coated in flour, fried and served with butter, lemon juice and parsley

trufas truffles (edible fungus)

trufas al jerez Haireth truffles in sherry

turbante de arroz toorbantay day arroth rice served with steak, sausage, peppers and bacon

turrón toorron nougat

turrón de Alicante aleekantay hard nougat

turrón de coco coconut nougat

turrón de Jijona HeeHona soft nougat

turrón de yema yayma nougat with egg yolk

txangurro changoorro spider crab cooked in its shell

uvas oobass grapes

vaca estofada baka stewed beef

verduras bairdoorass vegetables

vieiras bee-ay-eerass scallops

vinagre beenagray vinegar

yogur yo-goor yoghurt

zanahoria thana-or-ya carrot

zanahorias a la crema krayma carrots à la crème

zarzuela de mariscos tharthwayla day mareeskoss shellfish stew

zarzuela de pescados y mariscos fish and shellfish stew

Drink

Essential terms

beer la cerveza thairb**ay**tha

bottle la botella bot**ay**-ya

brandy el coñac kon-yak

coffee el café kaf**ay**

cup la taza t**a**tha

a cup of... una taza de...

gin la ginebra Heen**ay**bra

gin and tonic un gintónic Heent**o**neek

glass (wine glass) la c**o**pa

a glass of... un vaso de b**a**so day

milk la leche l**e**chay

mineral water el agua mineral **a**gwa meenair**a**l

orange juice (fresh) el zumo de naranja th**oo**mo day naran**Ha**

port el Op**o**rto

red wine el vino tinto b**ee**no t**ee**nto

rosé el vino ros**a**do b**ee**no

soda (water) la s**o**da

soft drink el refresco

sugar el azúcar ath**oo**kar

tea el té tay

tonic (water) la t**ó**nica

vodka el vodka b**o**dka

water el agua **a**gwa

whisky el wh**i**sky

white wine el vino blanco b**ee**no

wine el vino b**ee**no

wine list la lista de vinos l**ee**sta day b**ee**noss

another..., please **o**tro/**o**tra..., por favor fab**o**r

A–Z

agua ag-wa water

agua mineral meenairal mineral water

agua mineral con gas fizzy mineral water

agua mineral sin gas seen still mineral water

agua potable potablay drinking water

Alella alay-ya region near Barcelona producing red, white and rosé wines

Alicante aleekantay region in the south producing red and rosé wines matured in oak casks

Ampurdán region at the foot of the Pyrenees which produces rosé wine

anís aneess aniseed-flavoured alcoholic drink

año vintage

aperitivo aperitif

batido milkshake

batido de chocolate day chokolatay chocolate milkshake

batido de fresa fraysa strawberry milkshake

batido de frutas fruit milkshake

batido de plátano banana milkshake

batido de vainilla ba-eenee-ya vanilla milkshake

bebida drink

bebidas alcohólicas alcoholic drinks

bebidas refrescantes soft drinks

cacao kakow cocoa

café con leche lechay coffee with milk (large cup)

café cortado coffee with milk (small cup)

café descafeinado deskafay-eenado decaffeinated coffee

café escocés eskothayss black coffee, whisky and vanilla ice cream

café instantáneo eenstantanay-o instant coffee

café irlandés eerlandayss black coffee, whisky, vanilla ice cream and whipped cream

café solo black coffee

café vienés b-yenayss black coffee and whipped cream

caña (cerveza) kan-ya thairbay-tha 250cc of draught beer

carajillo karahee-yo black coffee with brandy

carajillo de ron black coffee with rum

carajillo de vodka black coffee with vodka

Cariñena kareen-yayna region in the north producing red and rosé wines

carta de vinos day beenoss wine list

Cava kaba Spanish champagne

cerveza thairbay-tha beer, lager

cerveza de barril draught beer

Chacolí fruity white wine produced in the Basque Country

champán champan champagne

champaña champan-ya champagne

chato glass of red wine

Cheste chestay region to the west of Valencia producing dry and sweet white wines

chiquito cheekeeto glass of red wine

chocolate caliente chokolatay kal-yentay hot chocolate

Cigales theegaless region in Valladolid producing light rosé wines

clara shandy

cóctel cocktail

Conca de Barbera barbaira region in Catalonia producing red and white wines

Condado de Huelva welba region in the south producing dry, mellow and sweet white wines

con gas fizzy, sparkling

coñac kon-yak brandy

corto (de cerveza) thairbay-tha 125cc of draught beer (1/2 caña)

cosecha vintage

cosechero kosechairo red wine of the last vintage

cubalibre koobaleebray rum and cola

cubata a spirit with a soft drink of lemon or cola

cubito de hielo yaylo ice cube

cucaracha kookaracha tequila and coffee-flavoured strong alcoholic drink

destornillador destornee-yador vodka and orange juice

espumoso sparkling

gaseosa gasay-osa lemonade

ginebra Heenay-bra gin

granizada/granizado graneethada crushed ice drink

hielo yaylo ice

horchata (de chufas) orchata day milk drink flavoured with tiger nuts

infusión eenfooss-yon herb tea

jarra de vino Harra day beeno jug of wine

jerez Haireth sherry

jerez amontillado amontee-yado pale dry sherry

jerez fino pale light sherry

jerez oloroso sweet sherry

jugo Hoogo juice

jugo de albaricoque day albareekokay apricot juice

jugo de lima leema lime juice

jugo de limón lemon juice

jugo de melocotón peach juice

jugo de naranja naran-Ha orange juice

jugo de piña peen-ya pineapple juice

jugo de tomate tomatay tomato juice

Jumilla Hoomee-ya region in the south producing dry, light red wines and sweet white wines

leche lechay milk

licor liqueur

licor de avellana day abay-yana hazelnut-flavoured liqueur

licor de manzana manthana apple-flavoured liqueur

licor de melocotón peach-flavoured liqueur

licor de melón melon-flavoured liqueur

licor de naranja naran-Ha orange-flavoured liqueur

limonada lemonade

lista de precios prayth-yoss price list

Málaga region on the south coast producing sweet and dry white wines

Mancha region of the interior producing mainly white, but also red wines

manzanilla manthanee-ya dry sherry-type wine; camomile tea

media de agua mayd-ya day ag-wa half-bottle of mineral water

menta poleo polay-o mint tea

Mentrida central region producing dark-coloured red wines

Montilla-Moriles montee-ya-moreeless region in Andalusia producing sherry-like white wines

mosto grape juice

Oporto port

orujo orooHo colourless, strong alcoholic drink made from wine

orujo de miel m-yayl orujo with honey

pacharán strong alcoholic drink made from sloes

Penedés penedayss region in Catalonia producing in particular sparkling white wines

Priorato pree-orato wine-growing region near Tarragona

refresco soft drink

reserva especial quality wine matured in casks

Ribeiro reebay-eero region in Galicia producing slightly sparkling red and white wines; type of white wine

Rioja r-yoHa region in the north producing some of the finest red and white wines

romeral wine

ron rum

sangría sangree-a mixture of red wine, lemonade, spirits and fruit

seco dry

semidulce say-mee-doolthay medium-sweet

sidra cider

sin gas seen still

sol y sombra ee brandy and anís

Tarragona region on the Mediterranean coast producing red and white wines

té tay tea

Tierra Alta t-yairra region in the province of Tarragona producing red and white wines

tila teela lime tea

tinto de Toro teento dry, red wine from Zamora

tónica tonic

tónica con ginebra Heenebra gin and tonic

Utiel-Requena oot-yeel-rekayna region in Valencia producing mild red and rosé wines

Valdeorras balday-orrass region in Galicia producing red and white wines

Valdepeñas balday-payn-yass central region producing pale and dark, fruity red wines; type of fruity red wine

Valencia balenth-ya region on the Mediterranean producing red and white wines

Valle de Monterrey ba-yay day montairray region in Galicia producing full-bodied red and white wines

vino beeno wine

vino blanco white wine

vino de aguja day agooHa slightly sparkling rosé and white wines

vino de jerez Haireth sherry

vino del país pa-eess local wine

vino de mesa maysa table wine

vino rosado rosé wine

vino tinto red wine

viñedo vineyard

Yecla region in the south producing smooth red and light rosé wines

zumo thoo*o*mo fruit juice

zumo de albaricoque day albareeko*k*ay apricot juice

zumo de lima *l*eema lime juice

zumo de limón lemon juice

zumo de melocotón peach juice

zumo de naranja naranHa orange juice

zumo de piña peen-ya pineapple juice

zumo de tomate toma*t*ay tomato juice

zurito thoor*ee*to 125 cc of draught beer (1/2 caña)

zurracapote thoorrakapo*t*ay wine with sugar and cinammon

Picture credits

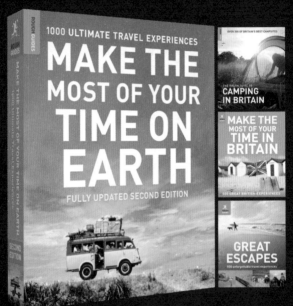

ROUGH GUIDES WORLD COVERAGE

ANDORRA Spain

ANTIGUA The Caribbean

ARGENTINA Argentina, Buenos Aires, South America on a Budget

AUSTRALIA Australia, Australia Map, East Coast Australia, Melbourne, Sydney, Tasmania

AUSTRIA Austria, Europe on a Budget, Vienna

BAHAMAS The Bahamas, The Caribbean

BARBADOS The Caribbean

BELGIUM Belgium & Luxembourg, Brussels

BELIZE Belize, Central America On a Budget, Guetemala & Belize Map

BENIN West Africa

BOLIVIA Bolivia, South America on a Budget

BRAZIL Brazil, Rio, South America on a Budget

BRUNEI Malaysia, Singapore & Brunei [1 title], South East Asia on a Budget

BULGARIA Bulgaria, Europe on a Budget

BURKINA FASO West Africa

CAMBODIA Cambodia, South East Asia on a Budget, Vietnam

CAMEROON West Africa

CANADA Canada, Toronto, Toronto Map, Vancouver

CAPE VERDE West Africa

CARIBBEAN The Caribbean

CHILE Chile, South America on a Budget

CHINA Beijing, China, Hong Kong & Macau, Shanghai

COLOMBIA South America on a Budget

COSTA RICA Central America on a Budget, Costa Rica

CROATIA Croatia, Croatia Map, Europe on a Budget

CUBA Cuba, Cuba Map, Havana, The Caribbean

CYPRUS Cyprus

CZECH REPUBLIC The Czech Republic, Czech Republic Map, Europe on a Budget, Prague, Prague Map, Prague Pocket

DENMARK Copenhagen, Denmark, Europe on a Budget, Scandinavia

DOMINICAN REPUBLIC Dominican Republic, Dominican Republic Map, The Caribbean

ECUADOR Ecuador, South America on a Budget

EGYPT Egypt, Cairo & The Pyramids

EL SALVADOR Central America on a Budget

ENGLAND Britain, Camping, Devon & Cornwall, The Cotswolds, Dorset, Hampshire & The Isle of Wight [1 title], England, Europe on a Budget, The Lake District, London, London Pocket, London Map, London Mini Guide, Walks in London & Southeast England, Yorkshire

ESTONIA Europe on a Budget, Estonia, Latvia & Lithuania [1 title]

FIJI Fiji

FINLAND Europe on a Budget, Finland, Scandinavia

FRANCE Brittany & Normandy, Brittany Map, Corsica, Corsica Map, The Dordogne & the Lot, Europe on a Budget, France, Languedoc & Roussillon, The Loire Valley, Paris, Paris Mini Guide, Paris Pocket, Provence & the Cote d'Azur

FRENCH GUIANA South America on a Budget

GAMBIA West Africa

GERMANY Berlin, Europe on a Budget, Germany

GHANA West Africa

GIBRALTAR Spain

GREECE Athens Map, Athens Pocket, Crete, Crete Map, Europe on a Budget, Greece, Greek Islands

GUATEMALA Central America on a Budget, Guatemala, Guatemala & Belize Map

GUINEA West Africa

GUINEA-BISSAU West Africa

GUYANA South America on a Budget

HOLLAND see Netherlands

HONDURAS Central America on a Budget

HUNGARY Budapest, Europe on a Budget, Hungary

ICELAND Iceland, Iceland Map

INDIA Goa, India, Kerala, Rajasthan, Delhi & Agra [1 title]

INDONESIA Bali & Lombok, South East Asia on a Budget

IRELAND Dublin Map, Europe on a Budget, Ireland, Ireland Map

ISRAEL Jerusalem

ITALY Europe on a Budget, Florence & Siena Map, Florence & the best of Tuscany, Italy, Italy Map, The Italian Lakes, Naples & the Amalfi Coast, Rome, Rome Pocket, Sardinia, Sicily, Sicily Map, Tuscany & Umbria, Venice, Venice Pocket

JAMAICA Jamaica, The Caribbean

JAPAN Japan, Tokyo

JORDAN Jordan

KENYA Kenya, Kenya Map

KOREA Korea, Seoul

LAOS Laos, South East Asia on a Budget

LATVIA Europe on a Budget

LESOTHO South Africa

LITHUANIA Europe on a Budget

LUXEMBOURG Belgium & Luxembourg, Europe on a Budget

MALAYSIA Malaysia, Singapore & Brunei [1 title], South East Asia on a Budget

MALI West Africa

MAURITANIA West Africa

MEXICO Mexico, Cancun & The Yucatan, Yucatan Peninsula Map

MONACO France, Provence & the Cote d'Azur

MONTENEGRO Montenegro

MOROCCO Europe on a Budget, Marrakesh Map, Morocco

NEPAL Nepal

NETHERLANDS Amsterdam, Amsterdam Map, Amsterdam Pocket, Europe on a Budget, The Netherlands

NEW ZEALAND New Zealand, New Zealand Map

NICARAGUA Central America on a Budget

NIGER West Africa

OVER 300 DESTINATIONS

NIGERIA West Africa
NORWAY Europe on a Budget, Norway, Scandinavia
OMAN Oman
PANAMA Central America on a Budget, Panama
PARAGUAY South America on a Budget
PERU Peru, Peru Map, South America on a Budget
PHILIPPINES The Philippines, Southeast Asia on a Budget
POLAND Europe on a Budget, Poland
PORTUGAL The Algarve Map, Europe on a Budget, Lisbon Pocket, Portugal
PUERTO RICO The Caribbean, Puerto Rico
ROMANIA Europe on a Budget, Romania
RUSSIA Europe on a Budget, Moscow, St Petersburg
ST LUCIA The Caribbean
SCOTLAND Britain, Camping, Europe on a Budget, Scotland, Scottish Highlands & Islands
SENEGAL West Africa
SERBIA Montenegro, Europe on a Budget
SIERRA LEONE West Africa
SINGAPORE Malaysia, Singapore & Brunei [1 title], Singapore, Southeast Asia on a Budget
SLOVAKIA Czech & Slovak Republics, Europe on a Budget
SLOVENIA Europe on a Budget, Slovenia
SOUTH AFRICA South Africa, South Africa Map
SPAIN Andalucia, Andalucia Map, Barcelona, Barcelona Map, Barcelona Pocket, Europe on a Budget, Mallorca & Menorca, Mallorca Map, Spain
SRI LANKA Sri Lanka, Sri Lanka Map
SURINAME South America on a Budget
SWAZILAND South Africa
SWEDEN Europe on a Budget, Scandinavia, Sweden
SWITZERLAND Europe on a Budget, Switzerland

TAIWAN Taiwan
TANZANIA Tanzania, Zanzibar
THAILAND Bangkok, Southeast Asia on a Budget, Thailand, Thailand Beaches & Islands
TOGO West Africa
TRINIDAD & TOBAGO The Caribbean, Trinidad & Tobago
TUNISIA Tunisia
TURKEY Europe on a Budget, Istanbul, Turkey
TURKS AND CAICOS ISLANDS The Bahamas, The Caribbean
UNITED ARAB EMIRATES Dubai, Dubai & UAE Map [1 title]
UNITED KINGDOM Britain, Devon & Cornwall, England, Europe on a Budget, The Lake District, London, London Map, London Mini Guide, Scotland, Scottish Highlands & Islands, Wales, Walks in London & Southeast England
USA Boston, California, Chicago, Chicago Map, Florida, The Grand Canyon, Hawaii, Las Vegas, Los Angeles & Southern California, Miami & South Florida, Miami Map, New England, New Orleans & Cajun Country, New York City, New York City Mini Guide, New York Pocket, San Francisco, Seattle, Southwest USA, USA, Washington DC, Yellowstone & The Grand Tetons National Park, Yosemite National Park
URUGUAY South America on a Budget
US VIRGIN ISLANDS The Bahamas, The Caribbean
VENEZUELA South America on a Budget
VIETNAM Southeast Asia on a Budget, Vietnam
WALES Britain, Camping, Europe on a Budget, Wales
WORLD COVERAGE Earthbound, Great Escapes, Make the Most of Your Time on Earth, Make the Most of Your Time in Britain Ultimate Adventures

ROUGH GUIDES DON'T JUST TRAVEL

COMPUTING Android Phones, Cloud Computing, Digital Photography, The Internet, iPad, iPhone, iPods & iTunes, Macs & OSX, Saving & Selling Online, Windows 7
FILM Comedy Movies, Cult Movies, Film, Film Musicals, Sci-Fi Movies
LIFESTYLE Babies & Toddlers, Brain Training, Food, Girl Stuff, Green Living, Happiness, Men's Health, Pregnancy & Birth, Psychology, Running, Sex, Weddings
MUSIC The Beatles, The Best Music You've Never Heard, Bob Dylan, Classical Music, Guitar, Jimi Hendrix, Nirvana, Pink Floyd, The Rolling Stones, Velvet Underground, World Music
POPULAR CULTURE Anime, The Best Art You've Never Seen, Classic Novels, Conspiracy Theories, Cult Football, FWD this link, Cult Sport Graphic Novels, Hitchhiker's Guide to the Galaxy, The Lost Symbol, Manga, Nelson Mandela, Next Big Thing, Shakespeare, Surviving the End of the World, True Crime, Unexplained Phenomena, Videogames
SCIENCE The Brain, Climate Change, The Earth, Energy Crisis, Evolution, Future, Genes & Cloning, The Universe

ROUGH GUIDES

Start your journey at **roughguides.com**